AF262748

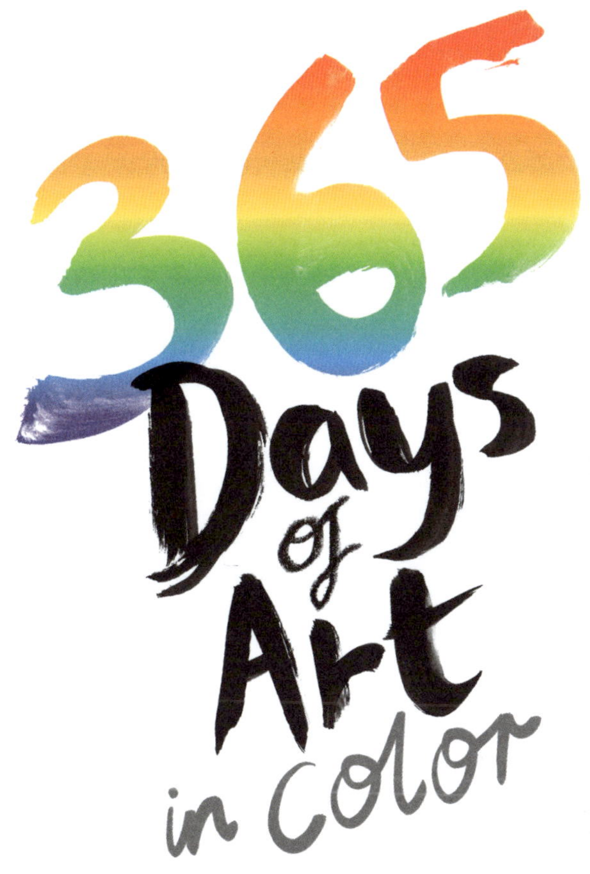

This book belongs to:

____

____

____

365 Days of Art in Color

CREATIVE ART PROMPTS FOR EVERY DAY OF THE YEAR

LORNA SCOBIE

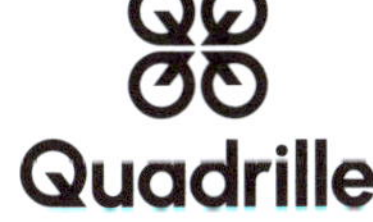

Quadrille

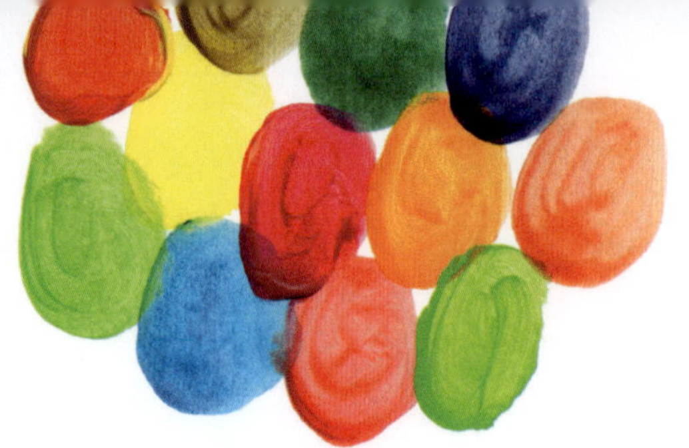

Welcome to 365 Days of Art in Color!

I absolutely love using color in my art—filling a page with vivid greens, blues, reds, and oranges brings me joy! In the past, however, I found using color a bit intimidating and I'd stick to colors that felt familiar and 'safe' rather than using the colors I loved. Through playful exploration and plenty of happy 'mistakes', I learnt to let go and fully embrace using a vast spectrum of color. I hope that this book encourages you to also feel excited and energized by color.

Or perhaps you already do! This is a book for people who love color and would like to use it more in their art, as well as a book for those who feel nervous about using color and unsure about where to start. Adding color can be daunting for any artist at first, as it can seem like there are so many decisions to make: which colors should I use, and where, and how? This book challenges the idea that there is a 'right' answer to these questions, and instead encourages you to make instinctive choices about color. As your confidence builds, you'll begin to trust your instincts and just go for it.

In these activities, I will introduce some elements of color theory, but mainly I'll create a safe space where you can relax, unwind, and have fun. As with all my *365 Days* art books, these tasks have been designed to be suitable for everyone—regardless of skill level, age, or prior experience.

Art has the power to make us *all* feel good. Although we often have the desire to be creative, it can sometimes be tricky knowing where to start. So I've provided a color-themed prompt for every

day of the year, sometimes with an example or a starting point. This book will encourage you to leave your comfort zone and try new colors, combinations, and themes, and through your exploration perhaps you'll discover fresh techniques to use in your art. I'd recommend trying activities even if they feel out of your comfort zone, as you may discover something new! You can also adapt the tasks in any way, so that they work best for you.

Approach these activities with confidence. Don't worry about making mistakes on the page—in my opinion there is no such a thing as 'bad' art, and if you've enjoyed the time spent creating, and perhaps even learnt something new, it was worth it! So just pick up a pencil, pen, or paintbrush, make a mark and enjoy the moment.

You can work through the book in order, or choose prompts based on how you feel in the moment. Be guided by your own intuition, and don't feel like you have to complete one every day—life is busy and there's no need to put extra pressure on yourself. Some activities can be accomplished relatively quickly, so you may like to squeeze one or two into a break during the day. Or perhaps you dedicate time once a week to spend on your art, really getting stuck in and letting your mind focus solely on creating. As you finish an activity, cross it off on the 'activities completed' grid to record your progress.

The activities are categorized to give you an idea about the nature of each task, and provide the opportunity to explore color in four key areas:

The **learn** tasks introduce color theory. You'll gain a greater understanding of how color behaves and how to mix colors, and the chance to explore what you've learnt. Definitions of color are sometimes used in a variety of ways and some words are interchangeable. I've used them in the way that works for me, but you might come across alternative definitions. Don't let the words and meanings hinder your creativity, use whichever terms work for you. And remember, in this book there's no right or wrong way to use color. It can be useful to learn the artistic conventions, but then it's up to you how you apply them in your art.

Some activities encourage you to **play**, forget the rules of color and be experimental! Challenge yourself to think differently and have fun without any fear of making a mess. Create art in an environment where you feel relaxed and free to be yourself, perhaps with friends, or while listening to music. This is a chance to let your imagination run wild, be mindful and enjoy the process.

There are activities that offer a chance to **observe** the colorful world around you. Rather than just seeing, practice actively *looking* at your surroundings. The observational tasks may require a little more time and concentration than others. Embrace taking these moments to focus entirely on your art without distraction, and at the same time you'll be building your artistic skills.

Different colors can evoke different feelings and moods, and we can harness this within our art. Explore this in the **feel** tasks. The emotions you experience will be personal to you—be guided by your own responses in these activities and enjoy thinking a little deeper when you create.

I believe *everyone* is creative, and thanks to the *365 Days of Art* community I have been lucky enough to see how art can bring happiness into people's lives, every day. Your art can be just for you and there's no need to share it, but if you do feel like it, do so with confidence! Use the hashtag **#365DaysOfArt** to share your art with the online community and see what else has been created.

Activities Completed

KEY: ■ Learn   ■ Play   ■ Observe   ■ Feel

1	2	3	4	5	6	7	8	9	10
11	12	13	14	15	16	17	18	19	20
21	22	23	24	25	26	27	28	29	30
31	32	33	34	35	36	37	38	39	40
41	42	43	44	45	46	47	48	49	50
51	52	53	54	55	56	57	58	59	60
61	62	63	64	65	66	67	68	69	70
71	72	73	74	75	76	77	78	79	80
81	82	83	84	85	86	87	88	89	90
91	92	93	94	95	96	97	98	99	100
101	102	103	104	105	106	107	108	109	110
111	112	113	114	115	116	117	118	119	120
121	122	123	124	125	126	127	128	129	130
131	132	133	134	135	136	137	138	139	140
141	142	143	144	145	146	147	148	149	150
151	152	153	154	155	156	157	158	159	160
161	162	163	164	165	166	167	168	169	170
171	172	173	174	175	176	177	178	179	180

181	182	183	184	185	186	187	188	189	190
191	192	193	194	195	196	197	198	199	200
201	202	203	204	205	206	207	208	209	210
211	212	213	214	215	216	217	218	219	220
221	222	223	224	225	226	227	228	229	230
231	232	233	234	235	236	237	238	239	240
241	242	243	244	245	246	247	248	249	250
251	252	253	254	255	256	257	258	259	260
261	262	263	264	265	266	267	268	269	270
271	272	273	274	275	276	277	278	279	280
281	282	283	284	285	286	287	288	289	290
291	292	293	294	295	296	297	298	299	300
301	302	303	304	305	306	307	308	309	310
311	312	313	314	315	316	317	318	319	320
321	322	323	324	325	326	327	328	329	330
331	332	333	334	335	336	337	338	339	340
341	342	343	344	345	346	347	348	349	350
351	352	353	354	355	356	357	358	359	360
361	362	363	364	365					

Materials

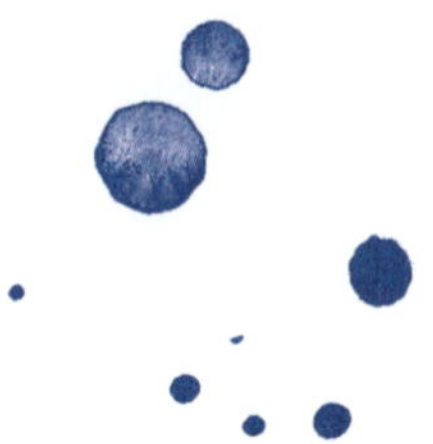

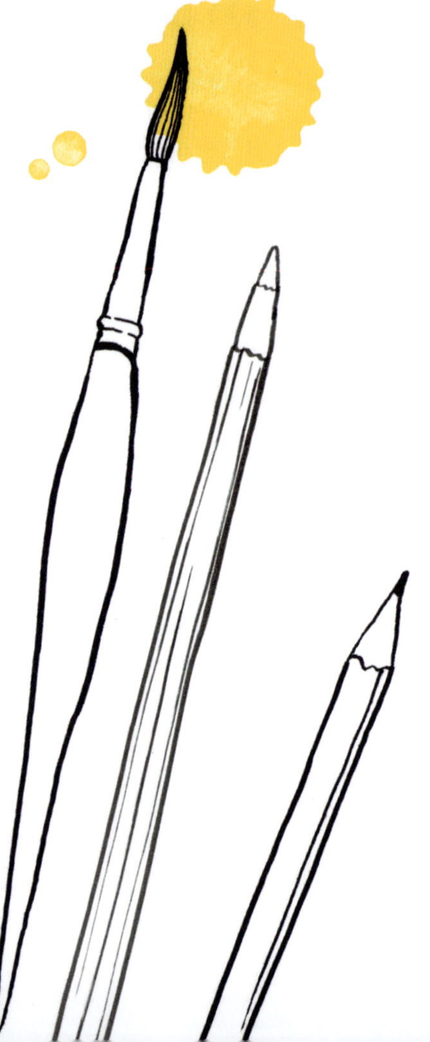

You can use any art materials you like to create colorful art. Complete the activities in this book with tools you already love, or take the opportunity to explore materials that you've always been interested to try. Through exploration, find what works for you, and if that means using something different to what is suggested in the activities, that's no problem at all! This is *your* book.

I like to prepare my art materials before I start creating, laying them out in front of me where I can see them. I find this inspires me to experiment, take more risks, and be bolder with my color choices. You could try this too. Embrace the way of working that feels natural to you and aim to work instinctively, grabbing colors that feel right.

There's no rush or need to spend lots to build your toolkit. I have suggested a few of my favorite art materials here, but I also recommend visiting art stores. Here you can see the vast array of pens, paints, and pencils available, and staff can offer advice on different materials to suit your needs. You could also browse online for recommendations, or swap tips, and discuss thoughts with friends and fellow creatives.

Ink pens and watery paints can bleed through paper. If you are concerned about this happening you can prime the pages of this book with **clear gesso** before you start an activity. Use a brush to apply the gesso over the page and allow it to dry before you start—you could use binder clips to keep your page open.

Pencils

Pencils and colored pencils are a great addition to your toolkit. There is a huge variety of colors to choose from, they are simple to use and are relatively mess-free. Drawing pencils range in softness, commonly from a 9B, which creates a soft black line, to a 9H, which is very hard and creates a sharp, light line. Colored pencils also range in softness, so I recommend trying out samples to find what you prefer before buying a full set. Pencils are also sold individually in stores—look out for colors that bring you joy!

Mechanical pencils can be useful for sketching. They contain a pencil lead, but feel more like a pen to hold as the casing is metal or plastic. I enjoy using the **Staedtler Mars Micro 0.5** and the **Pentel P205 0.5**. Mechanical pencils don't need sharpening, but you will need to buy extra lead refills for them. Make sure you choose the correct size refill (the mechanical pencil will give the lead refill size on its side).

I love to mix and match colored pencil brands based on which colors I am inspired by. I really enjoy the vast array of hues available in the **Faber-Castell Polychromos** range. Some colored pencils are water soluble, such as the **Caran d'Ache Supracolor** pencils, which have a soft lead and also come in a large range of colors. You can blend them with water and a paintbrush. I also enjoy the **Staedtler Ergosoft** pencils, which have a harder lead and produce very solid, bright colors.

If you are using pencils, it's worth buying a good eraser and sharpener from an art store.

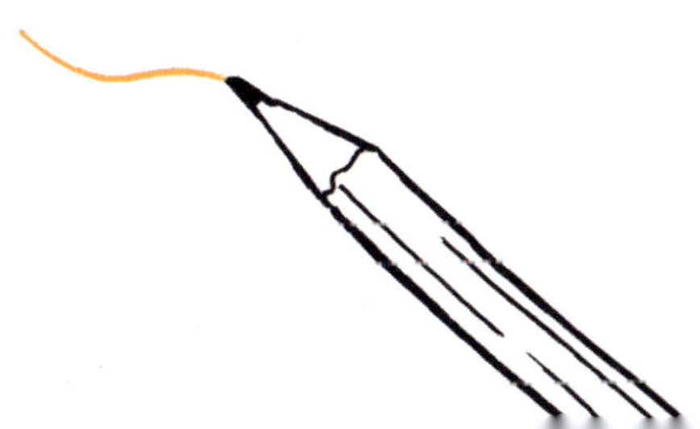

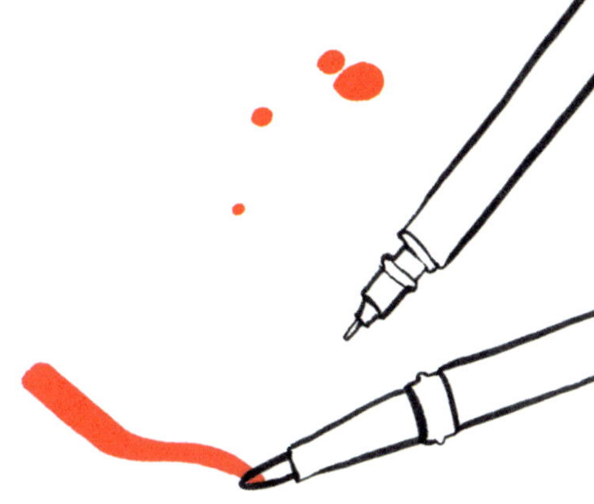

Brush tip pens

These are a great way to add color to a page quickly. I'd recommend water-based pens for this book—there are fantastic colors available, they are easy to use, and less likely to bleed through the paper. I enjoy using **Tombow ABT Dual Brush Pens**, especially for coloring backgrounds or creating bold shapes and marks.

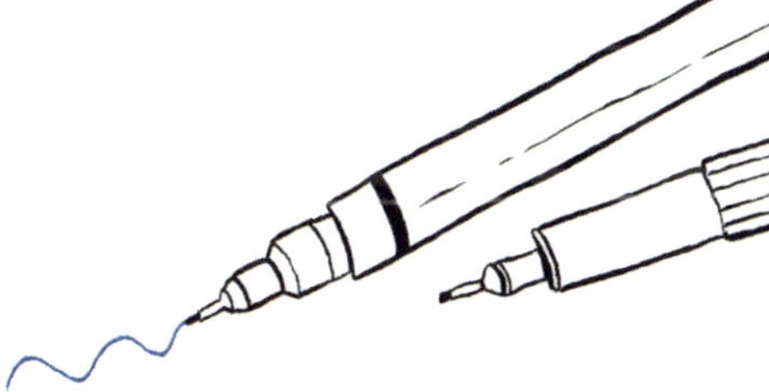

Fineliner pens

It's useful to have a few fineliner pens for jotting down notes and ideas, making quick sketches and adding detail to artwork. There is a wide range of brands, colors, and nib sizes to choose from, so I recommend experimenting with the testers in an art store. My favorites include **Uni Pin Fine Line** pens, **Pilot Juice Up** gel pens, **Sakura Pigma Micron** pens, and **Derwent Graphik Line Maker** pens.

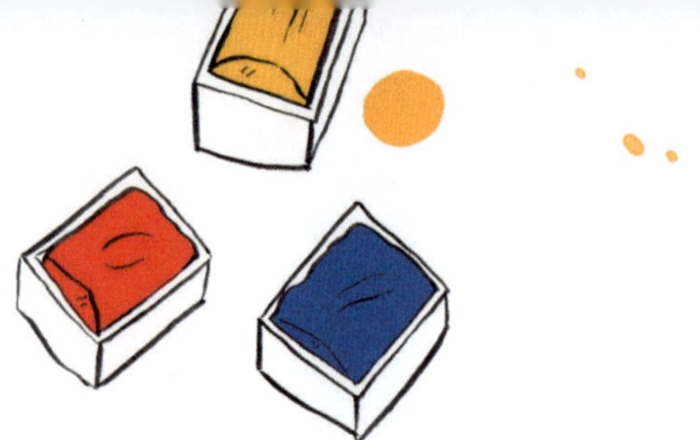

Watercolor paint

Watercolor paint is very versatile—it's not too messy, you can control the intensity of your color, it dries quickly and colors can be blended easily.

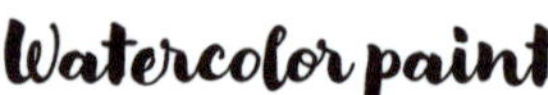

Daler-Rowney and **Winsor & Newton** both produce wonderfully vibrant colors in palettes or 'trays'. When you run out of a particular color (called a 'pan') you can purchase individual replacements so your tray of watercolors can last forever. For particularly rich colors, I enjoy using **Kuretake Gansai Tambi** paints. I like to use **Pentel Aquash Water Brushes**. These brushes come in a few sizes and can be filled with water, providing a useful alternative to a pot of water and paintbrush when painting with watercolors.

Paintbrushes vary greatly, and it's useful to have a range of brush sizes and shapes. Brush tips can be pointed, round or have a square-end, and each produces a different effect. Experiment with different types and see what you prefer. You'll also need a container for your water, and this can be anything from an old mug to an empty yogurt pot, and some paper towel for blotting water off your brush. You'll need a wet brush in order to pick up paint from the pan, and it can be a good idea to rinse brushes in water before changing color to keep colors clean.

Most watercolor palettes come with a space inside the lid to mix colors—a mixing palette. These can be revisited even when the paint has dried out, just by applying a bit of water from your brush.

Acrylic paint

Acrylic paint comes in an extensive range of vivid, pre-mixed colors that are highly pigmented. If you can't find a tube of the color you are looking for, you can also mix colors yourself. Acrylic paint dries quickly and can be watered down to make the consistency thinner or more transparent. I like to use **Daler-Rowney System 3 Acrylics** and **Liquitex Heavy Body Acrylic**.

As with watercolor, you'll also need brushes, a pot of water, some paper towel for blotting and a mixing palette. Be sure to wash your brushes once you've finished using them, as once the paint dries it can be harder to get off. You can use mixing palettes from art stores, or an old ceramic plate does a great job too. Paint will also dry quickly on the palette when exposed to air, but you can keep your colors from drying out so fast by sealing the whole palette in a zip lock bag.

Pastels

Wax and oil pastels are a fun material to use as they slide easily over paper, and you can cover large areas quickly when using them on their sides. Colors can be bought individually or in sets, and they can get a little messy. I like **Caran d'Ache Neocolor II Aquarelle** pastels, which are water-soluble. Just use a brush or sponge to add a little water to your wax pastel drawing for an interesting effect. **Sennelier Oil Pastels** are also lovely and creamy.

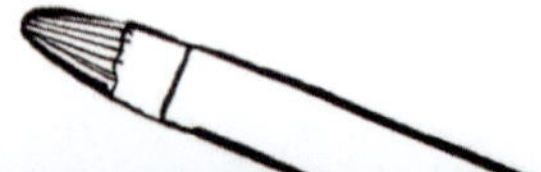

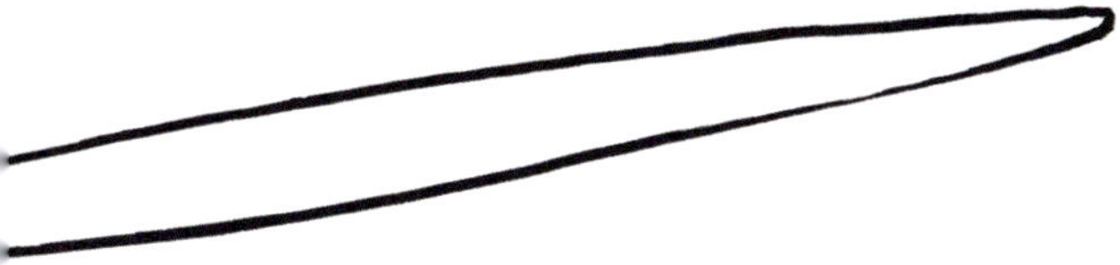

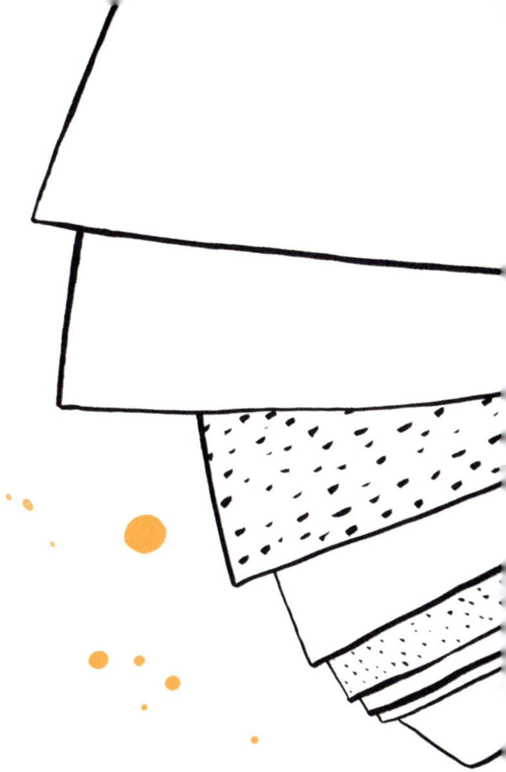

Colored paper

Keep aside any interesting colored, patterned, and textured paper—you can even use gift wrap or brown paper bags in your art. They are great materials to have in your kit for collage. You can build your own library of colored paper over time, and also paint your own sheets of colored paper to use. Origami paper is great as it is thin, easy to tear and cut, and often comes in a range of exciting colors and patterns.

Here are some other materials you may like to have in your art kit:

— **Sketchbooks:** Use these to continue your creative journey. They are a great place to experiment and record your ideas, and come in many different sizes and styles.

— **Watercolor paper:** Useful when using watery paint. You could choose to work onto sheets of watercolor paper for some activities, and then stick your artwork in your sketchbook.

— **Clear gesso:** A primer to apply with a clean brush to paper or board to prevent materials from bleeding through. Acts as a barrier between the paper and the art material.

— **Gouache:** These are water-based paints, similar to watercolor, but can provide a more intense color as they are more opaque. They dry quickly and are great if you're interested in layering colors.

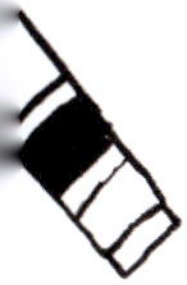

— **Scissors:** Useful for collages and cutting paper.

— **Glue:** PVA or a glue stick can be used to stick down collages. Water down PVA to make it less gloopy, and apply with a scrap of hard cardboard, or an old paintbrush.

— **Masking tape (low-tack sticky tape):** Handy for sticking things quickly, and easy to remove and draw on. Can also be used for straight lines; stick it down before you start painting, then peel off once finished to reveal a straight edge.

— **Tracing paper:** Use masking tape to stick this over drawings that are a bit messy, so marks don't transfer to the opposite page.

— **Fixative spray:** Apply on top of completed artwork to prevent smudging.

— **Binder clips:** Useful for holding back other pages while you work on an activity.

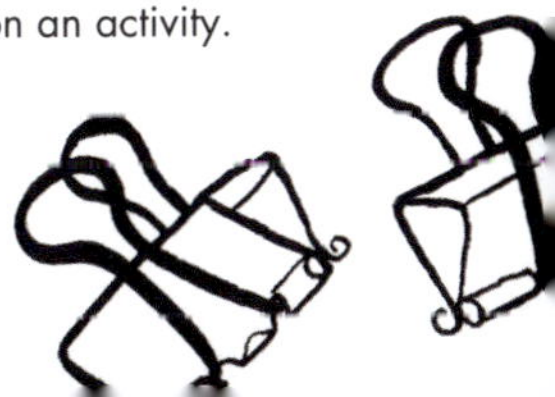

Referring to a color wheel whilst creating art can be really helpful—you can see the relationship between colors and also use it to decide which colors to use in your designs.

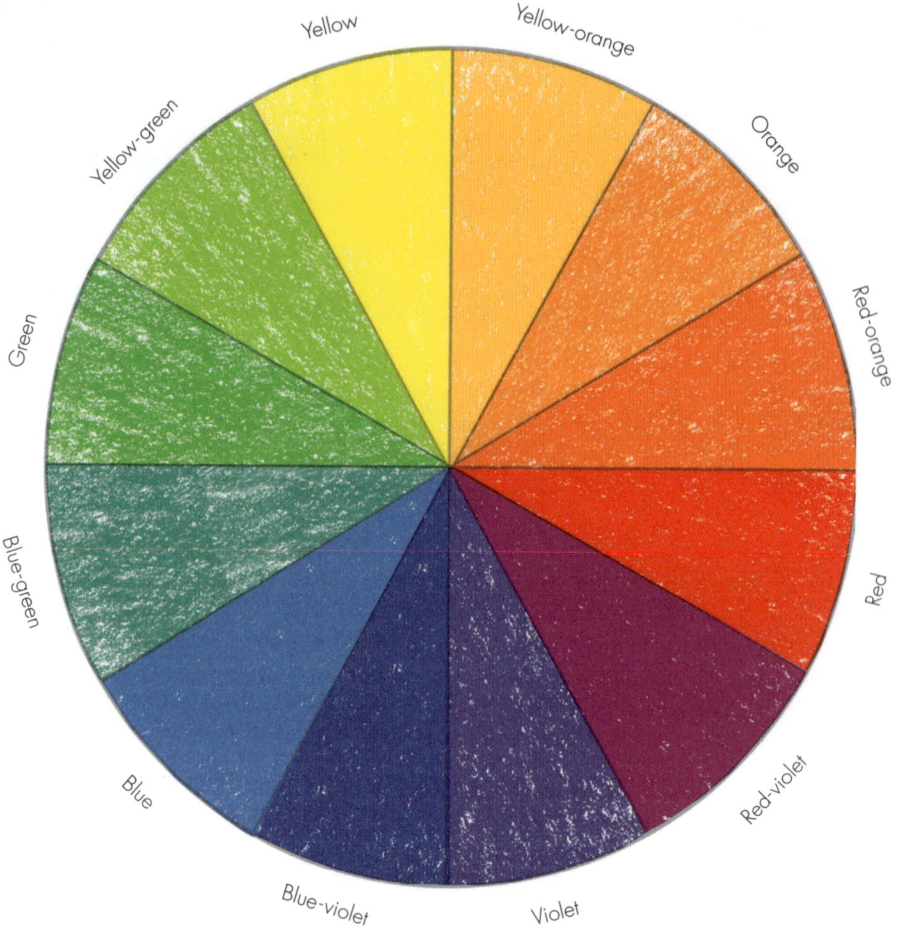

Yellow

Yellow-orange

Yellow-green

Orange

Green

Red-orange

Blue-green

Red

Blue

Red-violet

Blue-violet

Violet

Analogous colors are groups of three or more colors next to each other on the wheel. These often form a harmonious palette.

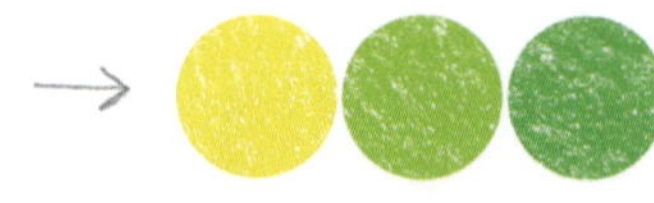

Complementary colors can be found opposite each other on the wheel, and these pairs will create striking contrasts within your work.

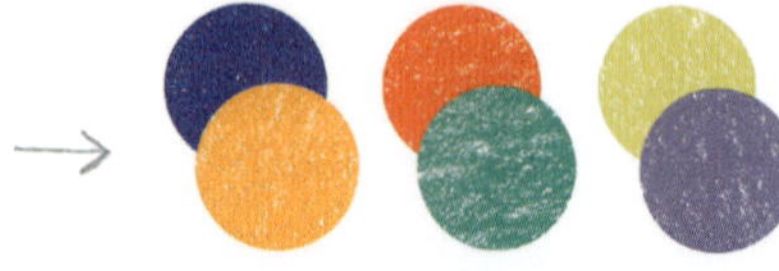

Create your own color wheel by adding colors to the segments below.
You can use any material you like.

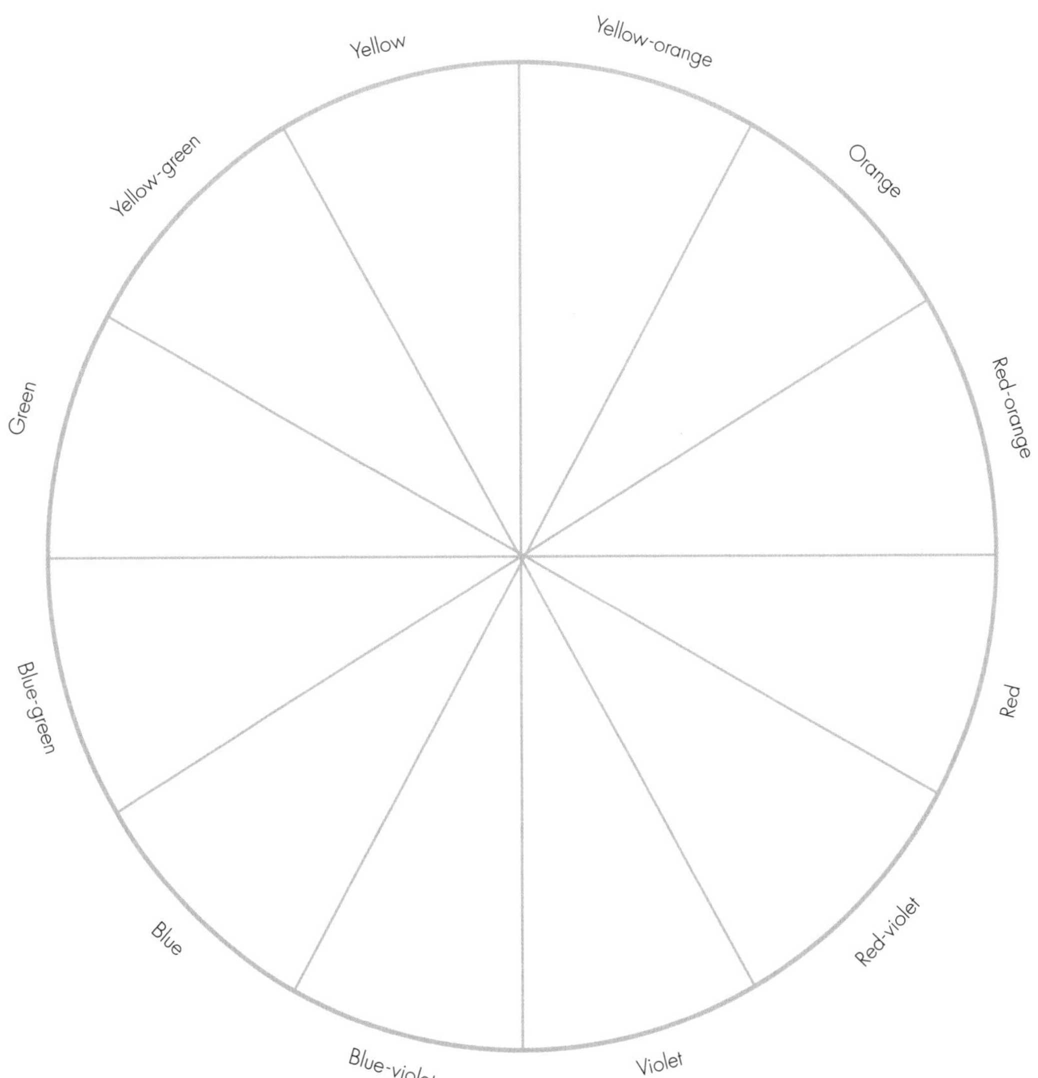

Tip: You may find it helpful to refer back to this color wheel when you are completing other activities. You could photocopy it, or create a separate one on a piece of paper and keep it with your art materials.

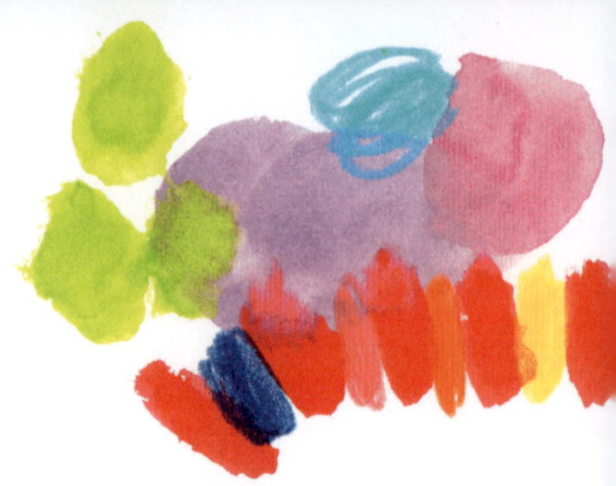

2 —————— Allow yourself to be bold and confident with your color choices. Create a lively page of color using any that appeal to you from your collection of art materials.

Tip: Enjoy the process of creation and the chance to be playful and messy. Get those colors on the page!

3

You can help turn a simple sketch into a colorful painting by taking color notes when you make the sketch. Look at a scene and make a quick drawing, noting down the colors you'd like to paint each area.

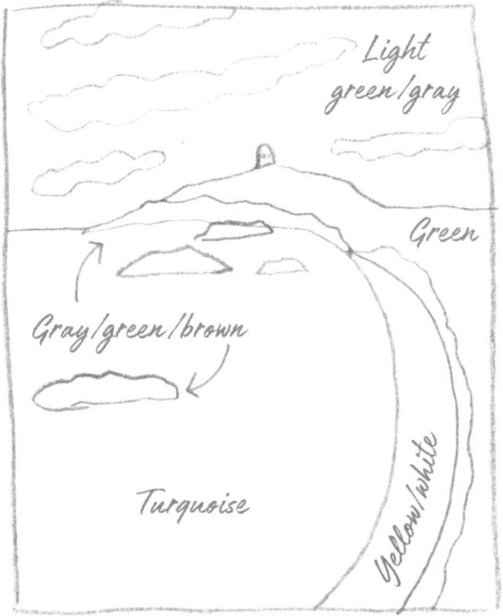

Then make a new color sketch, roughly mapping out each area of color based on your notes. If you feel inspired to create a painting based on your sketch, go for it!

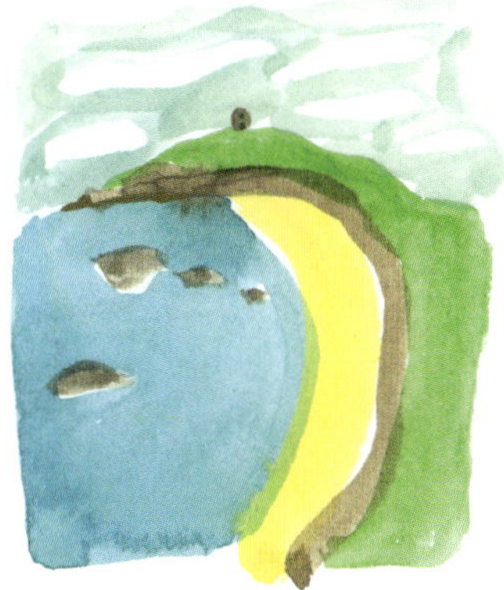

Tip: The image can evolve! Perhaps you discover you'd like to try alternative colors, or change the composition of your sketch—that's great! Go with whatever feels right to you.

Different colors can make us feel different things, and this can be a useful tool in art. Add splodges of many colors and consider the mood they evoke. Describe how each color makes you feel.

Tip: There is no wrong answer—it will be entirely personal to you.

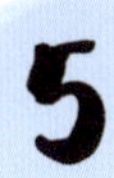

5

The primary colors are red, blue and yellow, and they cannot be made by mixing other colors. Broadly speaking, all of the other colors can be made by mixing different combinations and quantities of primary colors. The vast array of colors available to us can be overwhelming, so it can be a useful reminder that they all come from this starting point!

 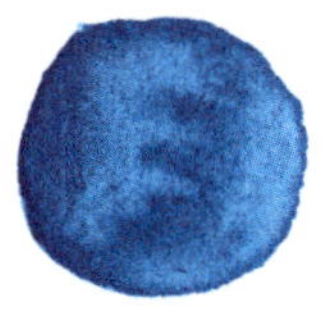 

For this activity you'll need paint. Add the three primary colors to a mixing palette (or you can use a plate). Mix as many different colors as you can on the palette, using different amounts of the primary colors (and also the new colors you've mixed from them). Record all the colors you create as swatches below them.

Tip: *It's worth noting that there are different reds, blues, and yellows, and each will create different colors when mixed together. Don't worry too much about finding a 'pure' red, blue, and yellow for this activity, instead just enjoy creating such a variety of colors from just three.*

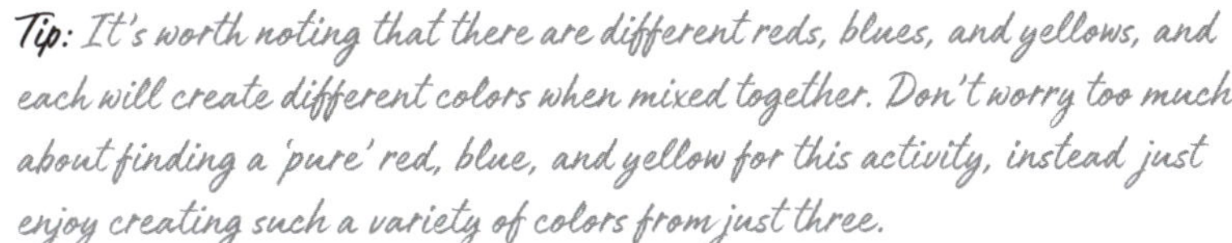

6 Add color to these vessels. Consider showing textures and reflections. Are they glass? Metal? Ceramic?

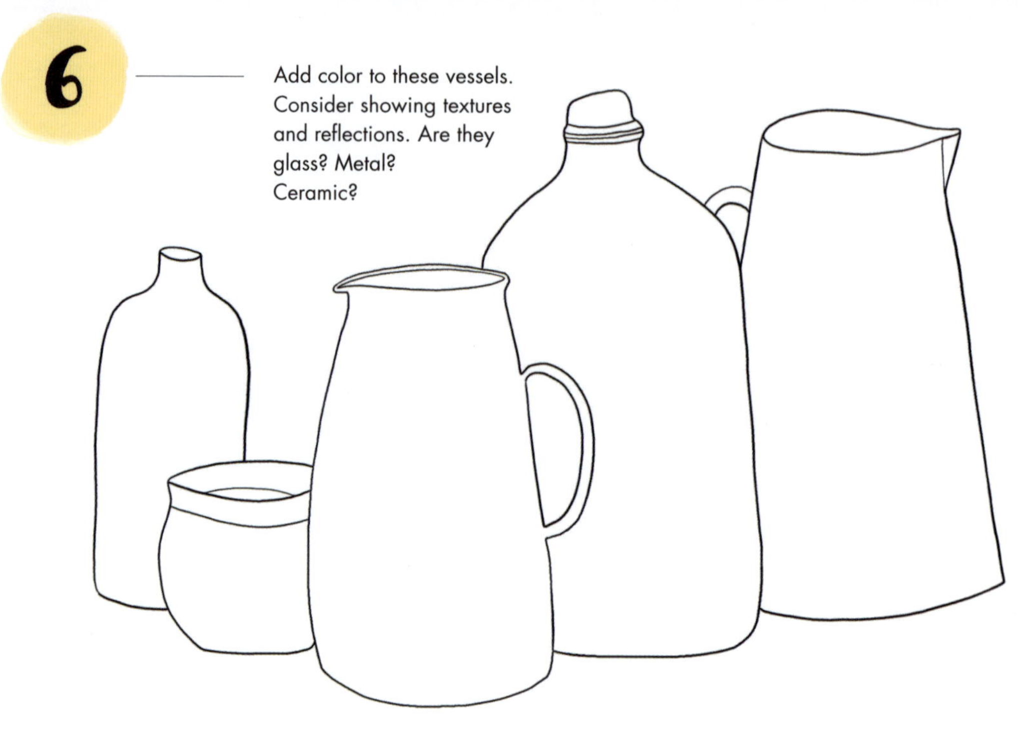

7 Never feel afraid to use bold colors in your art. Make a drawing of an object from your home using bright, bold colors. Don't worry about making a mistake … there's no such thing!

8 ——————— Oil or wax pastels are a brilliant material for making colorful
artwork because the colors are often rich and vibrant. You
can also get a lot of coverage, quickly. Explore using them by
creating an abstract, colorful design.

Continue adding lines of color to the page. Use a variety of art materials and choose colors you rarely use as well as those you enjoy.

10 —————— The color red can suggest anger, danger, confidence, heat, and love.
Be inspired by how red makes *you* feel and turn this shape into an image.

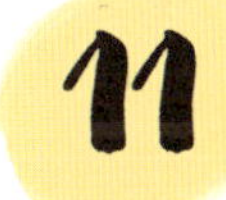

11 —————— Create a checkerboard pattern using pinks, reds, and purples.

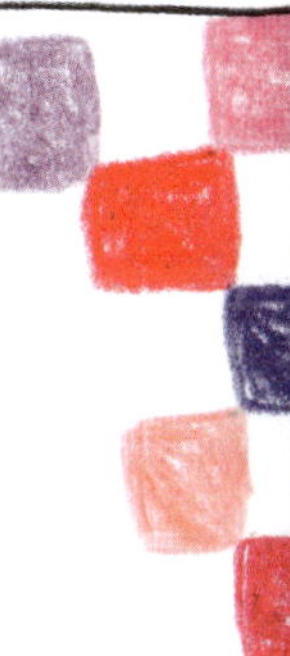

Part of learning to enjoy color is realizing the huge variety of colors and materials available to us which we can use in our art. Add swatches of as many colors as you can find, or mix colors yourself.

Tip: You could use found bits of colored paper, or fabric too.

Grass green	Dark green	Coral red	Turquoise	Mustard	Burgundy	Navy blue

13

Complementary colors are those found opposite each other on the color wheel. When used together, they can create striking images because they are contrasting.

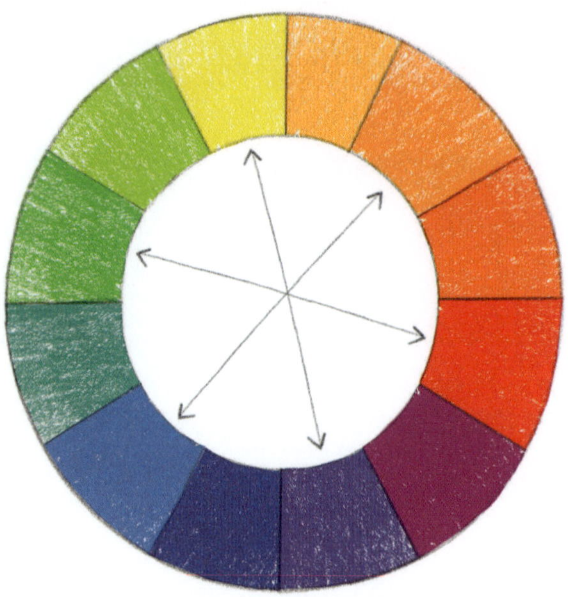

Fill the space with pairs of complementary colors using different art materials. Are there any pairings you particularly enjoy?

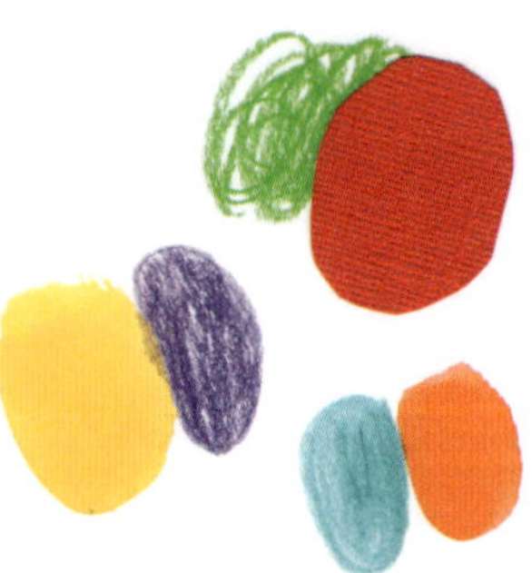

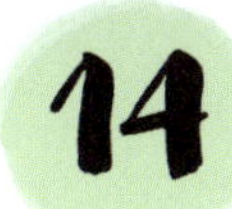

14 — Make a drawing of a person using a confident blue line to create a loose, joyful image.

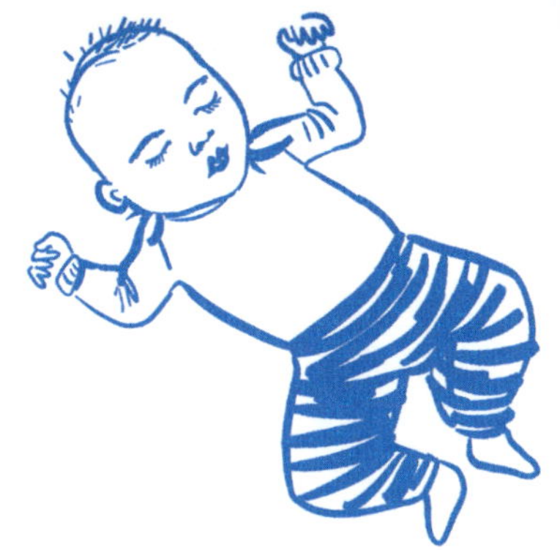

You can blend paint to create colorful artworks. Add colors here or create your own sheets of blended colors. You could then use these painted sheets for collages, or enjoy them as they are.

Tip: Blending is when you merge colors together when they are wet, but don't fully mix them. Watercolor works well to make blends.

16 ——————— Draw around your hand using a colored pencil, and create a piece of art inspired by this colorful outline. You could also draw around the hands of other family members or friends too.

Tip: You don't have to fit your whole hand on the page, you may choose to draw around your fingers, and create an abstract piece.

A 'tint' is a lighter version of a color, and a 'shade' is a darker version. Use the space on the right to explore mixing paints to create tints and shades of your colors. You can use any paints—you'll just need some colors, plus black and white, and you might find it easiest to mix your paints in a palette or on an old plate.

Tip: Using tints and shades can be especially useful when painting the light and shadow of an object—the 'tone'—because you can capture colors more effectively compared with using pure black or white .

To create a 'tint', add white to a color.

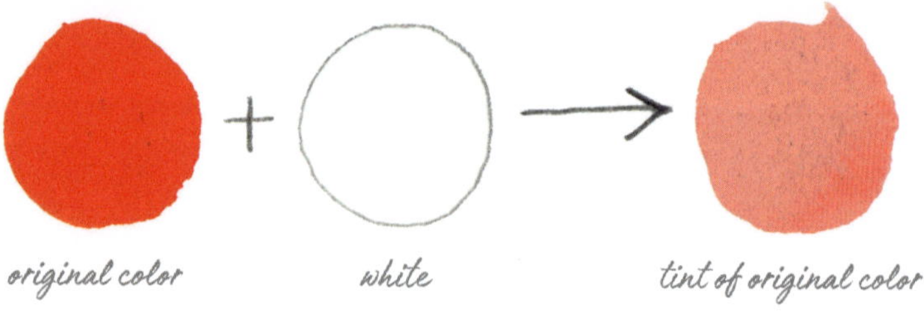

original color   *white*   *tint of original color*

To create a 'shade', add a small amount of black to a color.

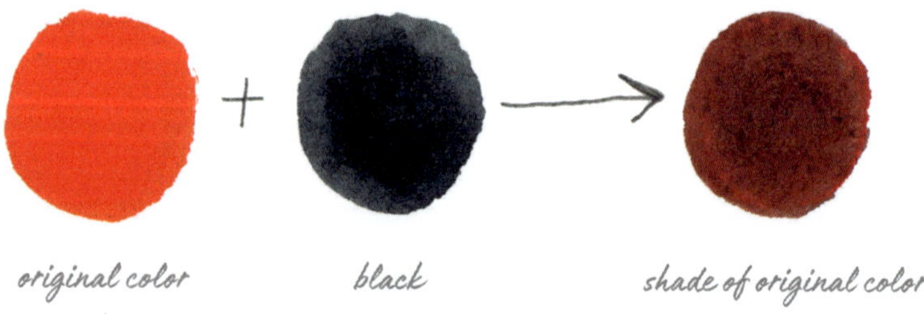

original color   *black*   *shade of original color*

Tip: You could try adding different amounts of black to get different shades of the same original color.

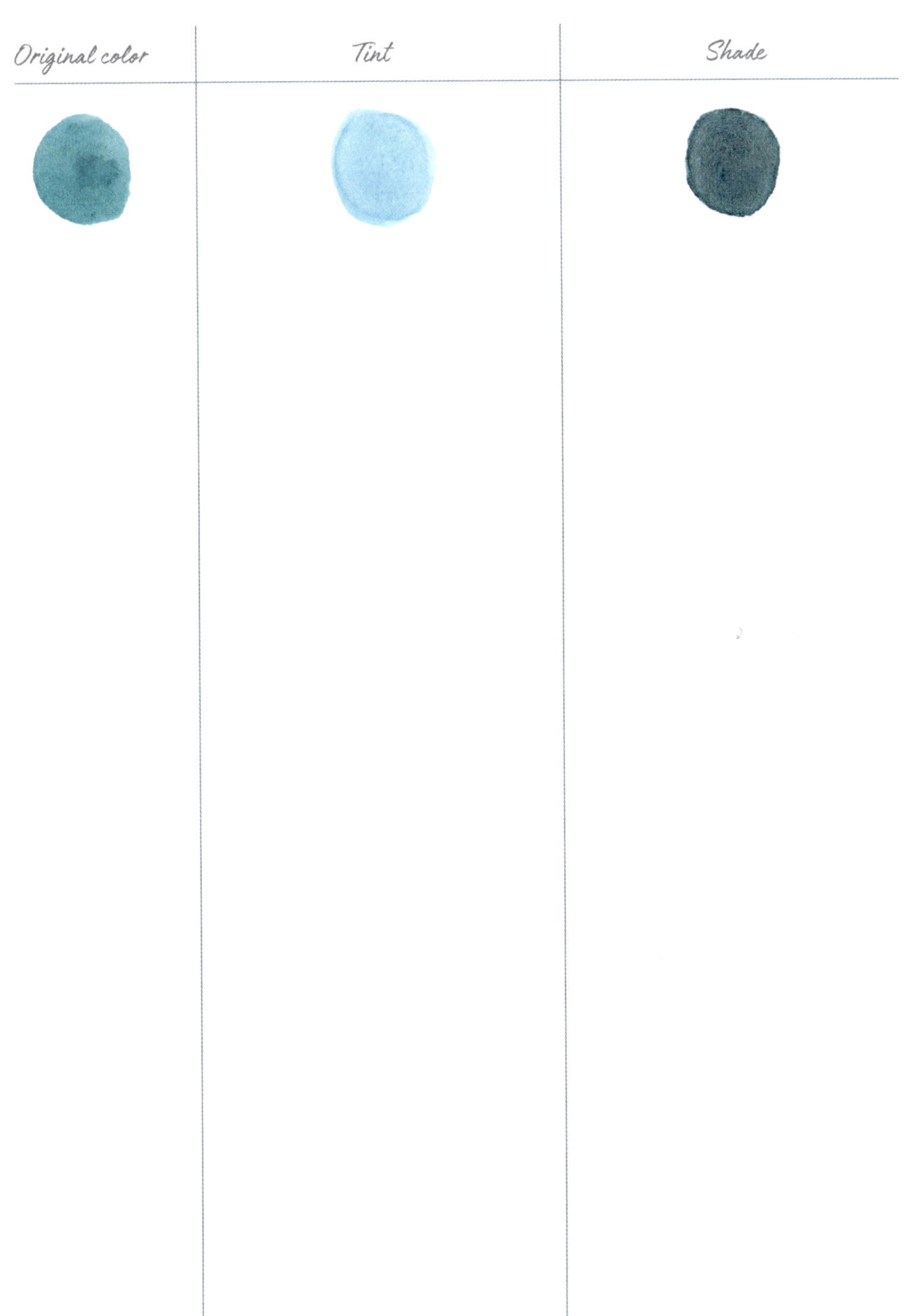

Original color
Tint
Shade

Drawing using a continuous line is a great way to practice looking at a scene in front of you, rather than just drawing what you *think* you can see. Choose a scene and three or four colored pencils that will help capture it. Each time you start a new color, keep the pencil on the page until you are ready for the next color. Try not to be tempted to lift the pencil from the page—embrace the challenge!

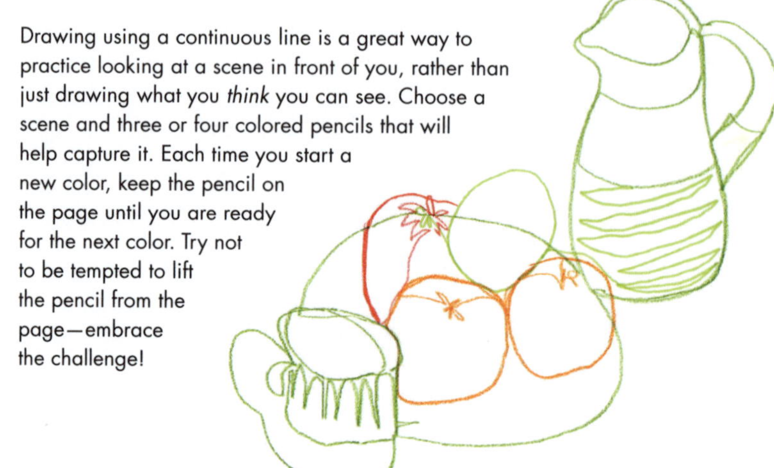

19

A color gradient is when a color gradually blends into another color. Make a gradient using watercolor paint; it doesn't need to be perfect. Start by selecting two colors that you'd like to blend.

Add a color at each end, cleaning your brush in between so the color stays pure.

Add a little more water to your brush and apply more of each color. It's alright if a little of the color from each end is left on your brush at this stage.

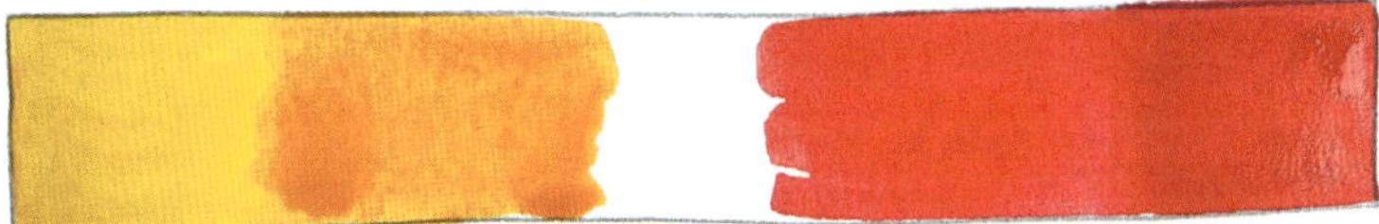

Then drag the paint from each side to fill in the middle section. You'll notice the colors start to run into each other and begin to blend.

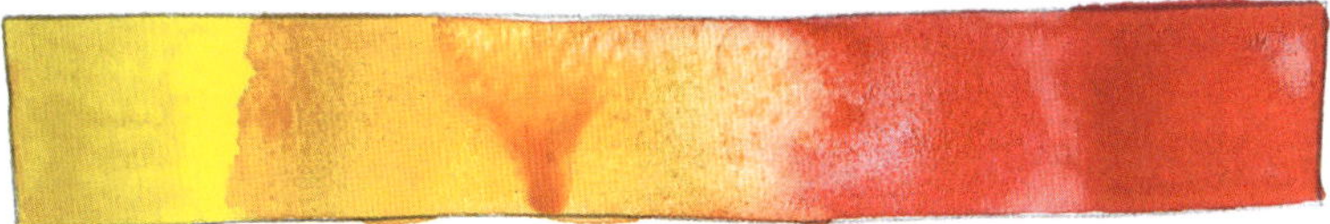

Continue blending the colors yourself, using gentle movements with your brush. It doesn't need to be perfectly smooth to still look effective.

Tip: If you are worried about the water bleeding through the page, you can prime the page first using clear or white gesso.

Create a colorful grid.

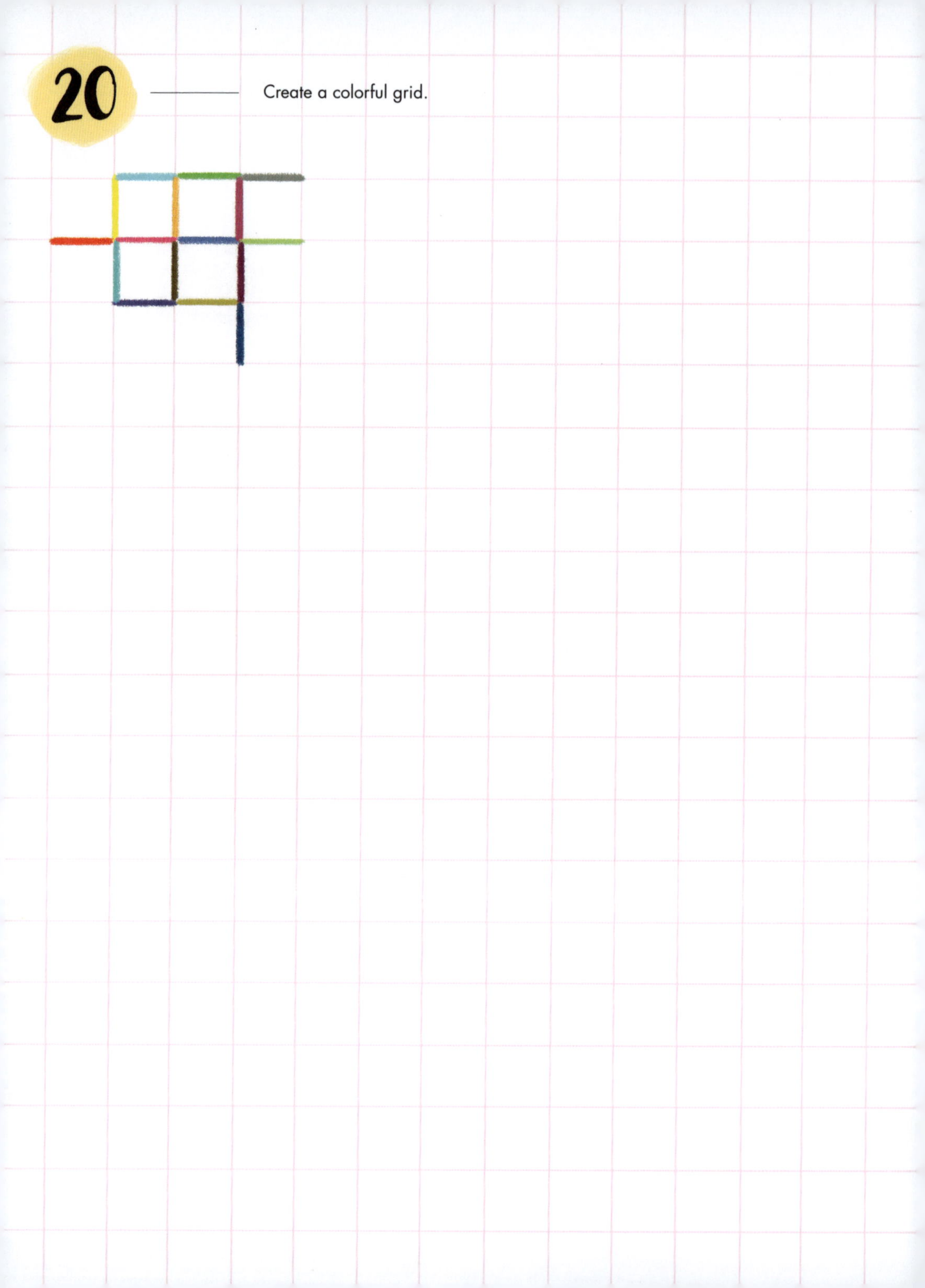

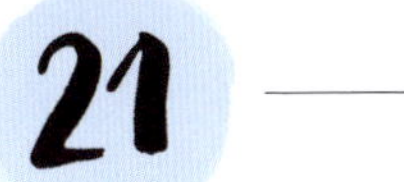

21 ——————— Practice blending colors together to create new hues. Use dry materials here, such as colored pencils, chalks, or pastels.

Tip: The colors can't be completely mixed like a wet material such as paint can be, so the effect can be quite beautiful as both colors show through!

Oil pastels   Colored pencils

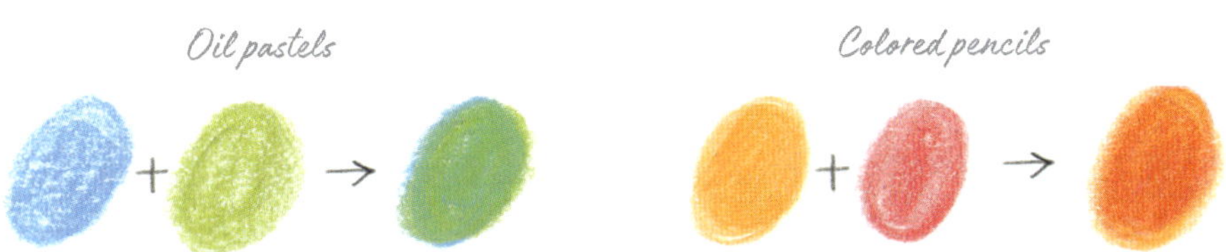

Tip: Try applying just a light amount of pressure to make your swatch, and alternate layers of color, e.g. a thin layer of green, then a thin layer of blue, then green again, then a bit more blue, until you are happy with the result.

Color palettes are collections of colors, which you can then use within your artwork and designs. Inspiration for color palettes can come from anywhere! You may see an outfit someone is wearing and think the colors look great together. Or perhaps some pink flowers look gorgeous next to a particular green. Spend time looking out for groups of colors you like, and create your own color palettes.

You could create grids and fill the boxes with your collection of colors—this can help you see how each color interacts with the others. Or you can just create swatches of color, loosely assembled in a group.

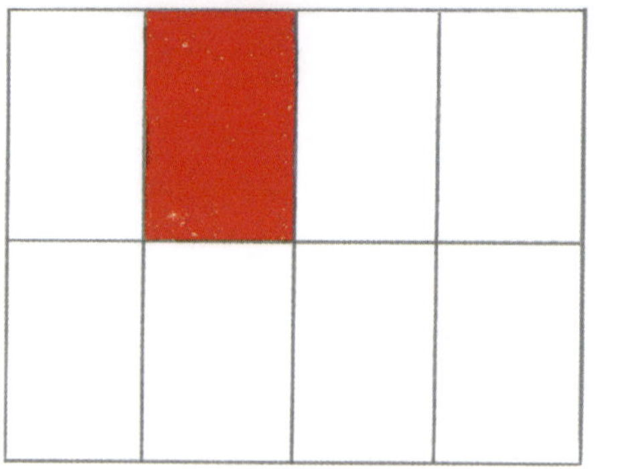 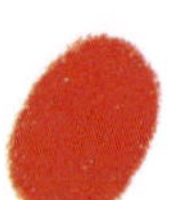

Select one color initially and build your palette around it. For a balanced palette, you can also include tints and shades of some of your selected colors, and perhaps consider introducing a complementary color too.

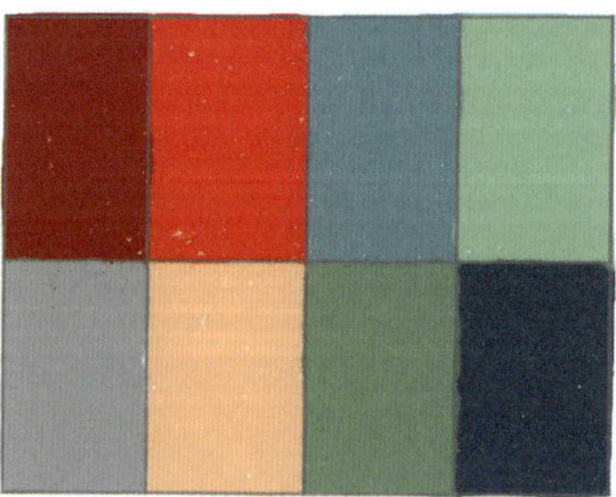 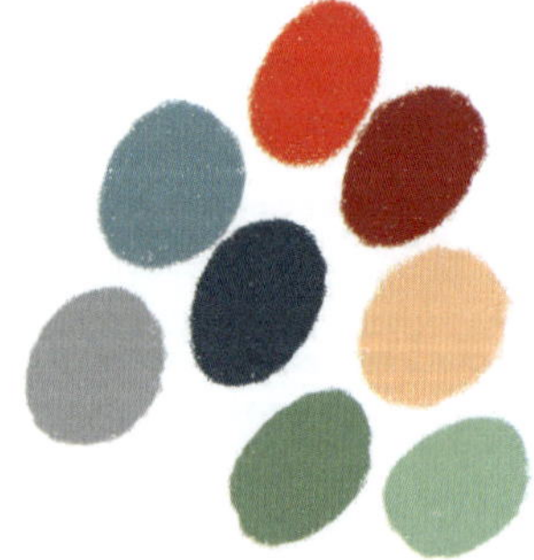

As well as including bright primary and secondary colors, think about which muted, neutral, and darker colors would look good in your palette too. Or just go wild and choose any colors you think look fun together!

23 — Practice using a small amount of bright, vibrant color on muted or dark backgrounds. Create little backgrounds using paint or cut paper. Once dry, add a flash of bright color, perhaps using wax pastel, colored pencil, or cut paper.

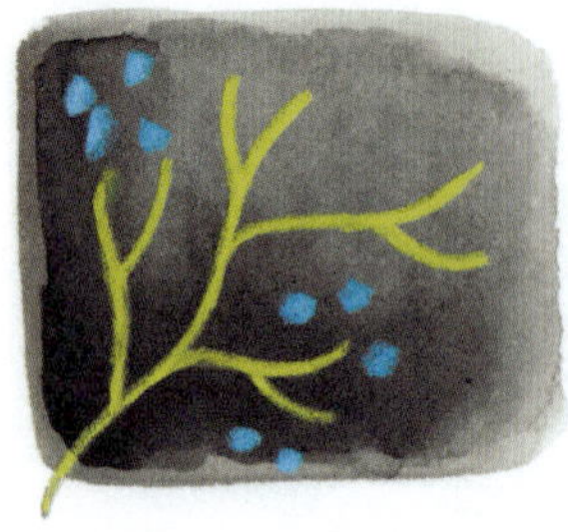 

Tip: You don't need to draw anything specific, just explore the effect of using bright colors alongside muted colors.

24 — Describe your feelings today using color. Perhaps the way you create the marks help express your feelings too—a calm mood might prompt you to make slow, sweeping marks, and any agitation might inspire you to make quick marks.

25 ———— Draw a colorful piece of clothing.

26 ———— Colors described as 'pastel' are pale, soft colors that appear creamy and subdued. They are often associated with tranquillity, and you can use them deliberately in your art to convey serenity. Make some swatches using pastel colors.

Analogous colors are found next to each other on the color wheel and can be used to create images that are satisfying to look at. For example, orange, yellow, and green are analogous and would produce a pleasing, fresh palette. Using your color wheel as a guide, create an abstract image using three analogous colors.

Continue drawing the pattern, and then add color to your design using only those in this palette plus one additional color of your choice.

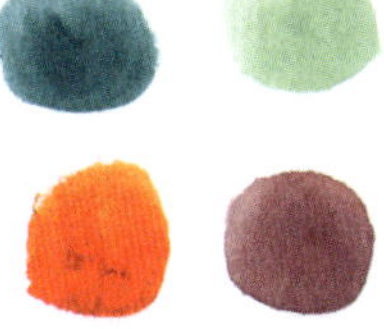

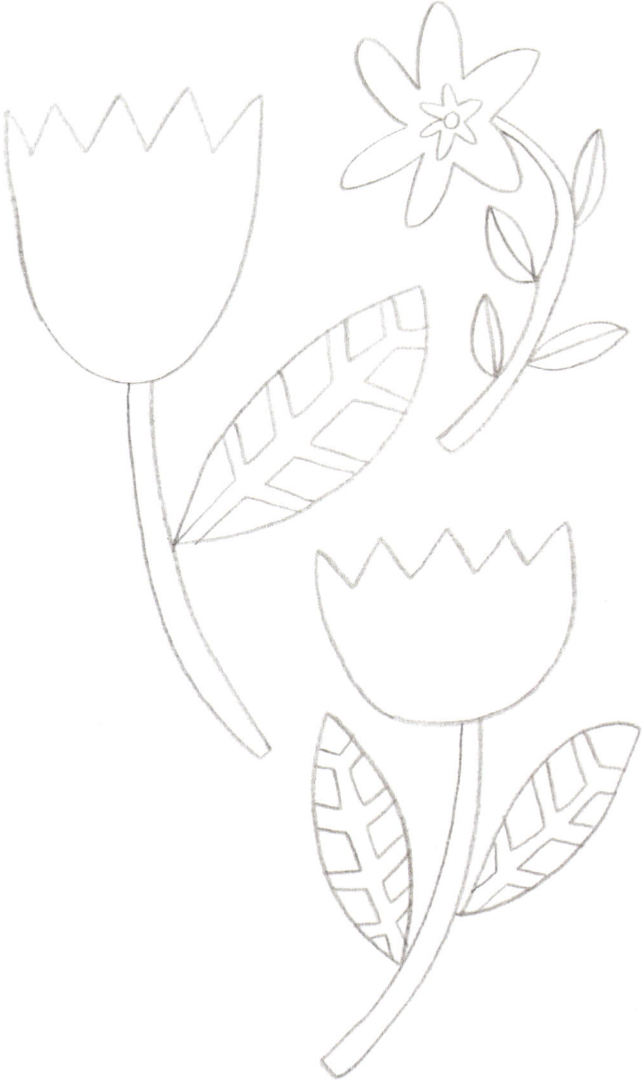

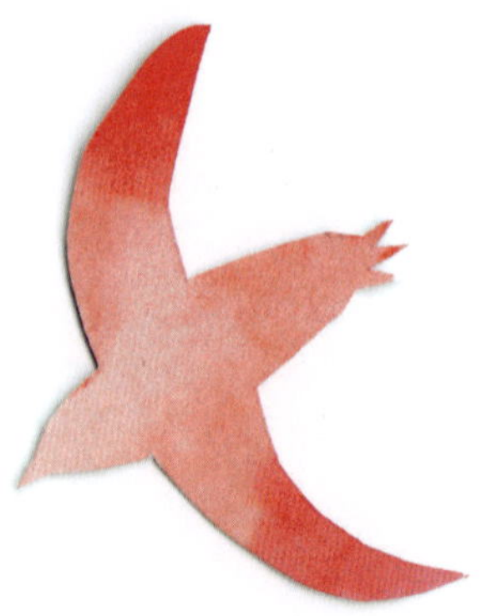

29 ———— Paint pieces of paper using colors inspired by different moods you feel. Use a separate sheet of paper for each mood. Once the paper has dried, cut out bird shapes and collage them here to create a flock of colorful birds.

Tip: You can keep any colored paper you don't use for future collages.

Creating a color palette can be a really useful starting point for pieces of art. Choose an image (perhaps a photo, or image from a magazine), and create swatches of the main colors that you can see. Once you've identified the colors, you could use your palette to create a drawing of your image or to inspire different artwork.

Tip: To make the swatches, try to find colors in your art materials that match those you see, or mix them yourself using paint.

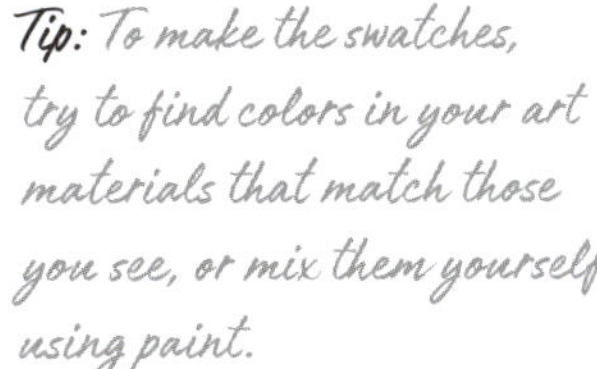

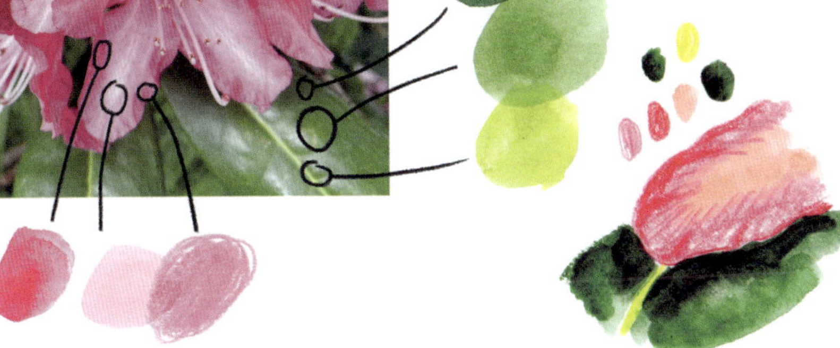

Look back at your color wheel and identify which colors are complementary (they will be opposite each other in the color wheel). Create different combinations of complementary colors, for example greens and reds or oranges and blues, using different materials. Are there any pairs you find particularly striking or appealing?

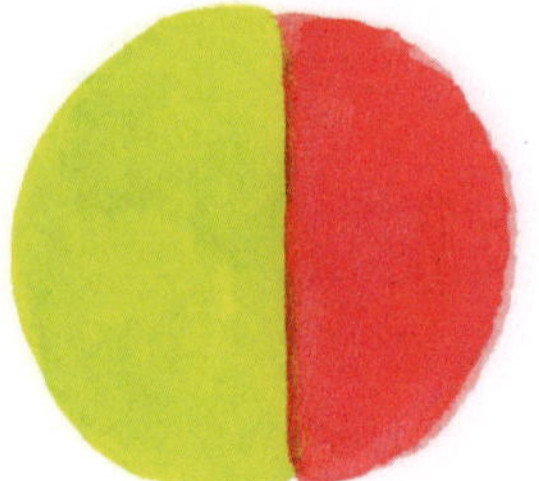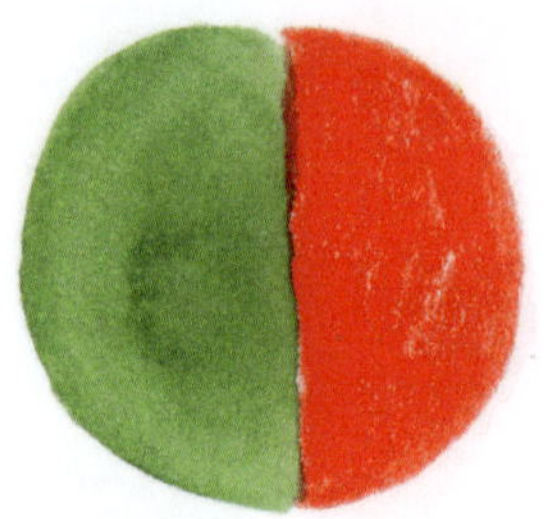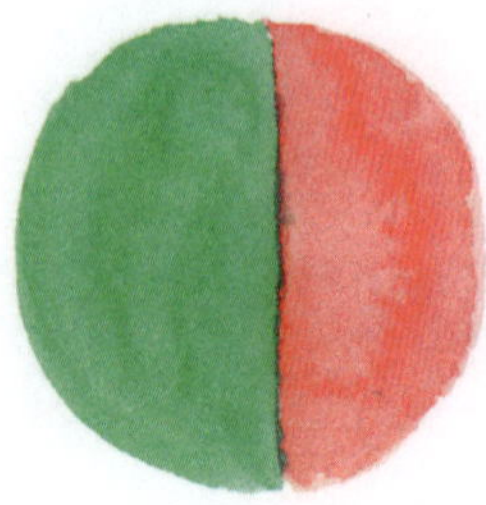

The sky isn't always bright blue, and grass isn't always green! Create a postcard of somewhere you love, but really think about what colors you can see in the landscape. Are there purples? Pinks? Yellows?

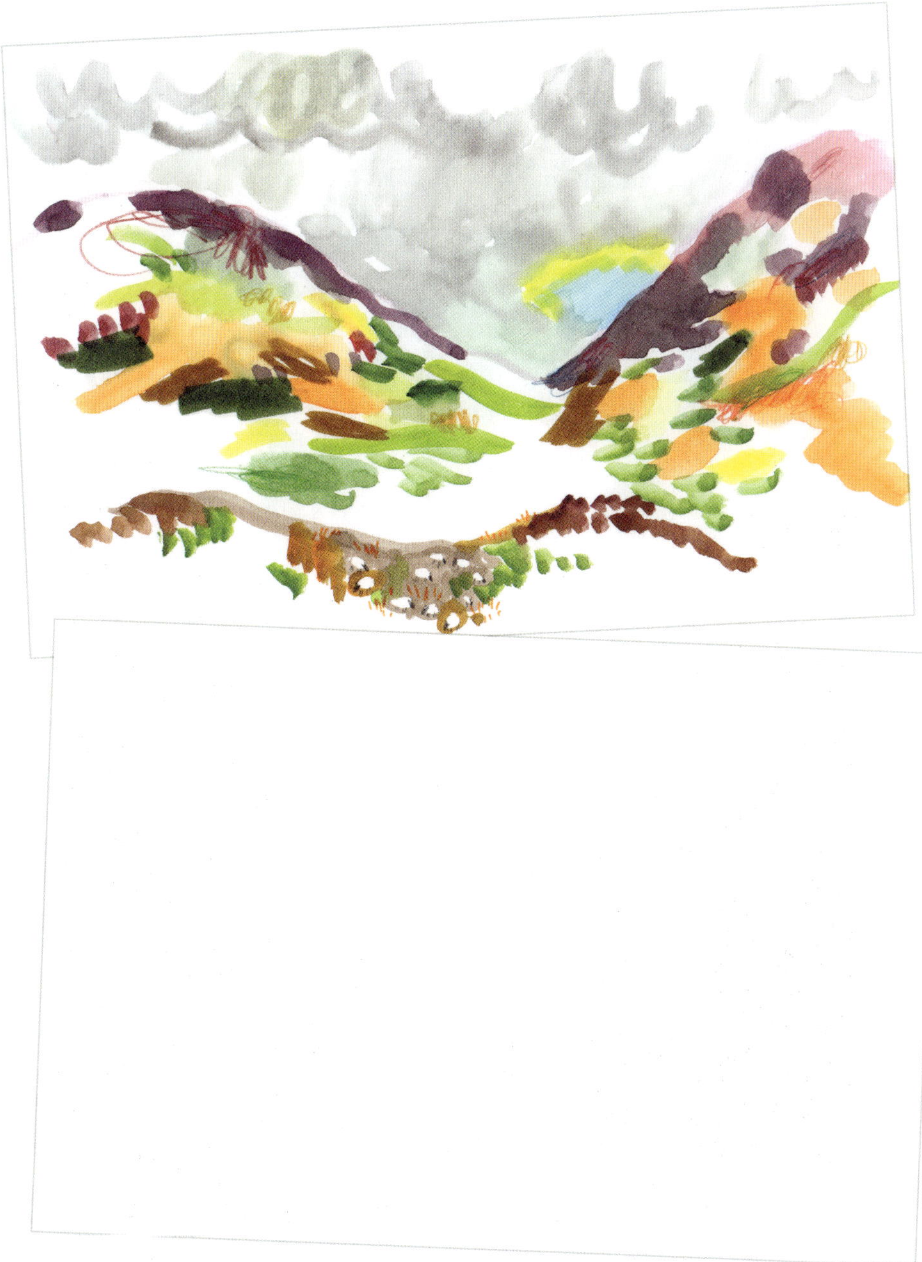

It can be fun to use a dark background as a starting point for observational drawing—it helps you take a fresh approach to your art, and light subtle colors suddenly pop! Create a drawing from observation on black paper. You could use pastels or coloring pencils.

Tip: Think about how the black can be used to make your image stand out— what object and colors will make for a good contrasting image?

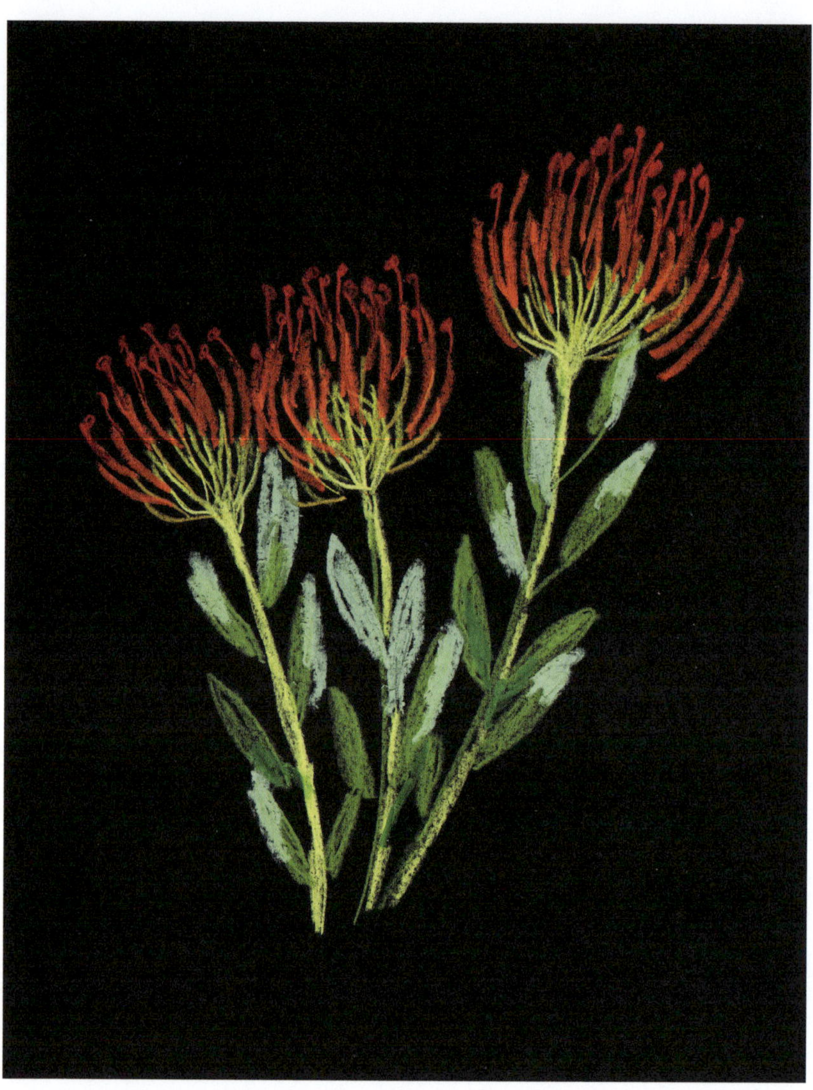

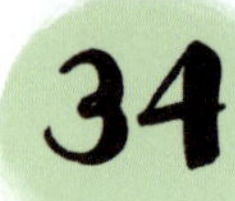

Find a piece of fruit and draw or paint it, seeing if you can avoid using outlines. Start by capturing the lighter colors in blocks, and then add the darker colors in blocks on top.

Tip: You could put your fruit on a brightly colored plate or piece of paper to make the colors stand out.

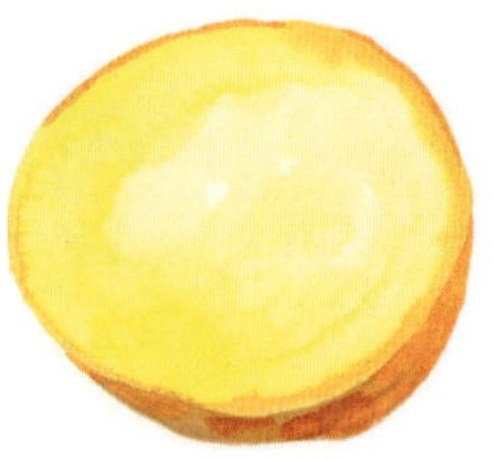

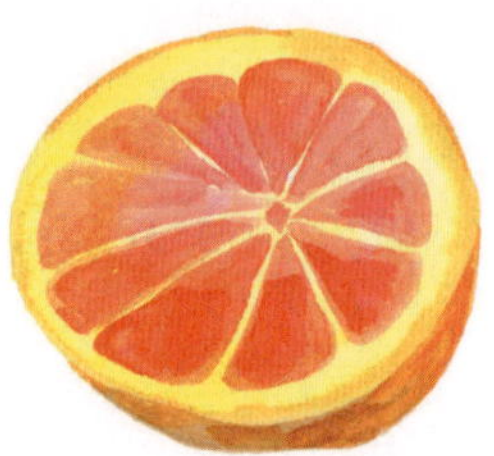

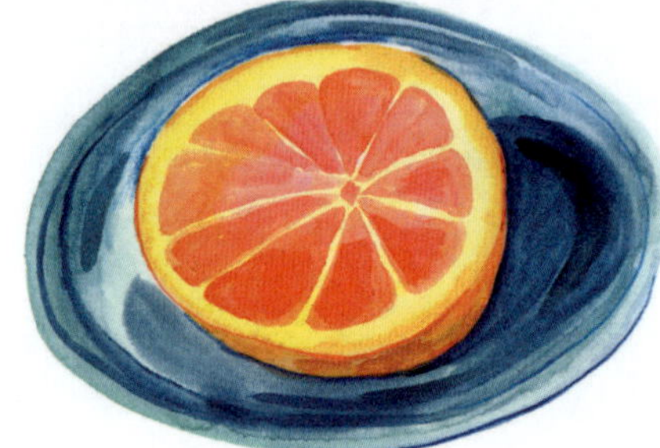

35 ———————— Write down ideas for potential colorful subjects in your artwork. For example: people, pets, things you enjoy looking at around your home, or perhaps things in nature that inspire you. Refer to this list in later activities, if you are needing a suggestion for a subject.

Tip: A 'subject' is the object or scene being represented in your art.

---

36 ———————— Which colors do you avoid using in your art? Encourage yourself to use them here, and consider why you avoid them.

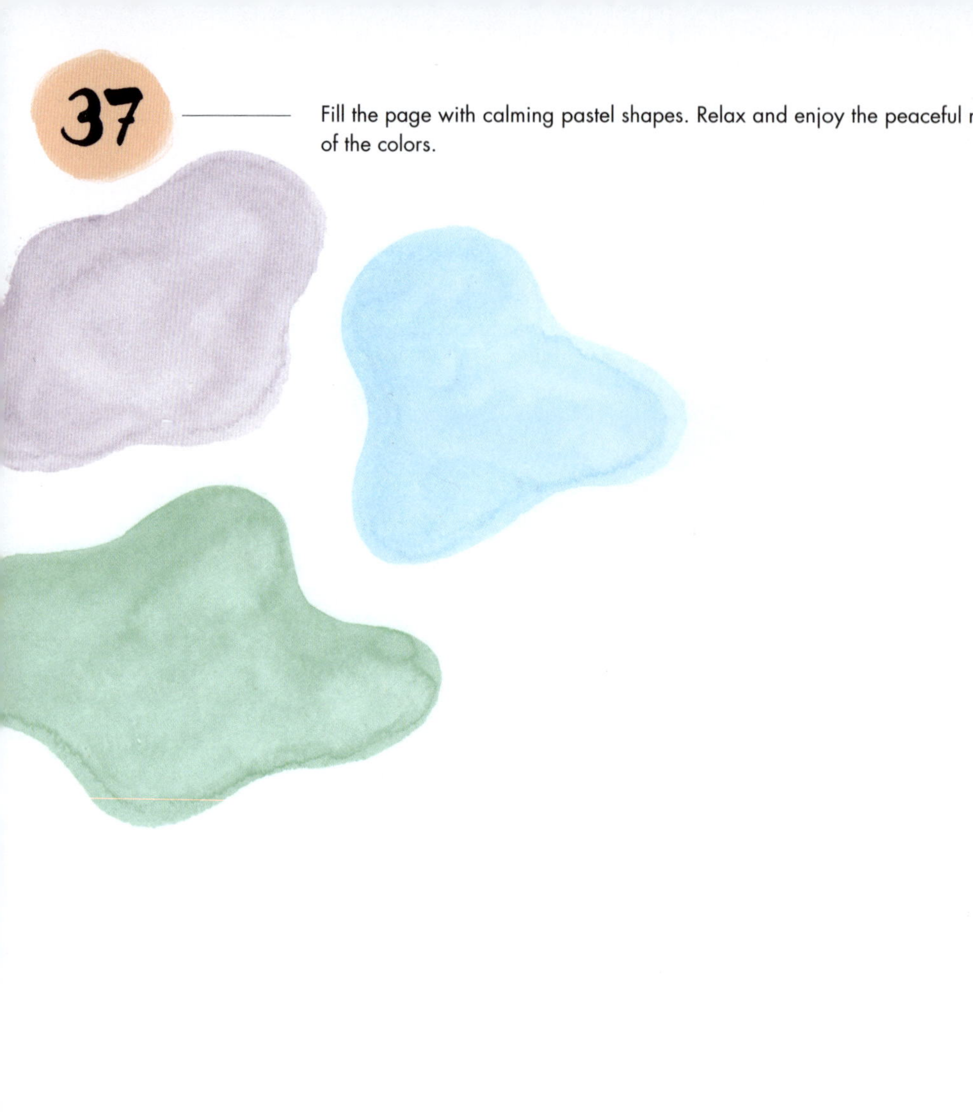

37 —————— Fill the page with calming pastel shapes. Relax and enjoy the peaceful nature of the colors.

The secondary colors are orange, green and violet, and are made by mixing two primary colors together. Slightly different reds, yellows, and blues will produce different hues of secondary colors.
Using paint and a palette to mix, create secondary colors here, noticing how varied the results can be depending on which red, blue, and yellow you use.

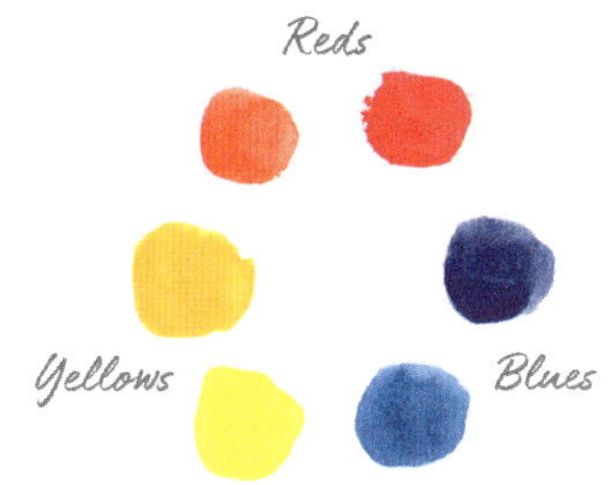

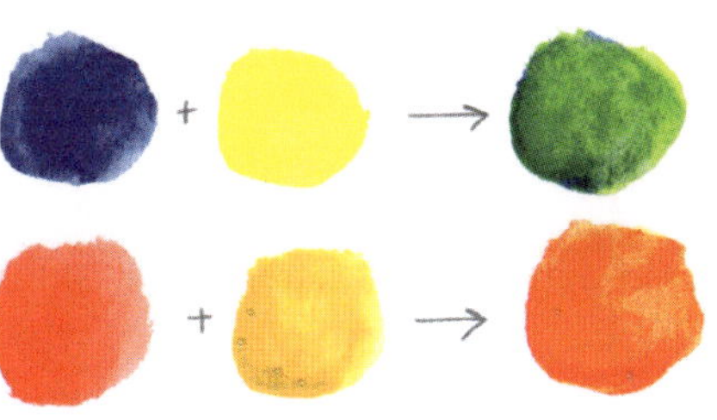

Add colorful scenes or designs to each colored background.

Draw some of your art materials and then color them in.

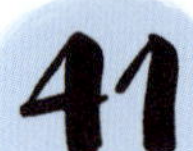

41

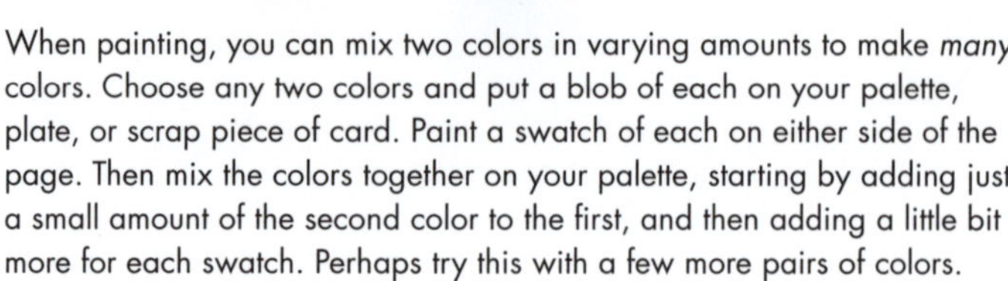

When painting, you can mix two colors in varying amounts to make *many* colors. Choose any two colors and put a blob of each on your palette, plate, or scrap piece of card. Paint a swatch of each on either side of the page. Then mix the colors together on your palette, starting by adding just a small amount of the second color to the first, and then adding a little bit more for each swatch. Perhaps try this with a few more pairs of colors.

Tip: Some of your swatches will only be subtly different!

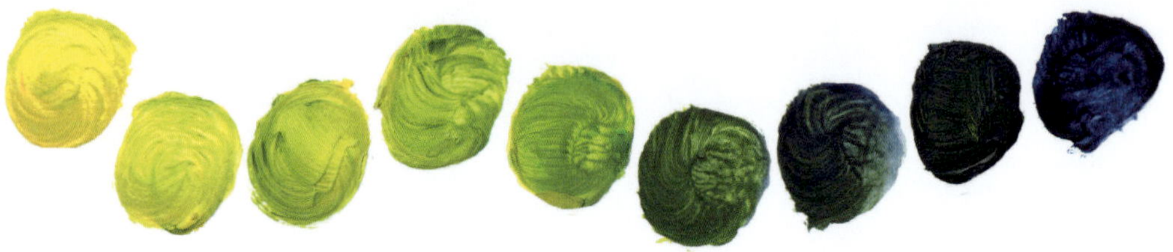

42 ———— Find an object that is your favorite color and draw it.

43 ———— Blue can evoke feelings of calm, healing, security, and consistency. Consider how blue makes *you* feel and create an image using this shape as a starting point.

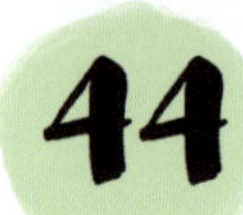

44

Find an object in your house which is comprised of complementary colors and draw it. You can work quite quickly, not worrying too much about accuracy, just enjoying the shapes you see.

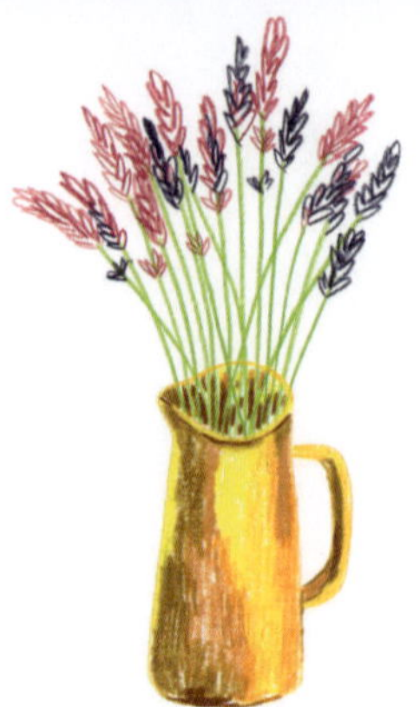

45

Add to the pattern to fill the page.

46 ——— Choose six things that you enjoy looking at.
Using any material, create palettes made
from the colors you see.

47 ———————— Design a pair of colorful sneakers.

48 ———————— Color this design.

49 ———— Create a portrait or self-portrait using collage. Use colored paper, cut-out magazines, or wrapping paper, or anything else you'd like.

Tip: The colors can be very abstract and bold, or you might try to match colors more closely to what you truly see—it's up to you!

Get messy! Put some paint in a mixing palette, or on a piece of card, dip your fingers in and make some fingerprints on the page! Once your prints are dry, turn the shapes into objects or little scenes.

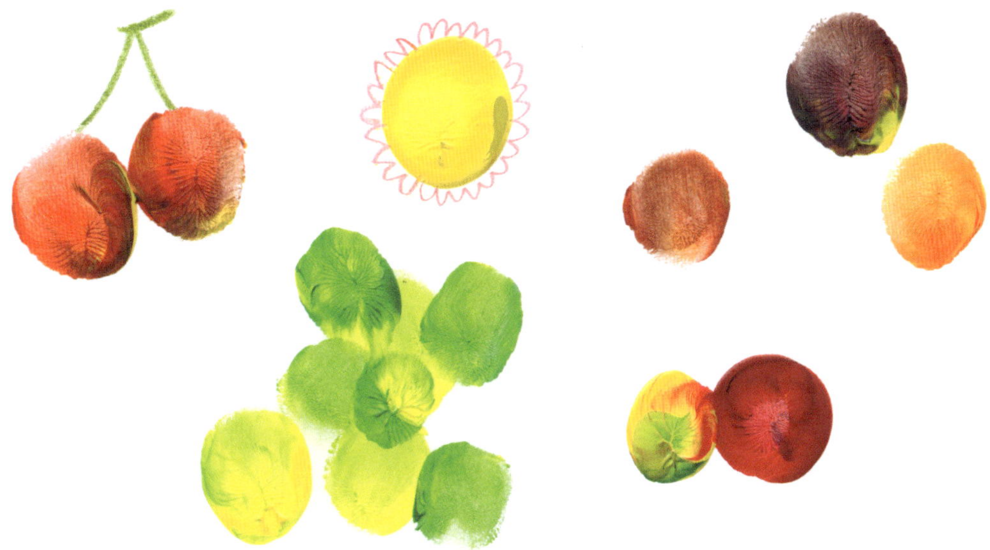

51

Make three drawings of a human figure using three different colors. Ask a friend or family member to model for you, and give yourself just one minute to draw them in three different poses! Work fast, trying to capture as much of the figure on the page as possible. You can layer the drawings on top of each other or draw them separately.

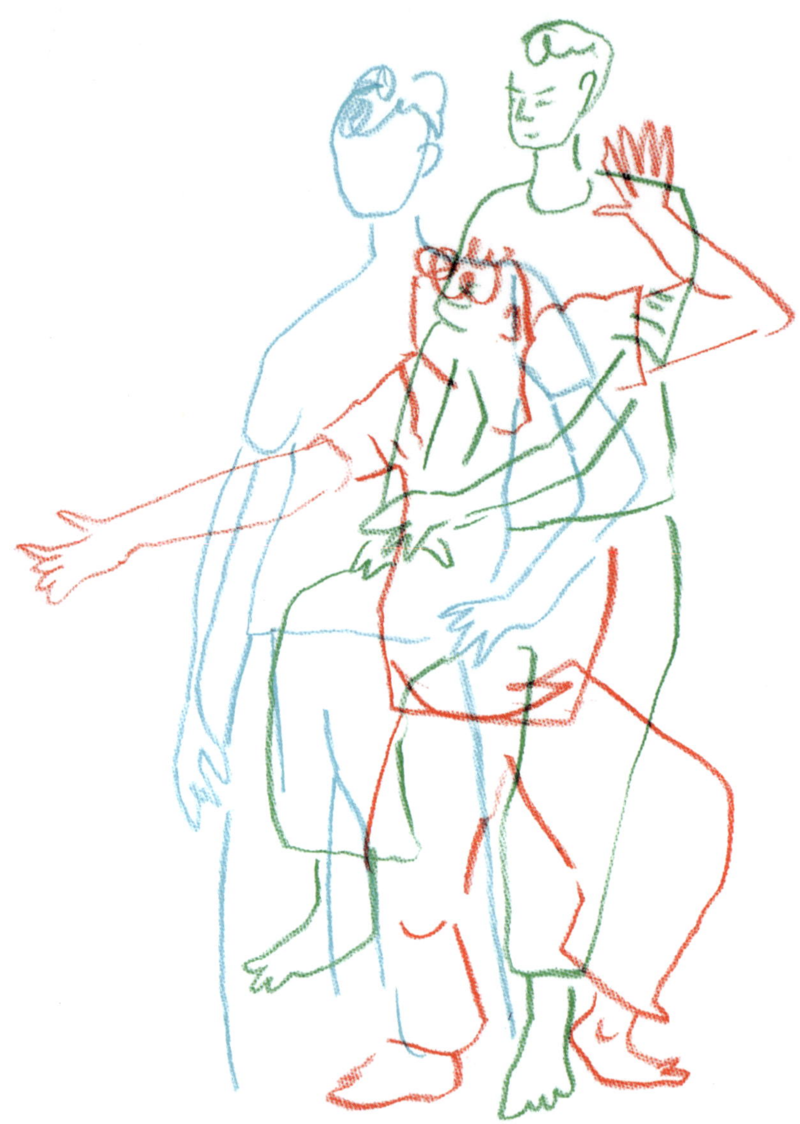

Tip: Using three random pre-selected colors means you will focus on the form of the figure, rather than worrying about choosing colors.

Gather some colored paints, a paintbrush, water, paper towels, and a clean mixing palette (or a clean, smooth plate), and use this space to practice combining paints to make specific colors. Try to match the colors below.

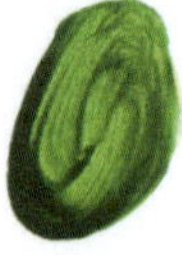 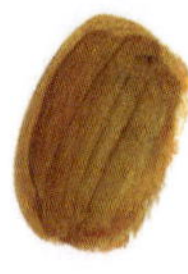 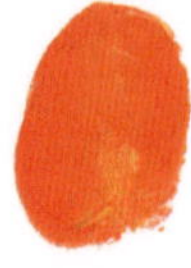 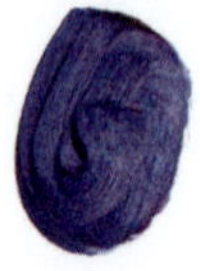 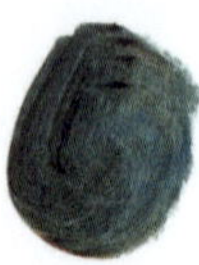

Tip: Start by guessing which colors might be in each color, then mix small amounts of paint together on your palette to see if it feels right.

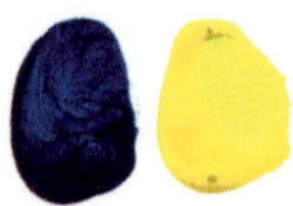 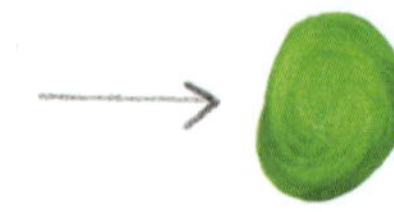

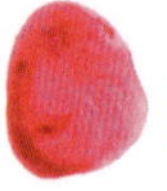 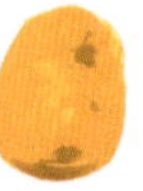 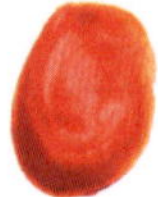

Mix blue and yellow to make green. Different blues and yellows will make different hues of green.

Mixing a small amount of magenta with yellow will make a cherry red.

Tip: Don't worry if you don't make an exact match for these colors—it's more about getting used to mixing colors and learning what results you can create.

Fill the page with colorful squares. Enjoy choosing which colors look good alongside each other.

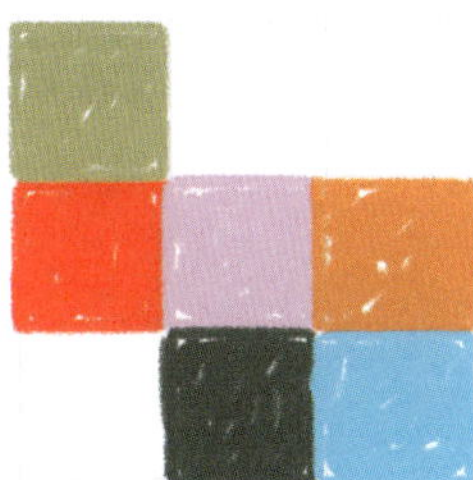

You can blend two or more coloring pencils to create new colors. These blended colors aren't truly mixed, as they are when you combine paints, and so they have a rich, textural appearance. Color each circle using a colored pencil to create blends where the circles meet.

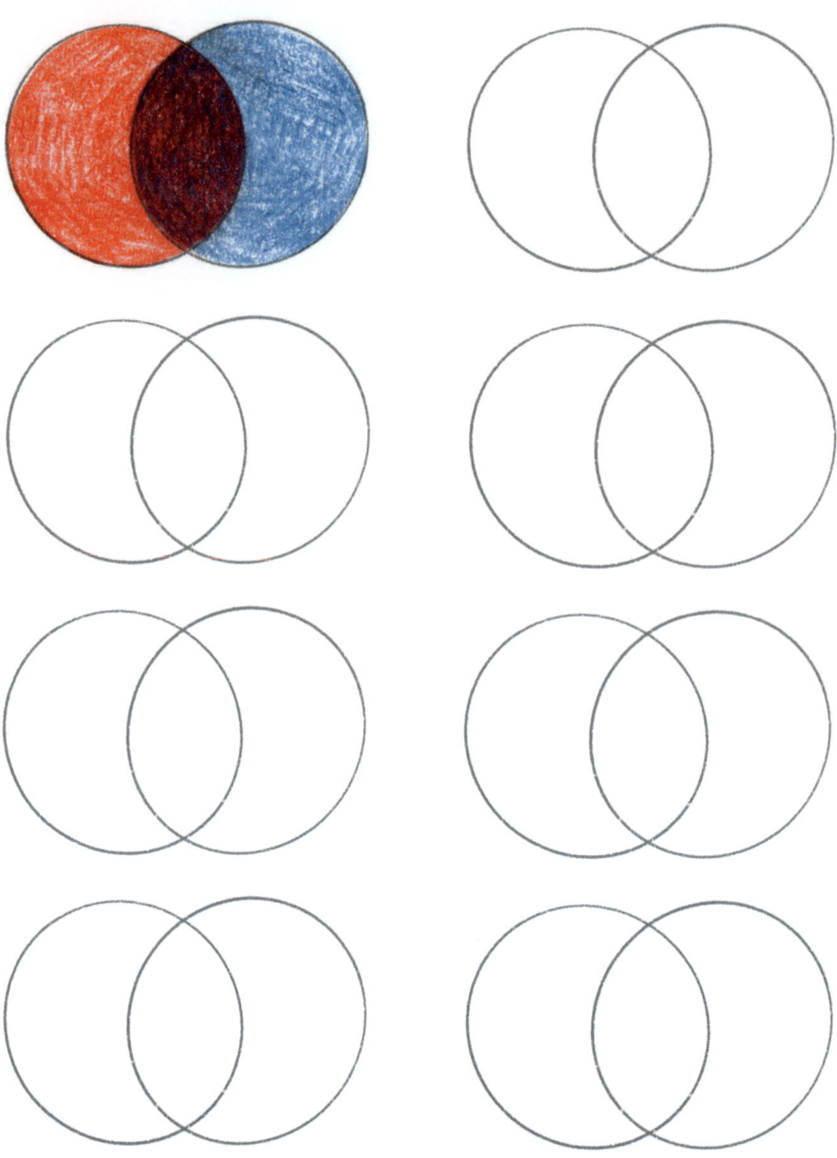

Tip: For a smoother, richer blend, add multiple layers of each color, alternating between the two different hues.

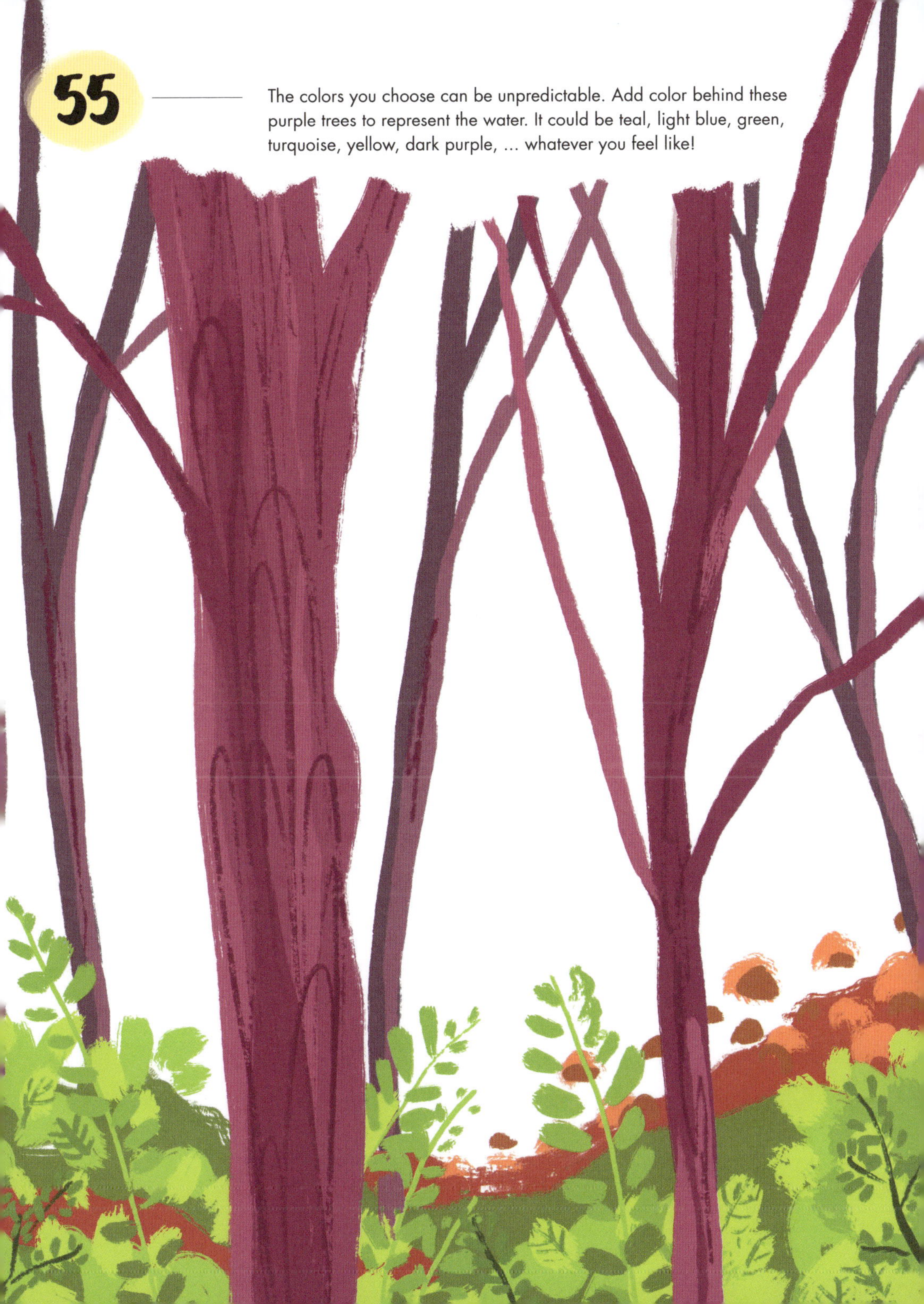

55

The colors you choose can be unpredictable. Add color behind these purple trees to represent the water. It could be teal, light blue, green, turquoise, yellow, dark purple, ... whatever you feel like!

56 ——— Off-white is a color too! There are so many variations of 'almost' white that you can use in your art. Paint lots of swatches of off-white. Consider how some have 'cool' undertones and some have 'warm' undertones, depending on how you make the white.

Tip: Mix very small amounts of color with white to create your off-whites. Try green, blue, red, yellow, … any colors you have to hand.

---

57 ——— Oranges and yellows can evoke feelings of warmth and joy. Create an abstract drawing using these two colors.

Create a painting around this image. Consider which colors will complement the orange.

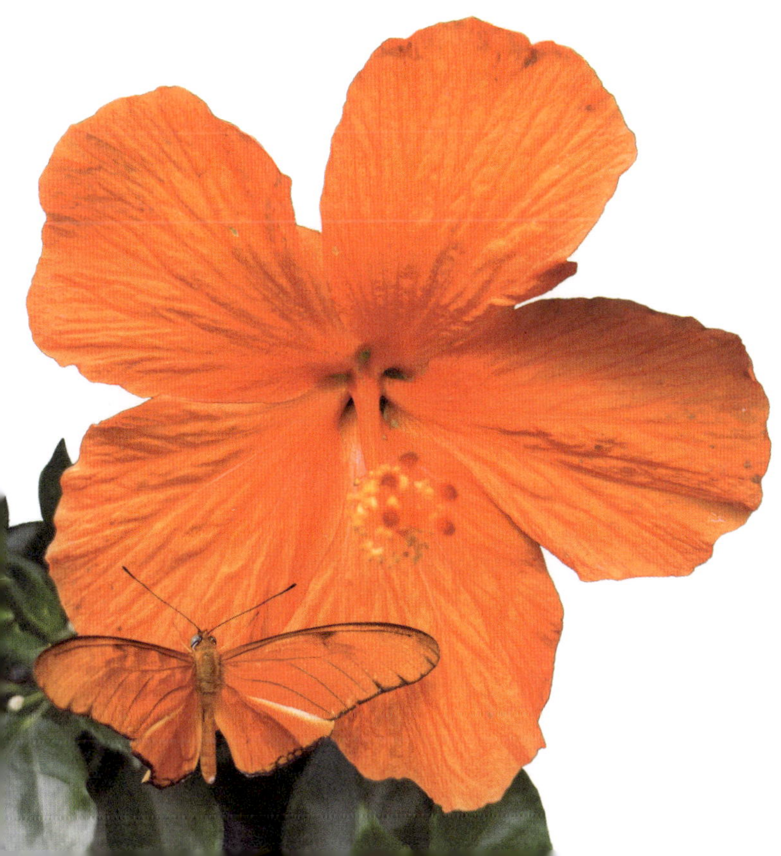

Neutral colors are earthy, natural colors—light tans, browns, olives, grays, and creams—and can be very calming.

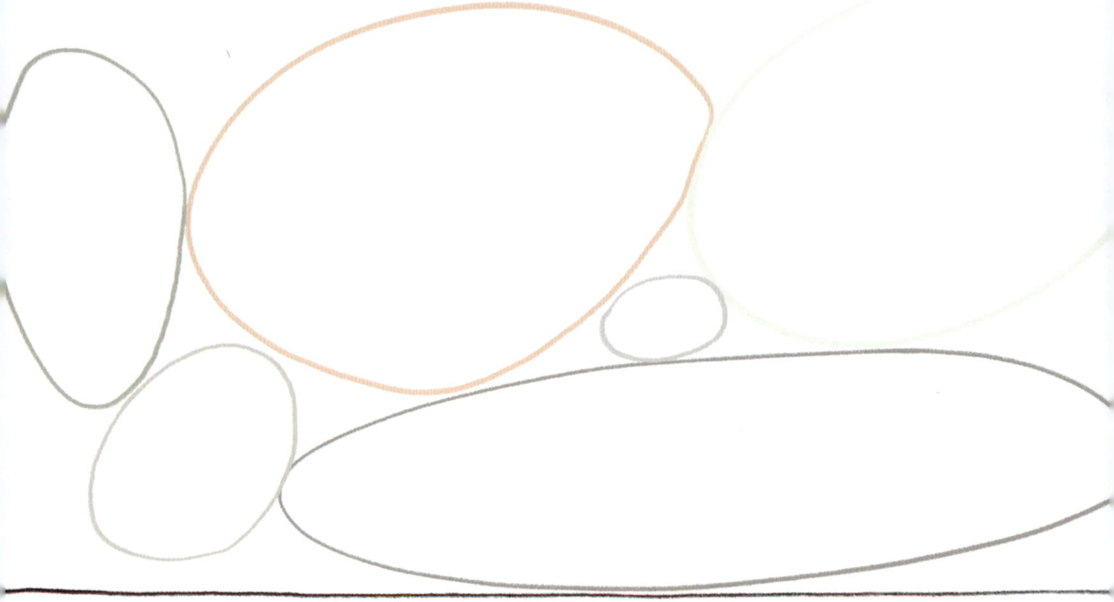

'Hue' is a word sometimes used interchangeably with the word 'color', although it specifically refers to *where* a color can be found on the color wheel in its purest form. A color's hue is a bit like the 'family' the color belongs to. Decide the hue of each of these collections of colors. (In your view, which family would the colors live with on the color wheel?)

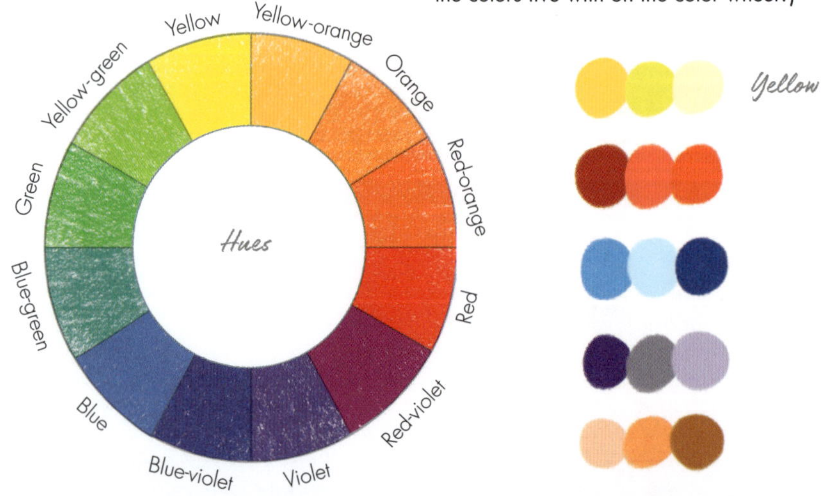

61

Put on relaxing music and create some abstract art, allowing yourself to be inspired by the music and how it makes you feel.

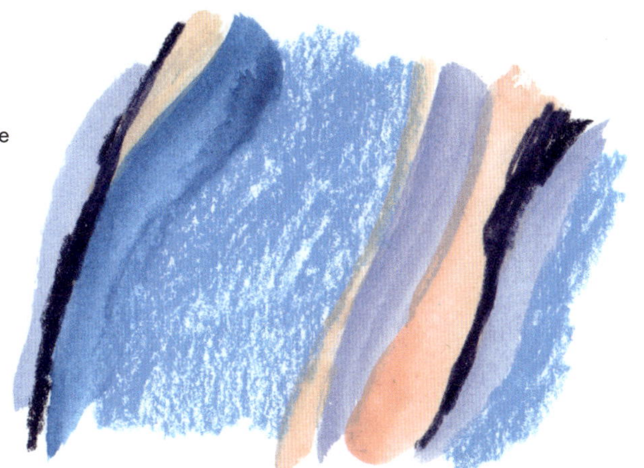

Draw some colorful houses.

63

Complementary colors, such as violet and yellow, are found opposite each other on the color wheel. By gradually mixing complementary colors you can make a complementary color scale. This scale can then become a harmonious palette to use in your art—any colors you choose from the scale will look good together. Mix a complementary color scale below using acrylic, watercolor, or gouache paint.

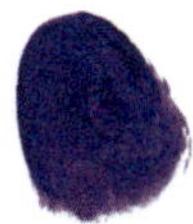

Choose two complementary colors from your color wheel and create swatches of them at either side of the page. Gradually mix a little of one color into the other and create a swatch below. Then add a bit more of the other color for your next swatch, and so on. Continue until your mixed color looks similar to your original complementary color. You may want to mix the colors in a clean mixing palette, and start by adding the darker color to the brighter one.

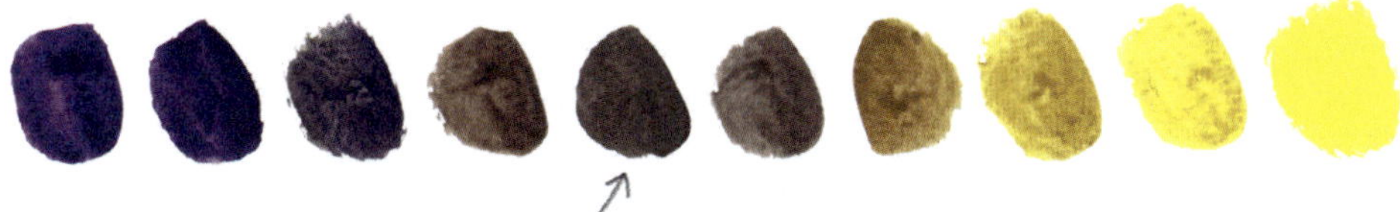

Tip: You can make browns and blacks by mixing complementary colors. All the colors on the scale are called 'neutrals' and when used alongside the pure complementary colors they originate from, the neutrals can form a calming background to help brighter colors stand out.

You can use the white of the page to add separation between colors in your art, and to help objects stand out. This is especially useful when the colors next to each other are similar. Make a piece of art, leaving a bit of white space between objects and the background.

Tip: Have a go at drawing the shapes you see as blocks of color rather than drawing the outlines. This will make it easier to leave a white outline around objects.

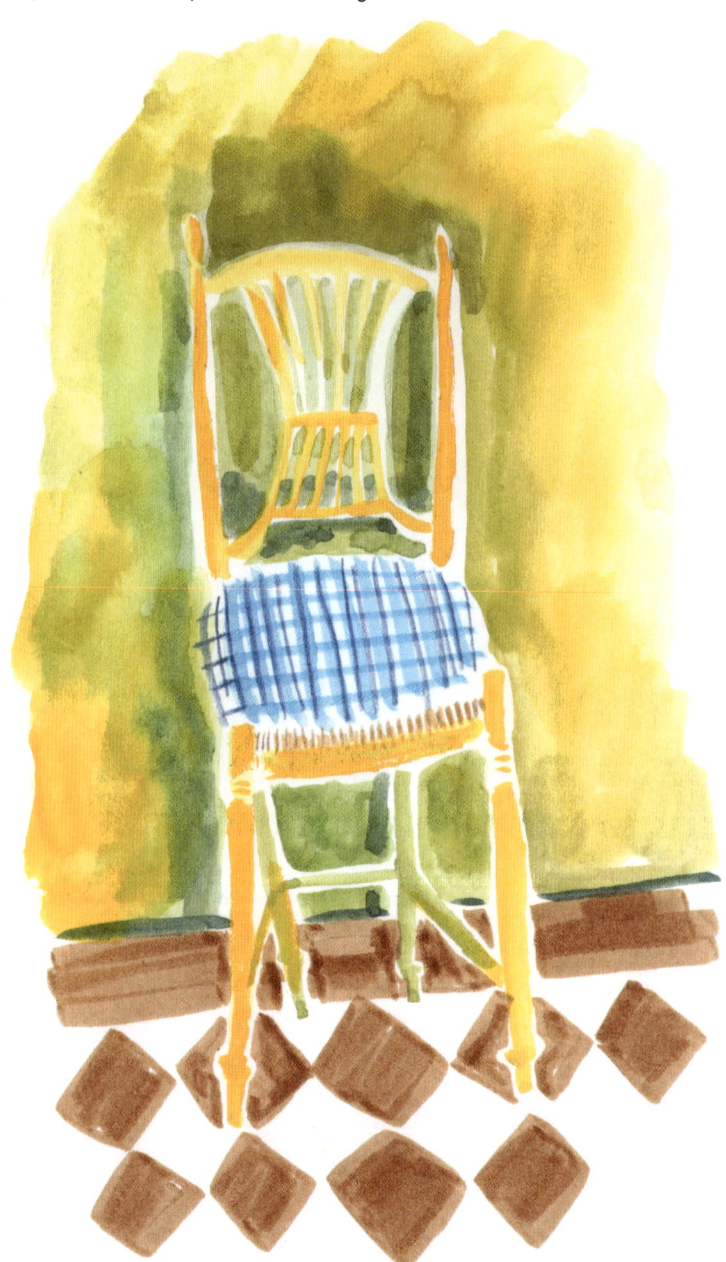

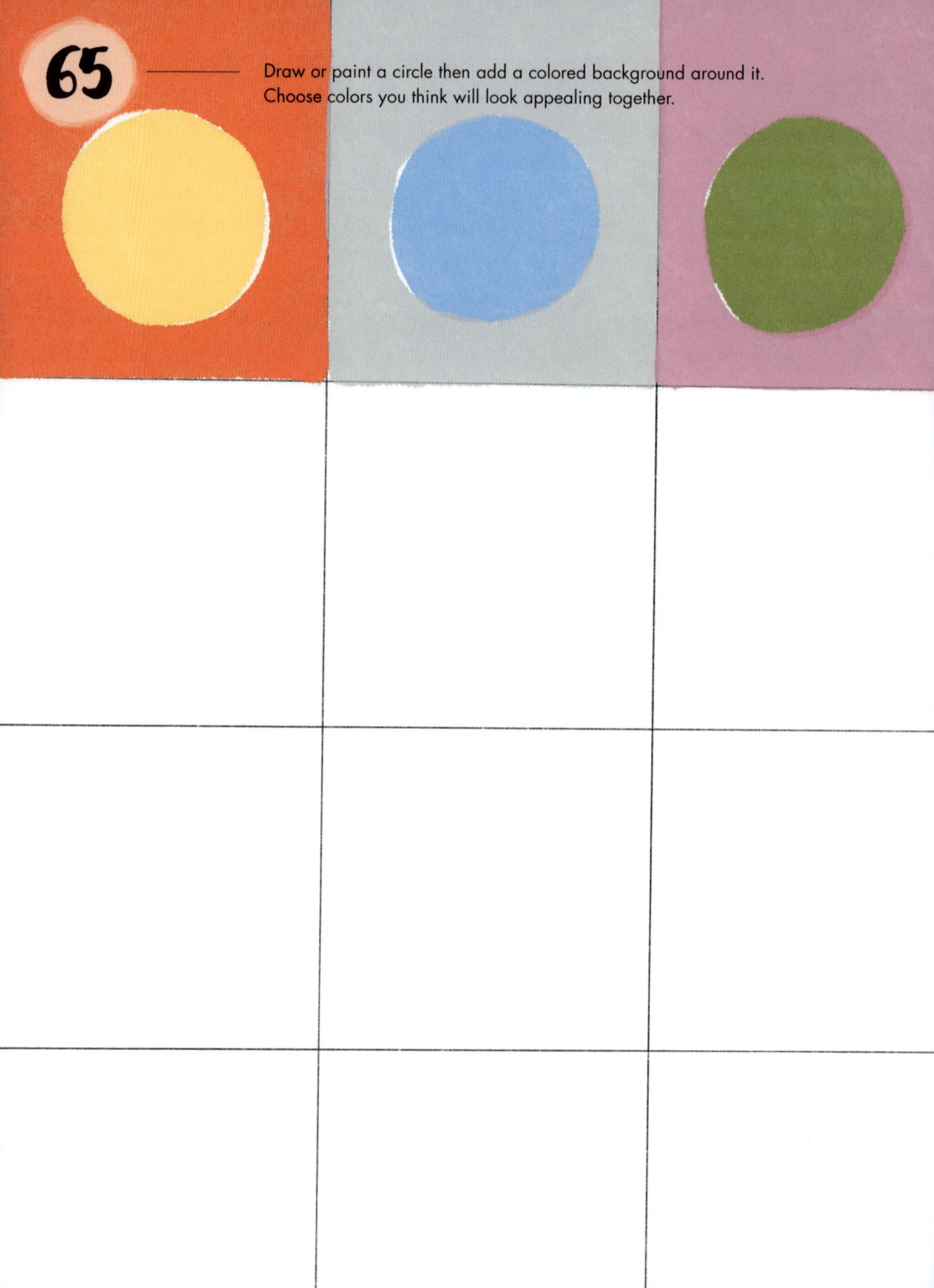

65
Draw or paint a circle then add a colored background around it.
Choose colors you think will look appealing together.

66

We can describe colors as having a 'temperature'. They can appear warm or cool depending on their position in the color wheel, and also their context (which other colors are near).

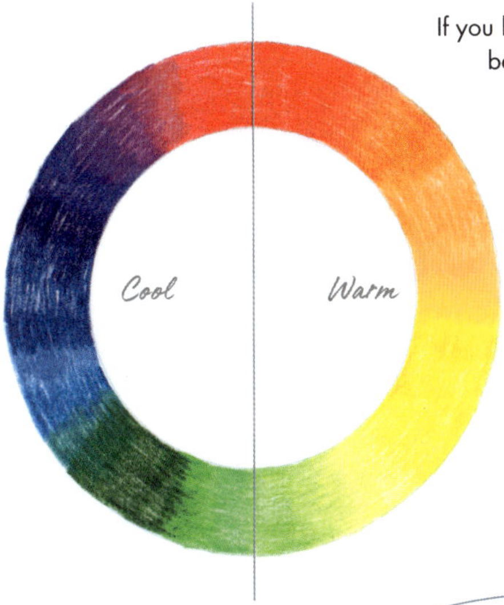

If you look at a color wheel, colors from red to green can be perceived as warm, and colors green to red can be seen as cool. Create your own color wheel and identify which colors feel cool and which feel warm. Have a go at blending hues.

Tip: This can be subjective. Perhaps you'll feel that some colors in the warm area look cool—such as a yellowy green. It's useful to know roughly which colors seem which temperatures, but you can make your own decisions about how you use them in your art.

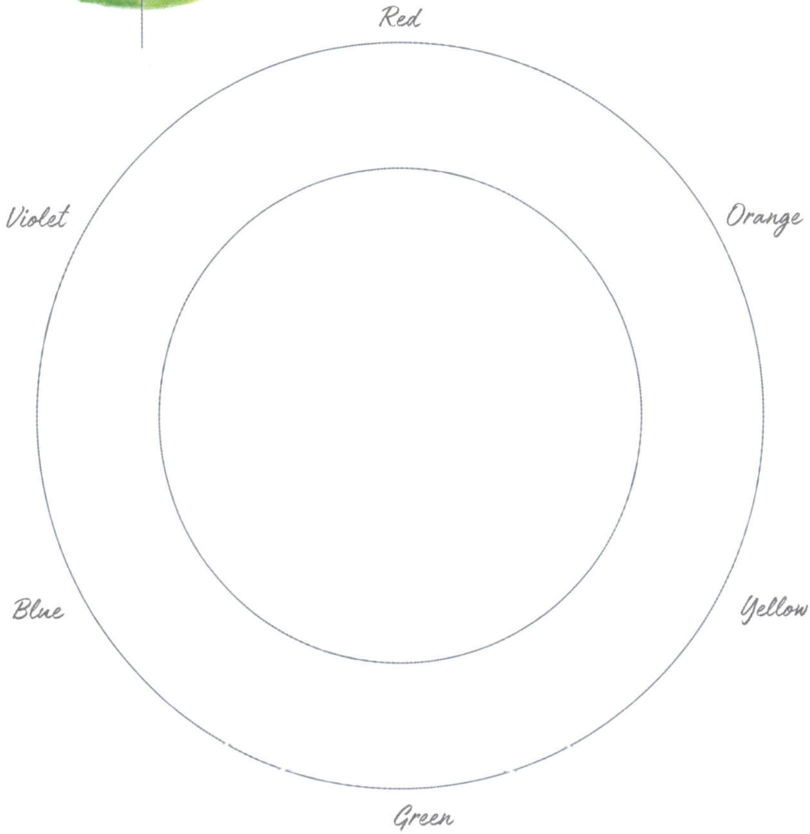

A color that appears very rich and pure is described as being saturated. A color that is more faded, as if some of the intensity of the color has been removed, is less saturated. We can make colors appear muted by mixing them with a little bit of their complementary color. Complete this diagram using paint to show pure colors, less saturated-colors and even further less-saturated colors!

Tip: Using a paint palette, mix a small amount of complementary color with the original color to make it less saturated.

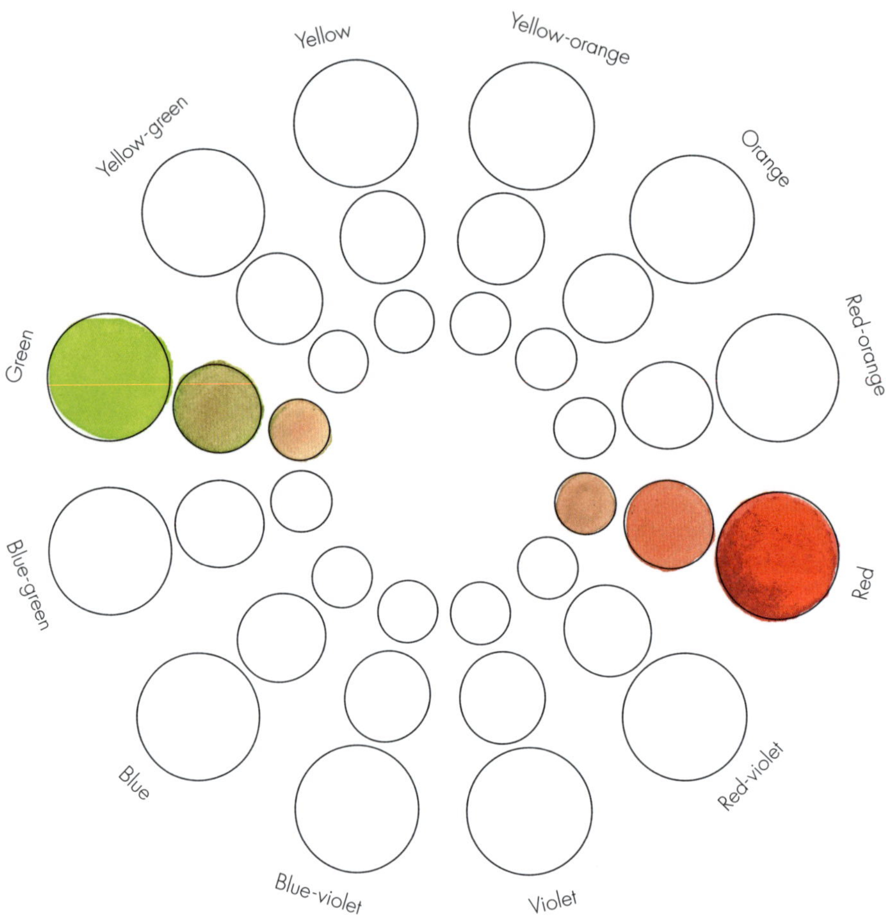

Tip: It's useful to know how to make colors less saturated as often, when looking at an object, you can see the pure, intense colors but also less saturated colors as a result of the light conditions around it.

Use different browns to create the form of a tree. You could add leaves in a variety of greens, or more trees to make a forest.

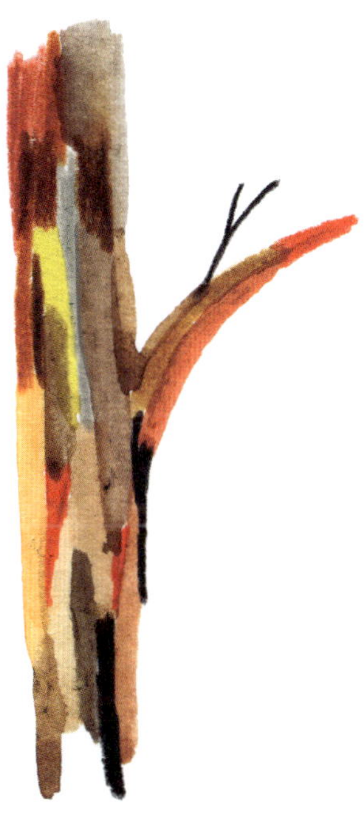

69 ——————— Paint a rainbow.

70 — Take some time to look for color around your home. Choose a corner and paint it, paying particular attention to the vibrant colors you can see, to create an energetic image.

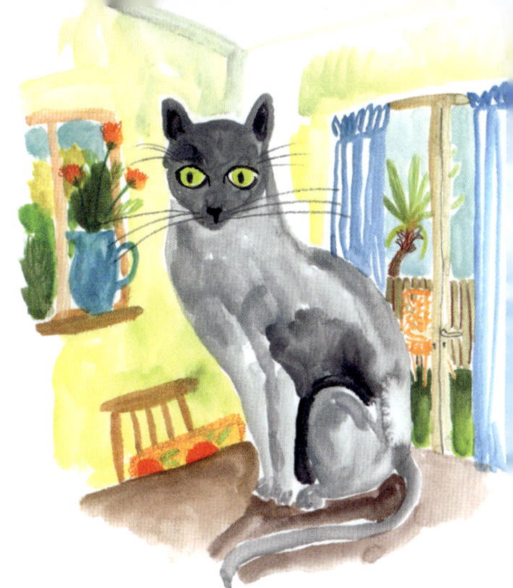

Frames don't have to be plain! Create some mini abstract artworks and then design colorful frames.

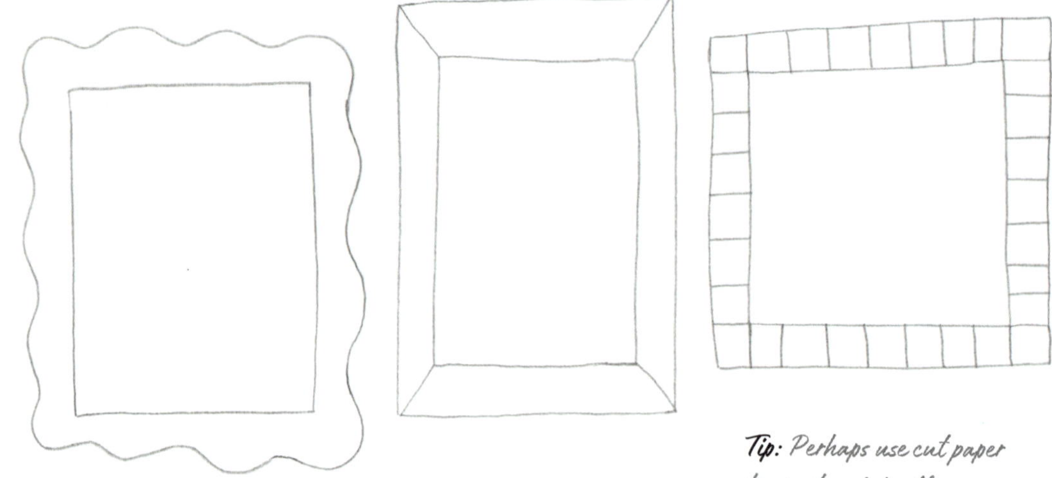

Tip: Perhaps use cut paper to create mini collages within the frames.

Paint or draw the sky you can see today, capturing all the colors you notice.

Different colors can suggest different emotions—and there's no right or wrong answer as it depends on how *you* perceive them. Consider the emotion each of these colors could be representing, and draw an expression to match.

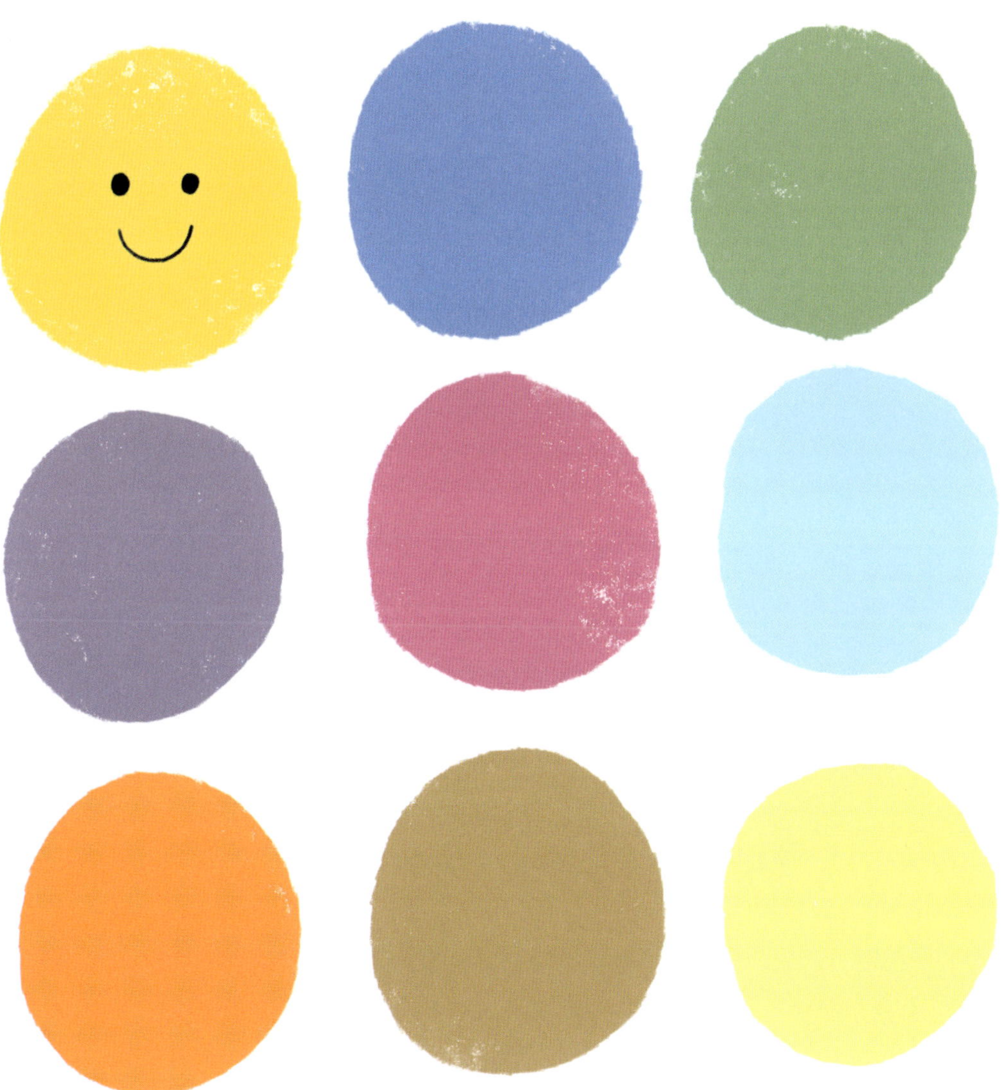

Create a painting of an object using three colors. Combine your three colors in a mixing palette to create new hues.

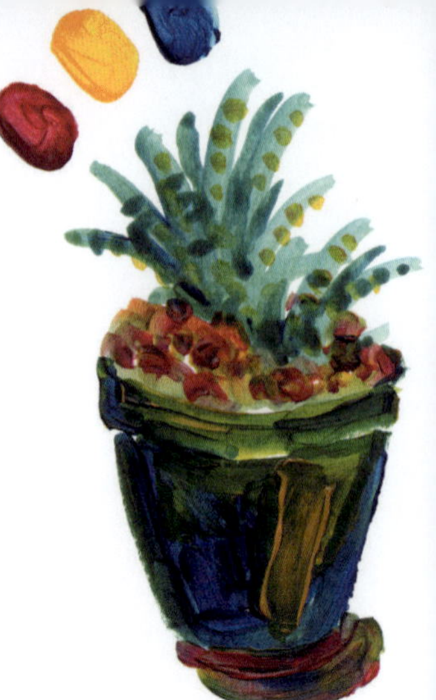

'Clean' colors are those that look fresh and pure, and 'dirty' colors are muddy, muted colors. It can be useful to identify and use clean *and* dirty colors in art. They can be used alongside each other to create balance, and using dirty colors around a clean color will make it stand out. Decide whether the colors you have are clean or dirty, and add them to the grid.

Clean colors	*Dirty colors*
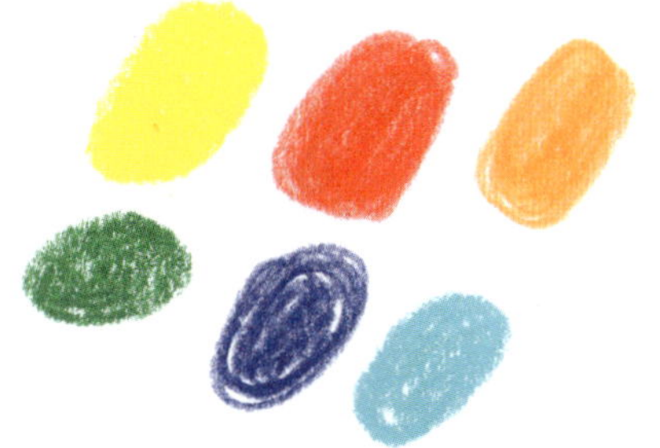	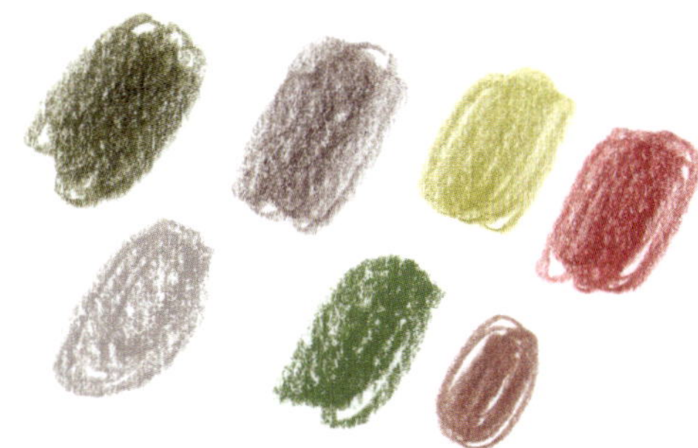

Tip: Whether a color is clean or dirty is subjective—there's no wrong answer.

76

Paint a portrait using patches of bold color as your starting point. You could look at a photograph or observe from life.

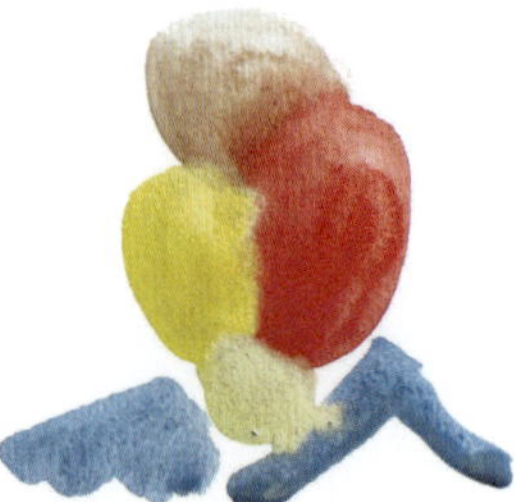 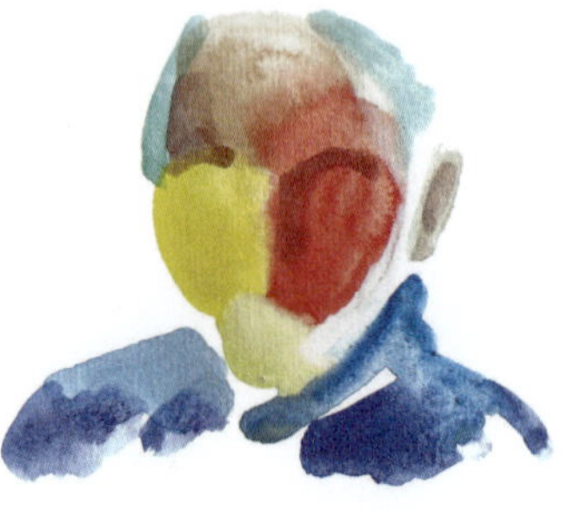 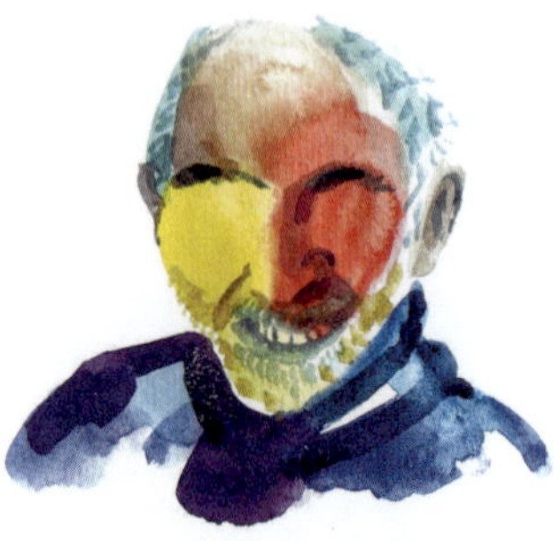

Begin by drawing blobs of color, roughly marking out the areas of the face. Choose darker colors for areas of the face that are in shadow.

Then add more definition to the face with colored marks— map out the key features and some areas of tone.

Continue adding detail, perhaps in a material that allows you more precision— a colored pencil or pen.

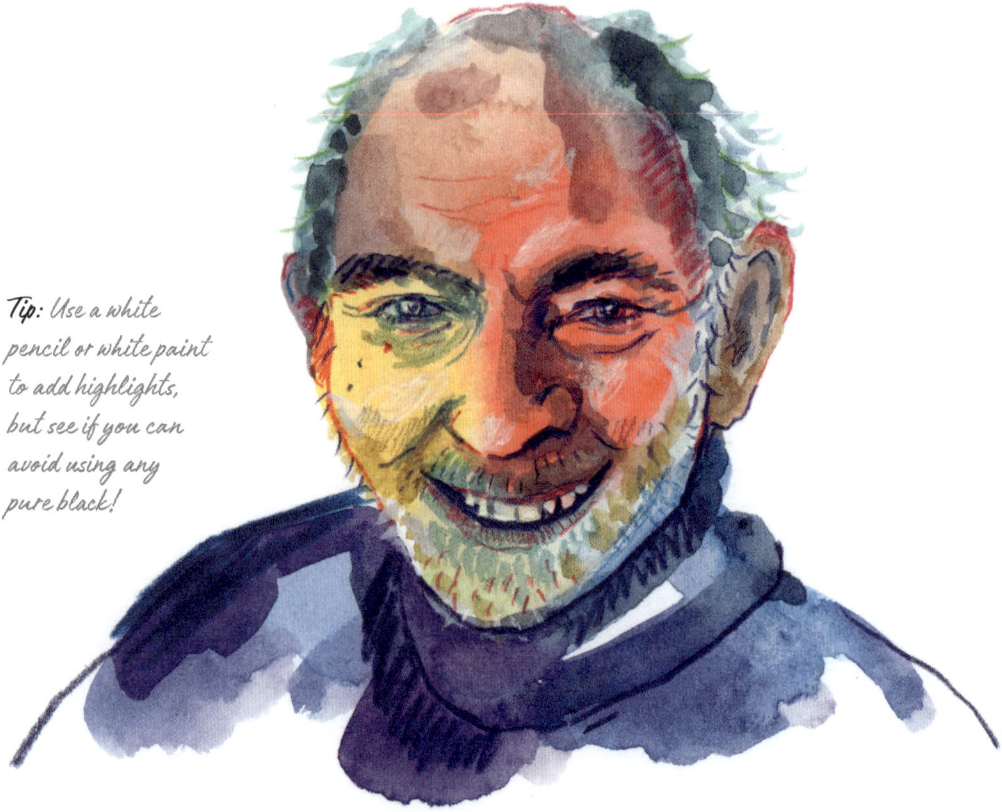

Tip: Use a white pencil or white paint to add highlights, but see if you can avoid using any pure black!

77 ———— Create a wallpaper design using three to five colors.

78 ———— Think about how you could introduce more color into a room in your home. Perhaps a small glass or vase of flowers, or putting a colorful postcard in a clipframe. Write down some ideas here.

79 — Use this swipe of blue paint to inspire a picture.

80

Paint a beautiful view, enjoying and exaggerating the variety of colors you can see. Paint the colors in blocks to create a tapestry of color.

Tip: You could use an image from the internet, draw from life or from a photo.

Notice how the shadow on an object usually isn't just gray or black, but a darker, less-saturated tone of the color of the object. Choose a simple object such as a cup, and make a tonal drawing of the colors you see.

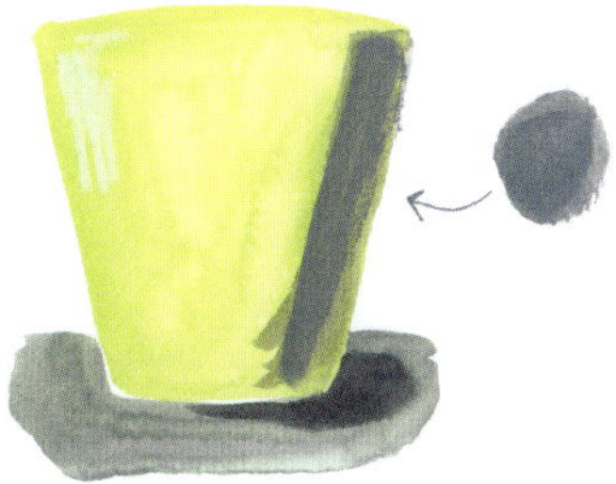

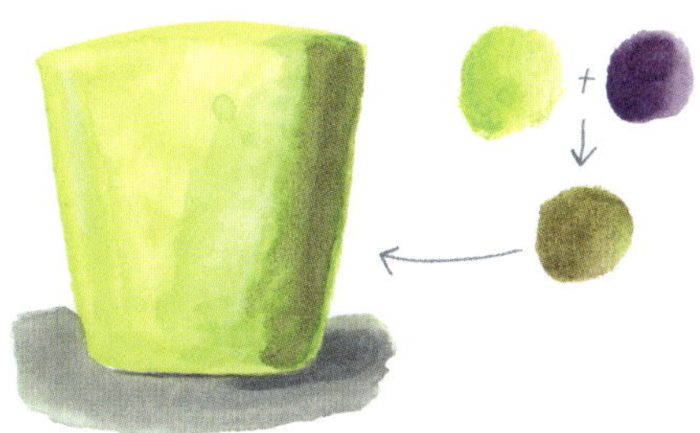

If the object is colored, using gray or black for the shadow will make the image appear flat and lifeless.

So instead, mix the brightest color you see with its complementary color and use this tone for the shadow. It will create a more harmonious image, as well as being a more accurate color.

Design some colorful mugs based on different moods.

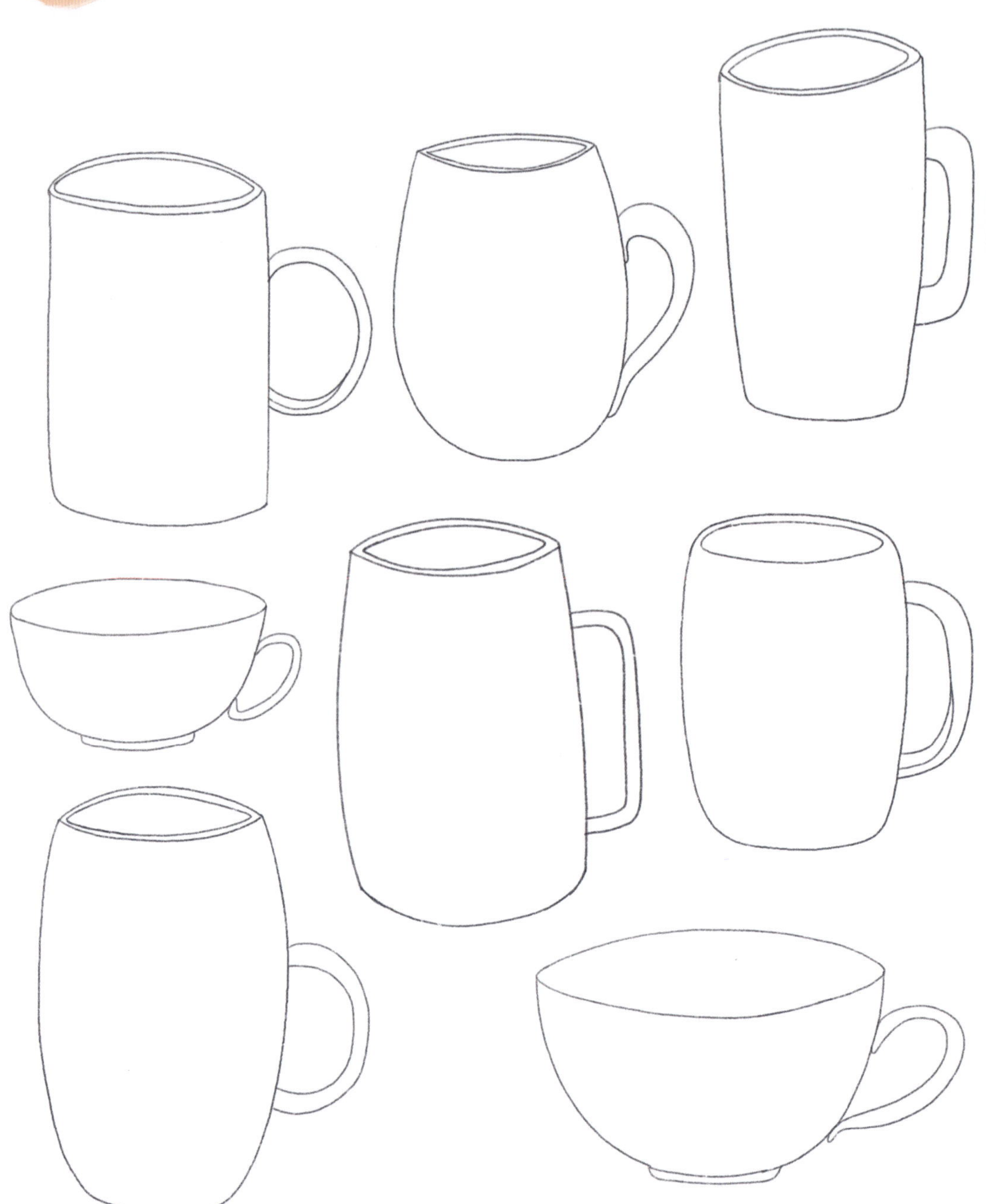

Color and print can be used as a disguise. Draw an animal hiding in foliage of a similar color and pattern, so it appears camouflaged.

Paint the weather that you experienced today.

All of these colors could be described as having a green hue.

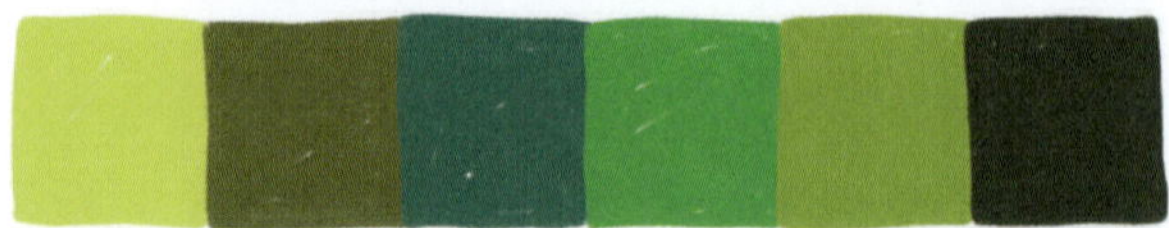

Choose a hue from the color wheel and enjoy recording as many different colors as you can. You could make a pattern.

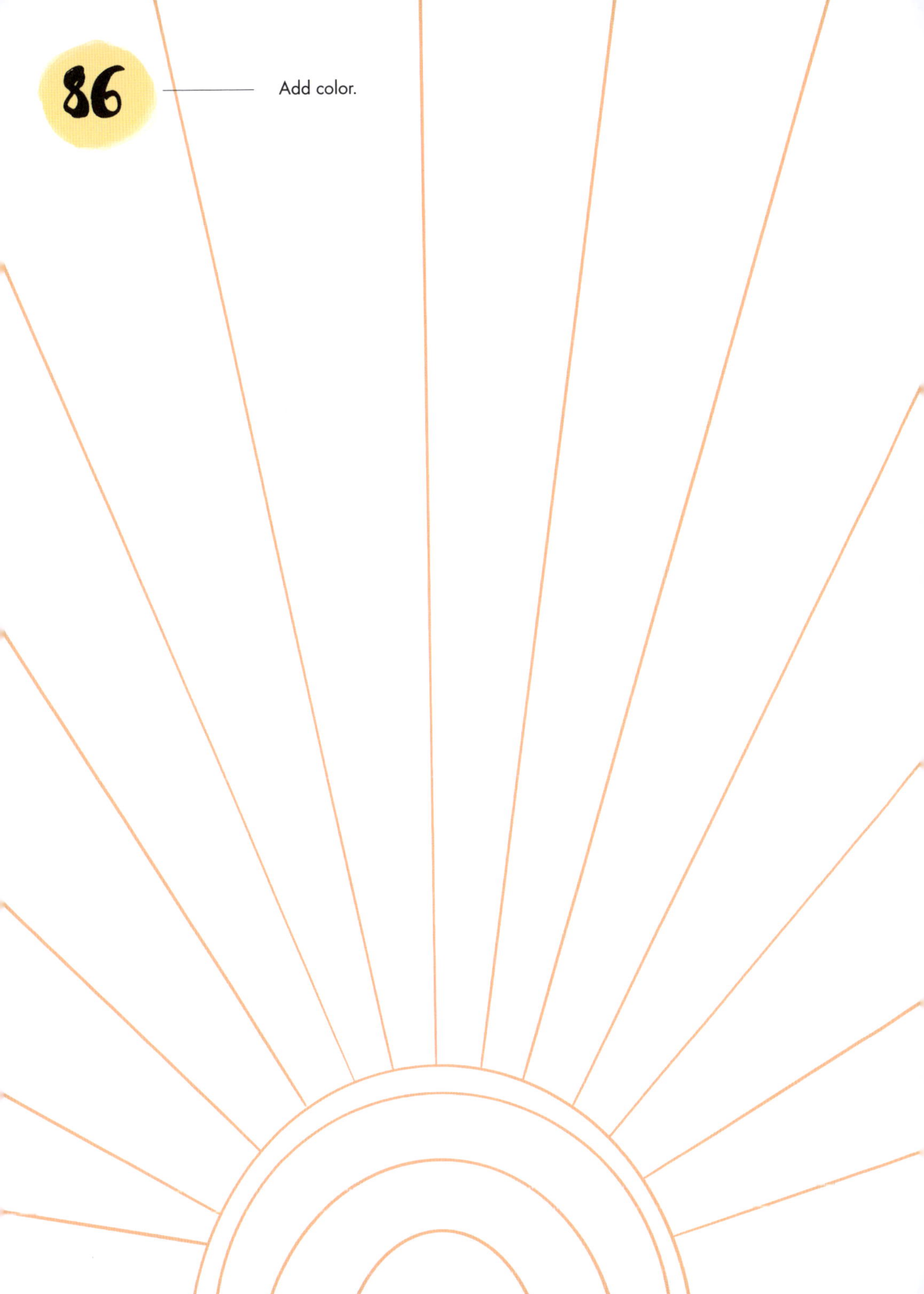

86
Add color.

Fill the page with painted circles, allowing colors to blend into each other.

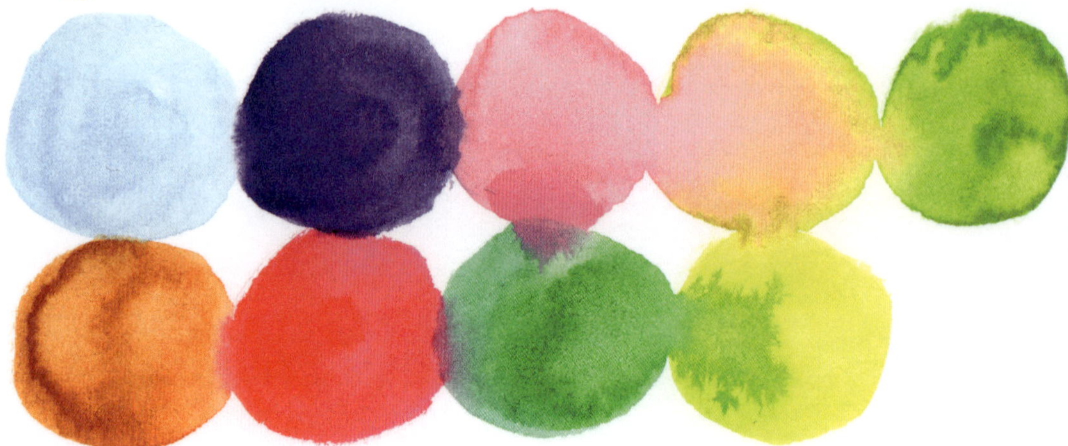

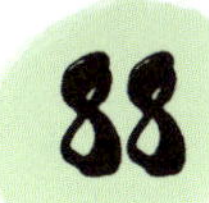

Place a simple object and some colored pencils in front of you. Look carefully at your subject—it's not just one color, but made up of lots of colors depending on the lighting in the room and the colors of the object. Make a drawing of it carefully including all the colors you can see.

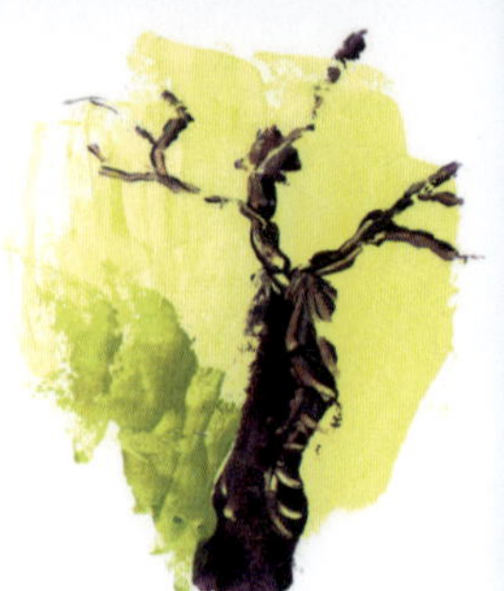

89 ———— Make an image where you explore complementary colors. Perhaps a violet tree against a yellow sky, a person wearing a blue outfit on a red chair, or a blue-green car on a red-orange road.

90

Refer back to your color wheel in activity 66.
Create a winter scene using cool colors.

Tip: An absence of color can also appear cool. You may like
to use neutral colors too, or try using tints of white.

91 ——————— Colors like orange, red, bright pink, and bright blue can be used to create bold, eye-catching imagery that feels positive and energetic. Use colors that you find positive to design a graphic or poster. You could choose a phrase you like, and illustrate that in color.

Paint some colored shapes, then, once these have dried, draw a pattern on each shape using contrasting colors.

 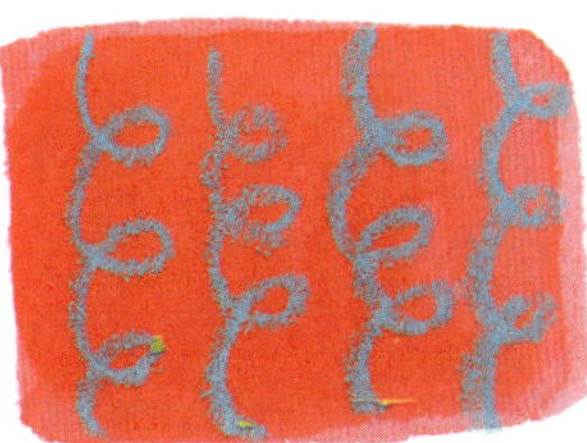

The 'negative space' refers to the empty area around or between objects. If you have a light-colored object, you may choose to fill the negative space with color rather than the object itself. The paper can become the white of your object. Choose a white or light-colored object and add color to the negative space to create a striking, contrasting image.

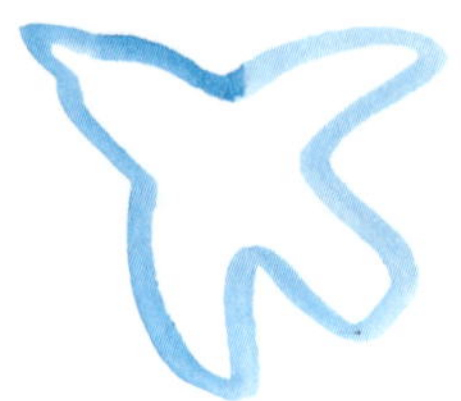 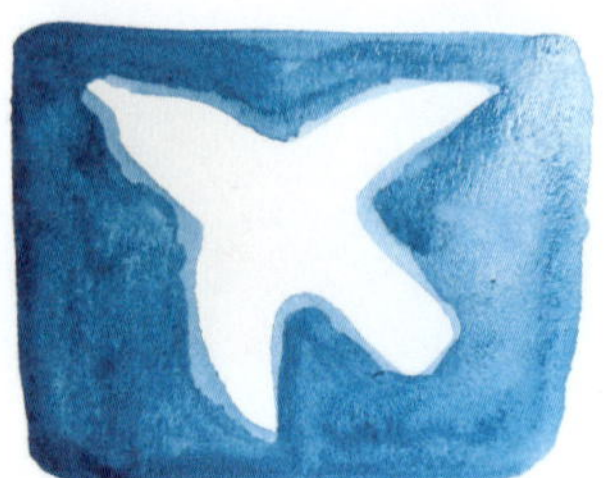 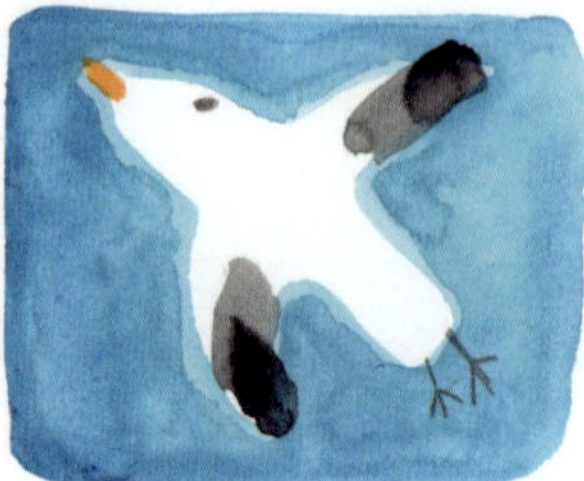

94

Triadic color schemes are those that use three colors found evenly spaced on the color wheel, for example yellow-green, red-orange and blue-violet. You can use triadic color schemes to create appealing combinations. Make some triadic color schemes below. You don't have to use the colors at their full intensity—you could use tints of the colors too.

Tip: Refer to activity 17 as a reminder of how to mix tints.

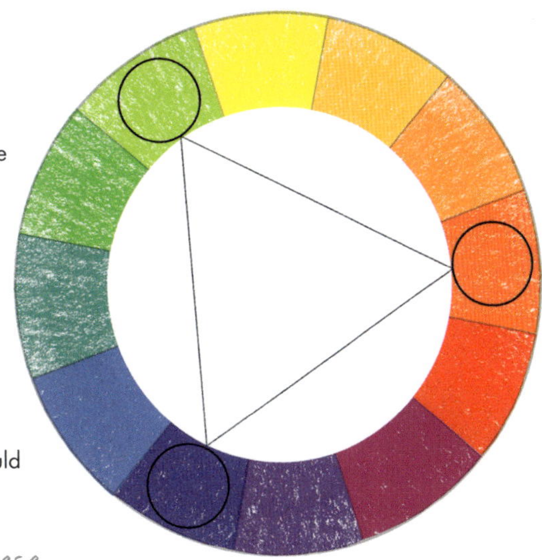

Tip: When using a triadic color scheme, you don't have to use all three colors equally. Perhaps make one color more dominant than the other two.

Yellow can suggest joy, energy, warmth, and ease. Be inspired by how yellow makes *you* feel and turn this shape into an image.

Add color to the shapes.

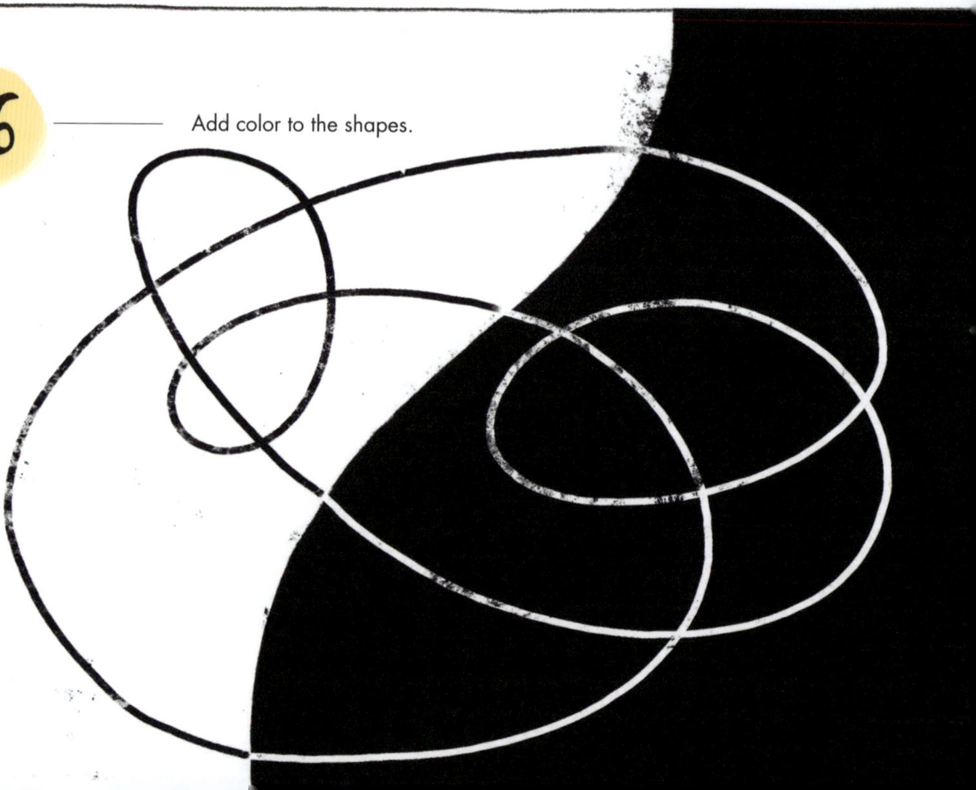

Mix as many colors as you can from three paint colors. Once you've mixed two together, what happens if you mix this with another of your colors? You should find that all of these mixed colors form a cohesive palette and would go together beautifully in a piece of art.

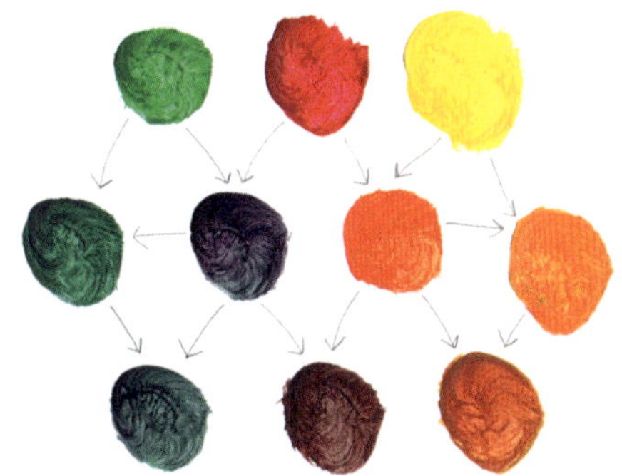

98 ———— Draw a vivid fire using yellows, reds, oranges, and any other colors that evoke warmth and coziness.

Layer oil pastel shapes over each other
and enjoy the color blends you create.

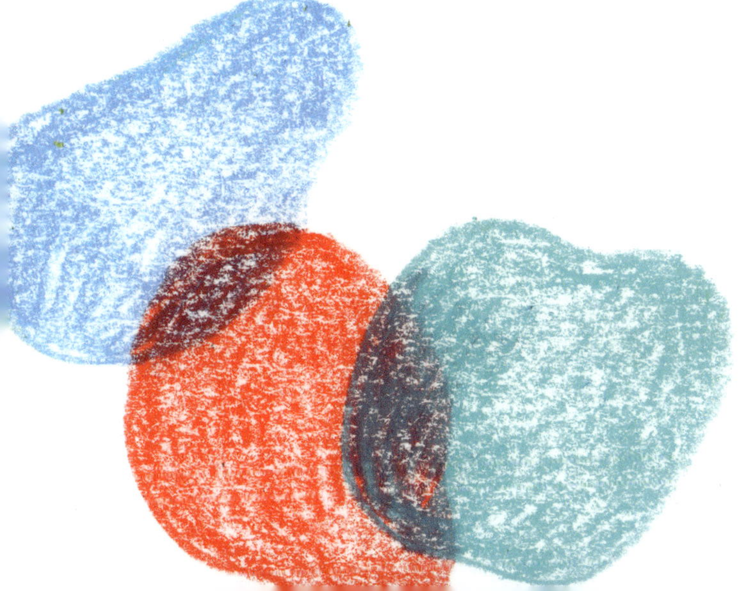

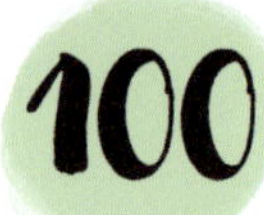

100 ———— Create a colorful drawing of a location you experience today. There's no need to match the colors exactly as you see them, just enjoy getting lots of color down onto the page and exploring different materials to capture the moment.

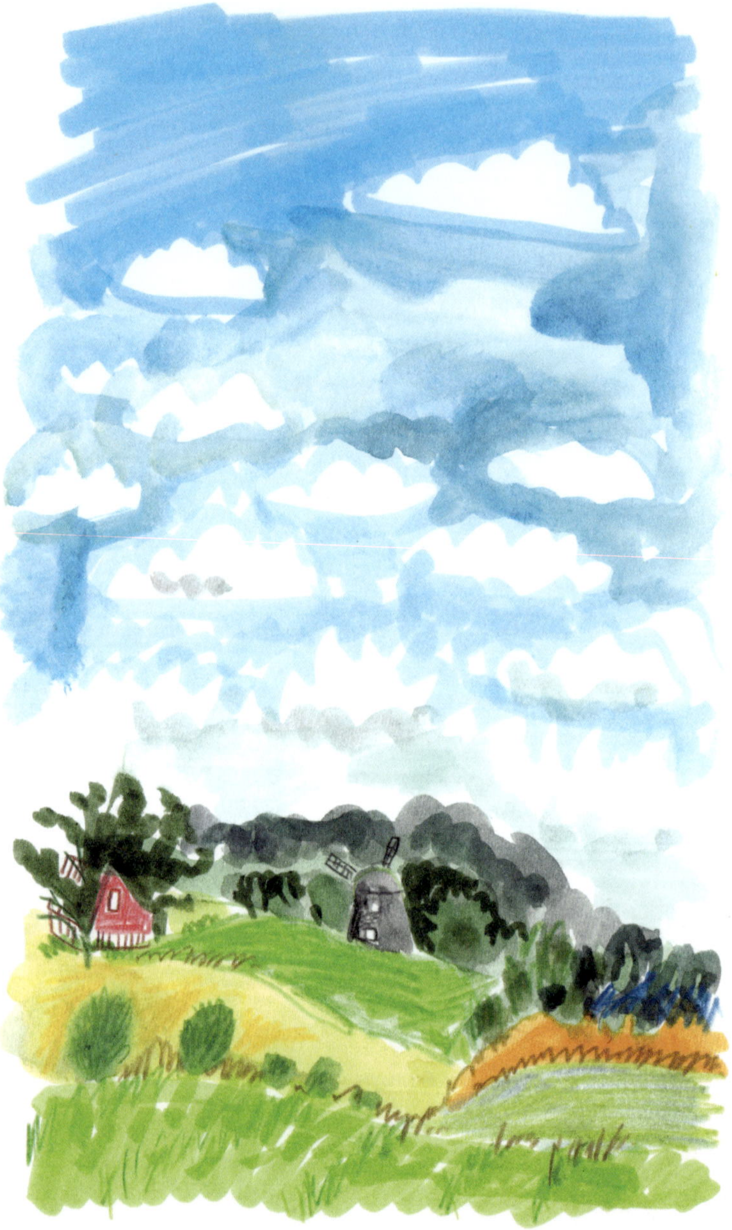

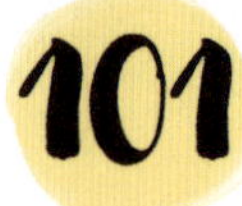

101

Continue adding circles of color to the page, enjoying the effect of all the colors together. The many small parts form one cohesive whole, whichever colors you choose!

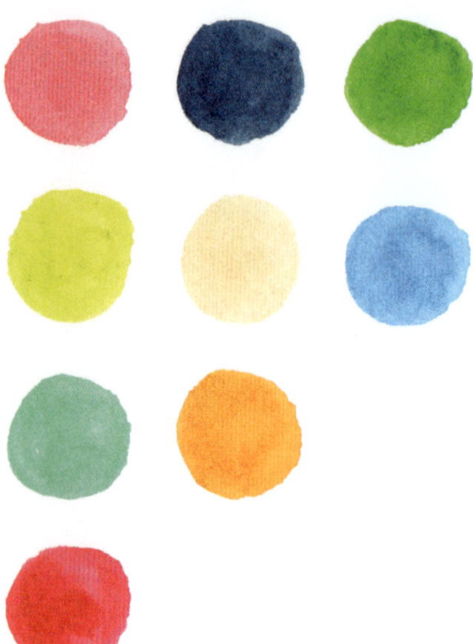

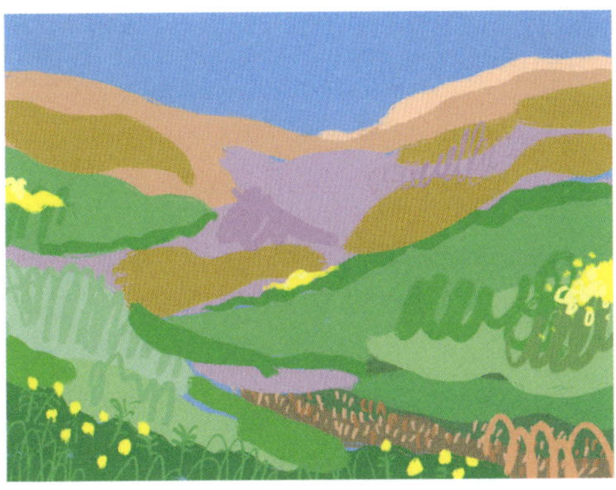

When looking at a landscape, there are sometimes so many colors that the thought of painting them all can feel overwhelming. It can be useful to start by breaking down the image into just a few colors and see the scene in sections. Perhaps there is a large bright green section at the front, or you notice big areas that look ocher. Look at a landscape (your local park, a garden, some fields, or even buildings) and map out the colors you see in big, simple areas.

Add details afterwards if you like, and perhaps some pops of bright color using paint or collaged paper.

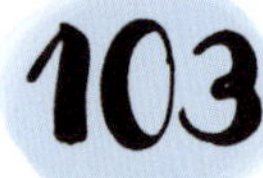

103 ———— Explore using clean colors alongside dirty colors to create interesting combinations. Remember—whether the color appears clean or dirty is your own personal interpretation, there is no right or wrong.

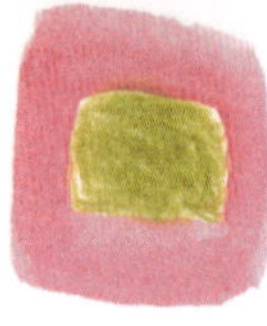

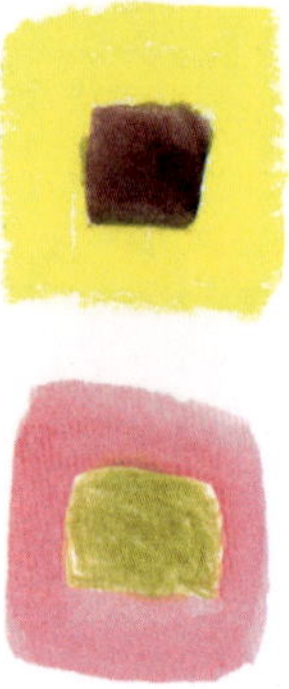

104 ———— Add color to this design.

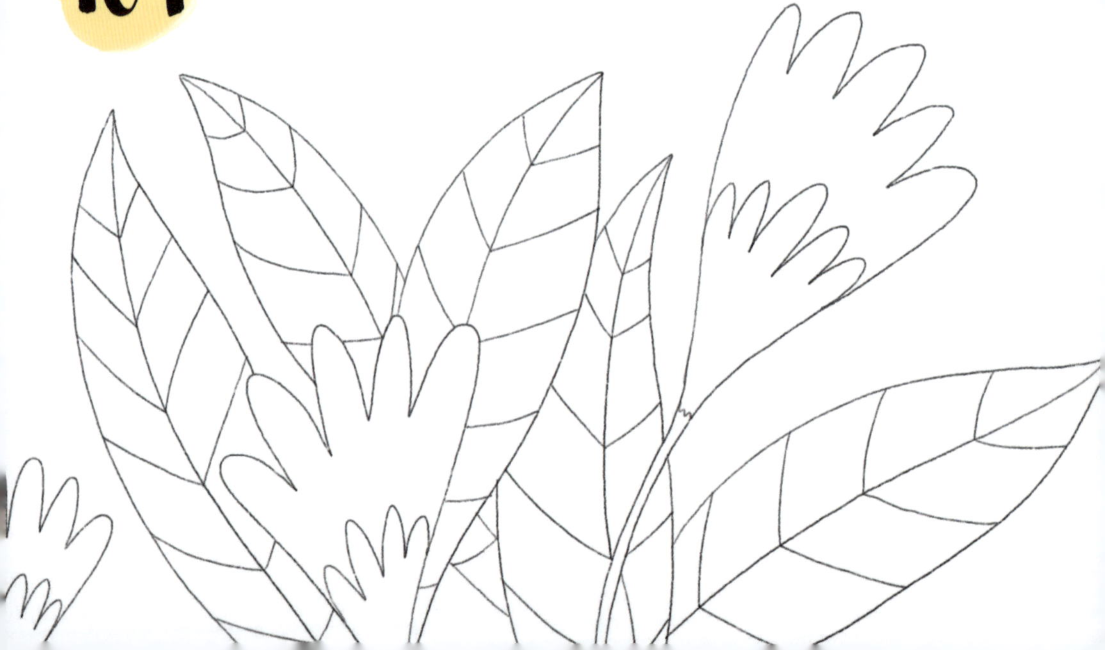

105

Red can be seen as an aggressive color. It can evoke passion, fire, or strong emotion, and can be used in a deliberate way in your art. Create two or three abstract designs where you use red with lots of energy and confidence. What is the atmosphere of the pictures you have created?

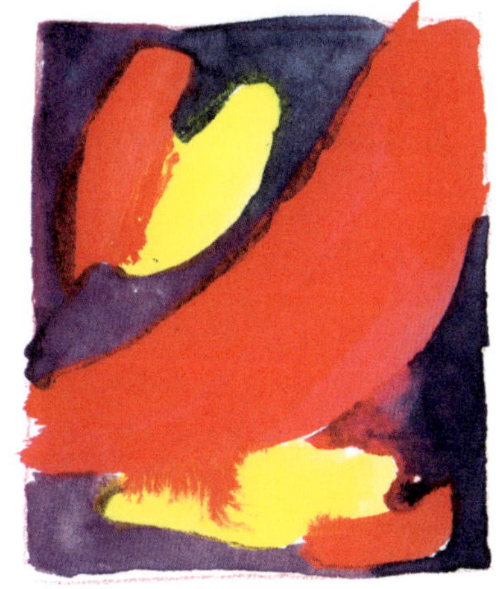

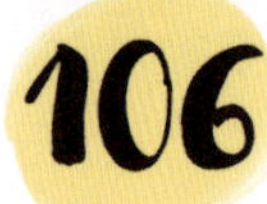

Create a collage using bold semicircle shapes. You could add lots of the same color paper to each semicircle, or approach the activity in any way that inspires you.

107

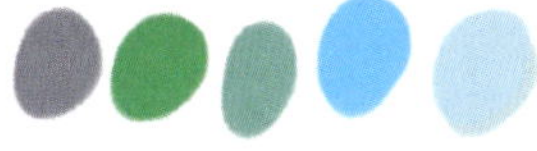

Create a scene using a few analogous colors. This will result in a soothing, relaxed image.

Tip: Analogous colors are those that appear next to each other on the color wheel.

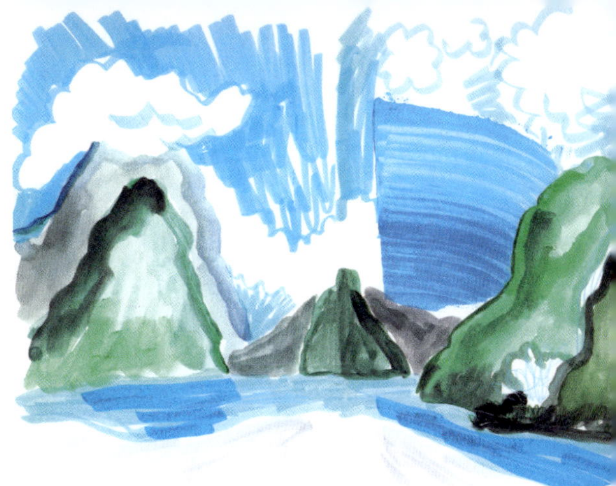

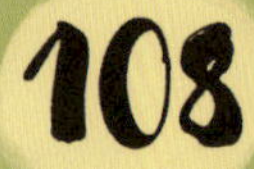

108 —————— Add more colors to this design to create a harmonious abstract. Consider how big you make each shape—perhaps you use a very bright or very dark color in small amounts.

109 —————— Draw a leaf, noticing the variety of colors you see.
Perhaps add a colored background.

110 —————— If you are finding the idea of drawing in color
daunting, you can simplify it. Start by creating
a simple drawing in pencil. You only need to
think about the forms. Then draw it again in
color … just using colors you love.

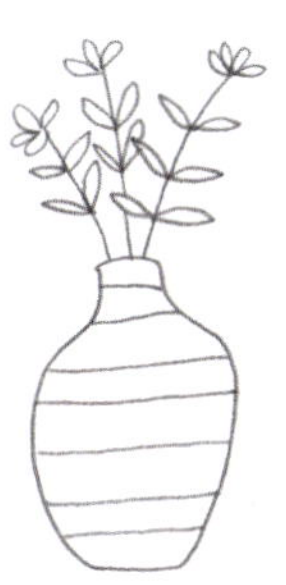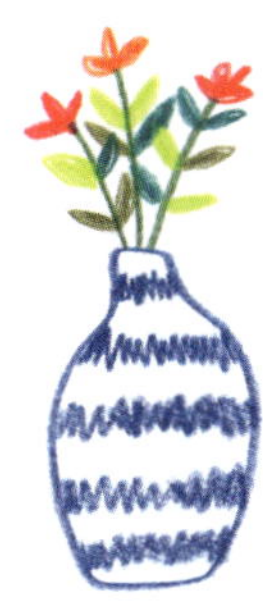

Draw a portrait of yourself using only warm colors.
How does the image make you feel?

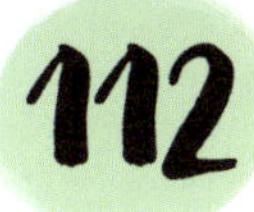

112

Draw a landscape using lines of color.

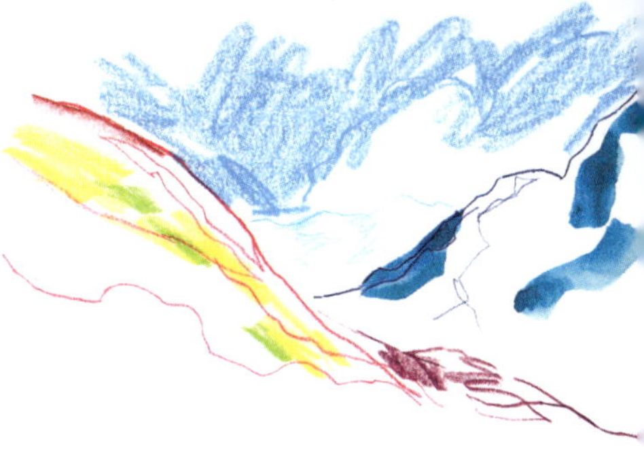

Mixing clean colors together can create interesting dirty colors. Create your own dirty colors here, and then make a pattern using your favorites plus one clean, bright color.

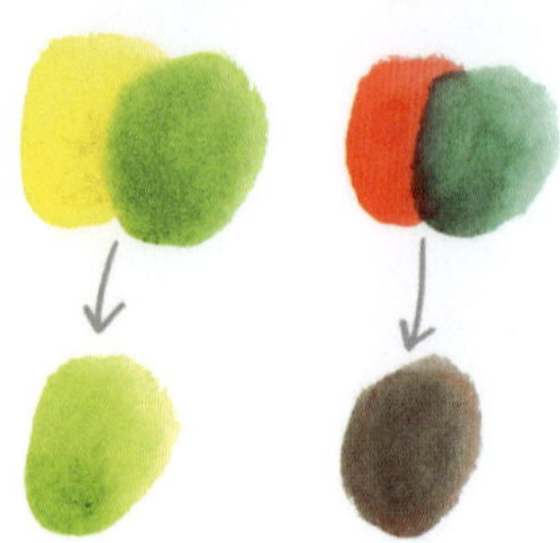

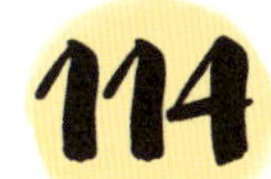

114 ——— Continue adding color to the page to produce an undulating patchwork.

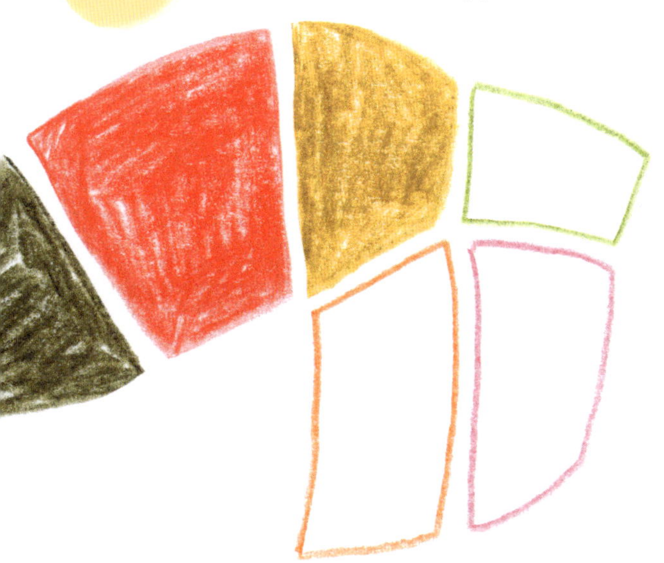

115

Using a lot of blue in a piece of art can make for a peaceful image. Paint a scene where blue is the predominate color. You could start by painting a blue background, or perhaps using a blue piece of paper.

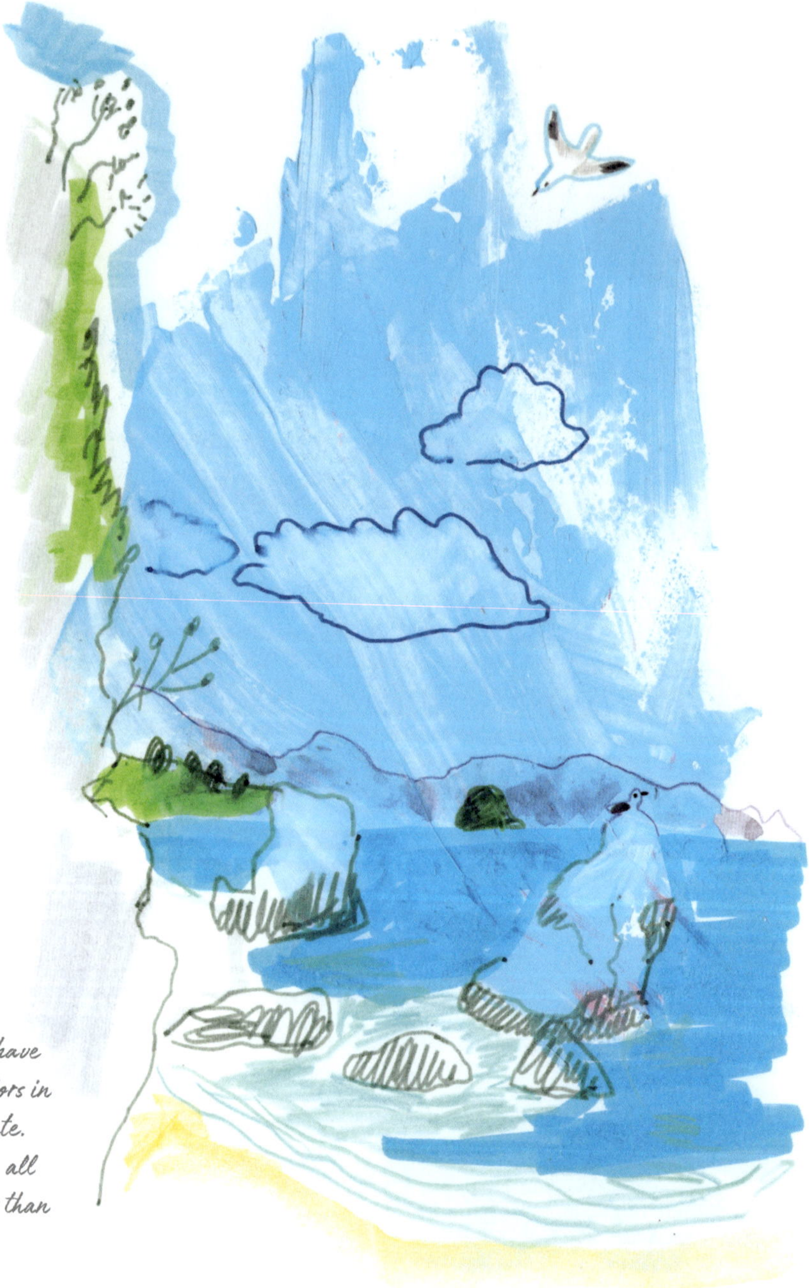

Tip: You don't have to make the colors in your art accurate. Explore making all the colors bluer than they really are.

116 ———————— Draw an object using only four colors.

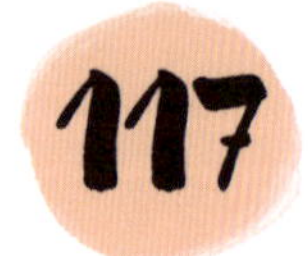

117 ———————— Put on some energetic music and create an abstract design based on how the music makes you feel.

118 Create patterns using blue.

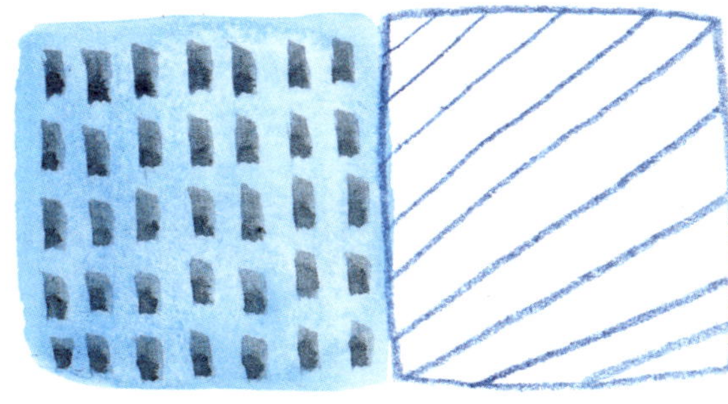

119 Draw dots using as many different colors as you can. You could mix colors too.

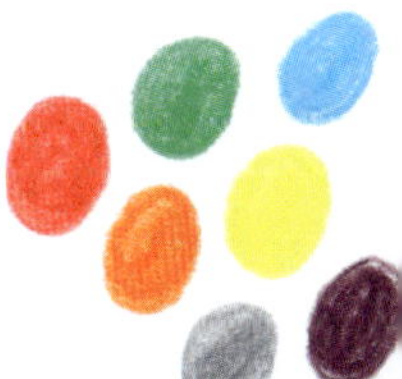

120

Start by painting a shape of color using watercolor. Then paint another shape of color next to it, watching as the colors bleed together in the middle. Repeat as many times as you like, perhaps filling the page. Notice how each pair of colors blends differently—and enjoy how wonderfully unpredictable paint can be!

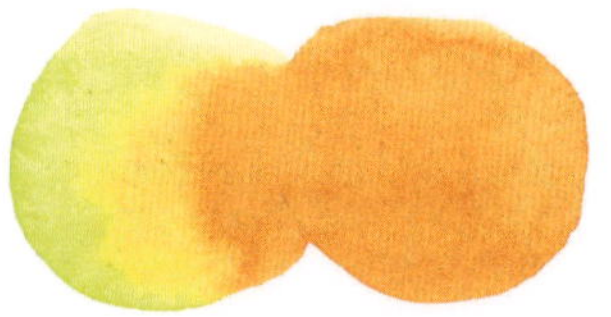
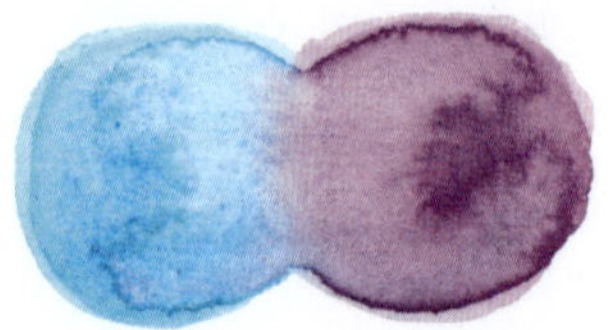
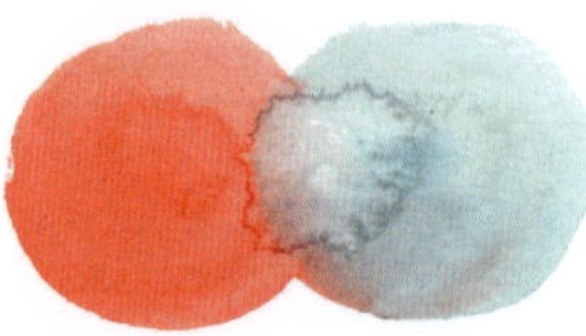

121

Paint or draw a view from observation using the most vibrant colors you have.

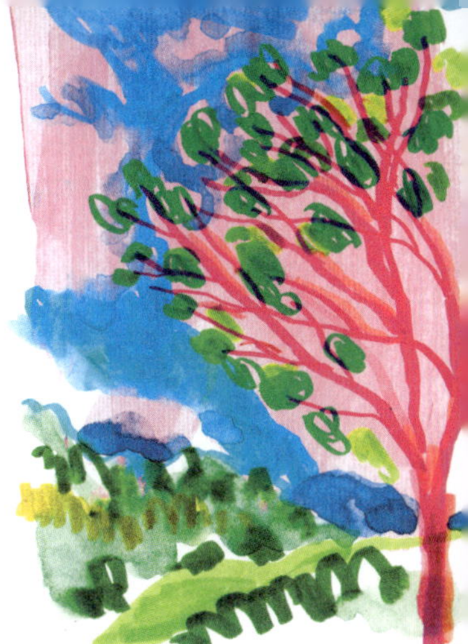

Create an abstract piece of art using colors that represent a specific feeling. This can be totally personal to you.

123 ———————— Enjoy creating some color
palettes. Consider including
clean and dirty colors, and
think about how you might use
these palettes in future pieces
of art.

Tip: It can be useful
to keep a color palette
sketchbook—a book
entirely dedicated to your
collections of colors.

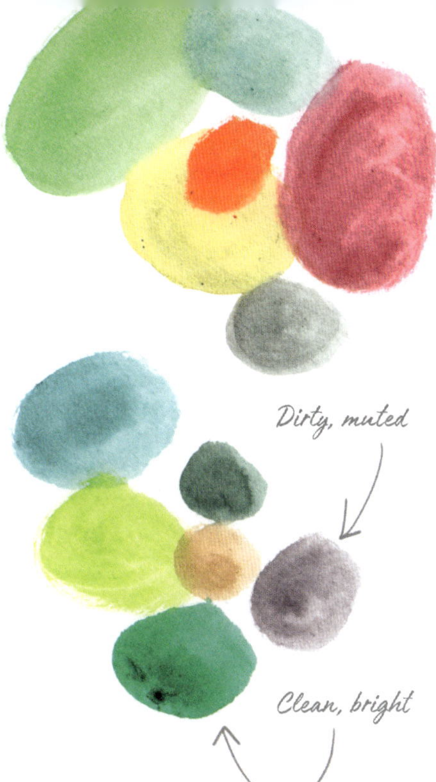

Be inspired by the energy and color of this paint mark, and use it as a background for a piece of art. It could be a scene, a portrait, an abstract ... anything you like.

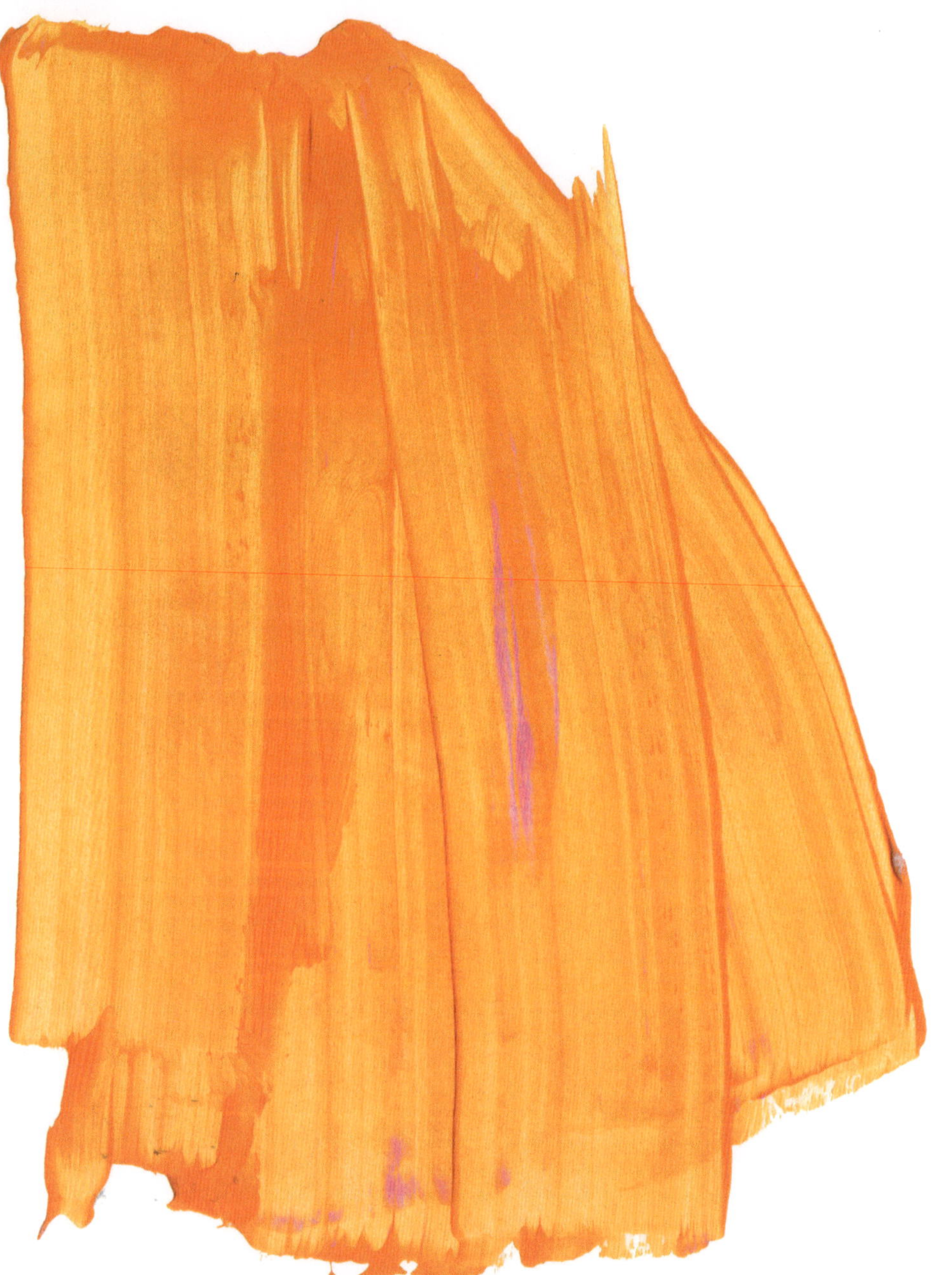

Design a colorful blanket pattern that you could use in your home.

Create thumbnail color studies of the land and sky, starting with colors you expect to see, and then exploring more unusual color combinations. These could be colors that you've seen or imaginary combinations.

Tip: Exploring color palettes beyond what we expect can encourage us to be braver about using color in a more daring way generally. Perhaps one of your thumbnails will inspire you to create a larger piece of art.

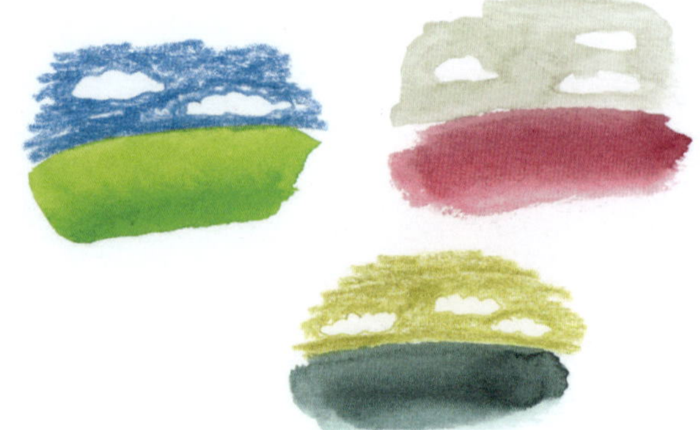

Draw nature-inspired shapes using calming, neutral colors.

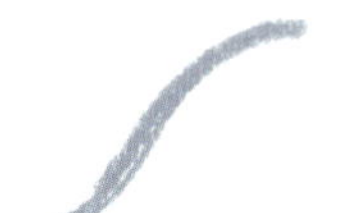  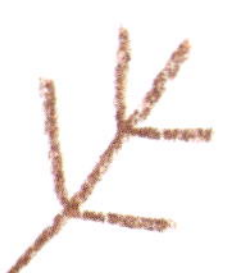 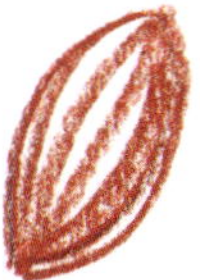 

128

Make some small paper collages of everyday objects. The nature of collage means your art can be bold and graphic, so enjoy this and exaggerate the shapes you see. Consider what the elements would look like in their simplest forms, and enjoy being playful with the color choices and shapes.

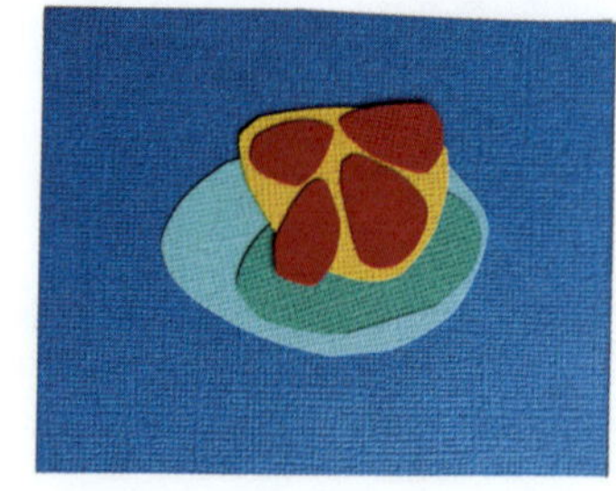

Tip: If you don't have paper in the colors you need, you can paint paper and cut this up once dry.

Based on your color wheel in activity 66, add cool colors to these squares. Consider the atmosphere of the piece once completed.

Look through a window and draw the shapes and colors you see, without drawing the window frame—instead leave this as white space.

Tip: You could sketch the window frames lightly in pencil first.

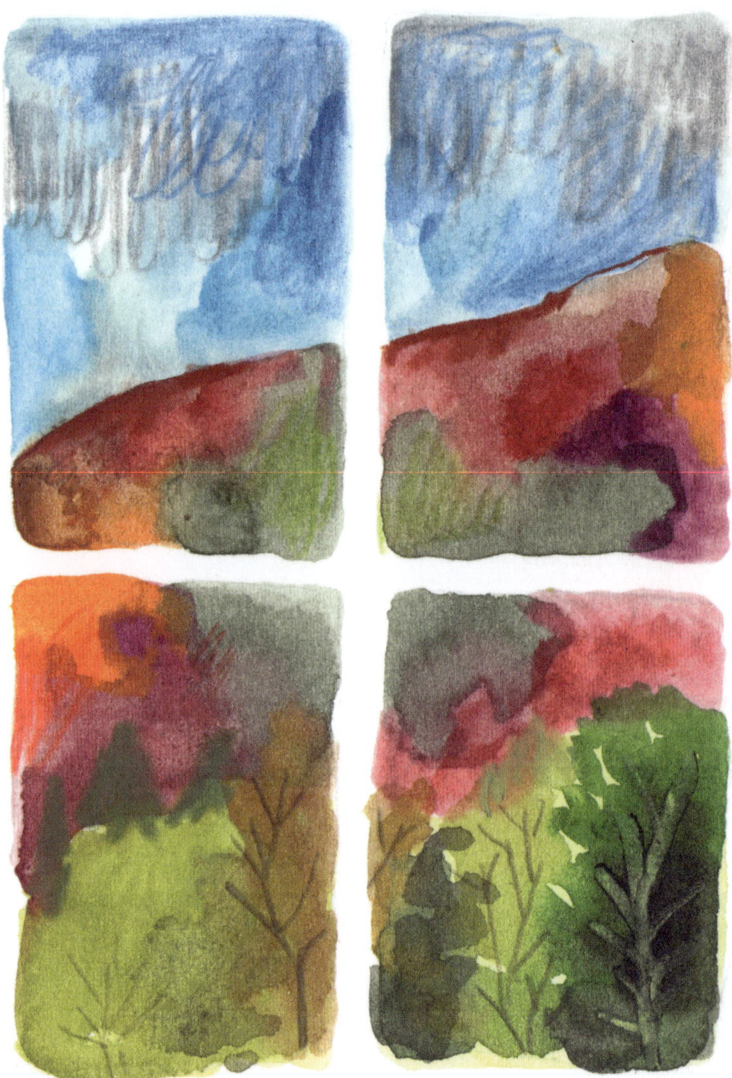

131

Add some more lines and shapes to this design and then introduce color and pattern—perhaps spots, stripes, and waves.

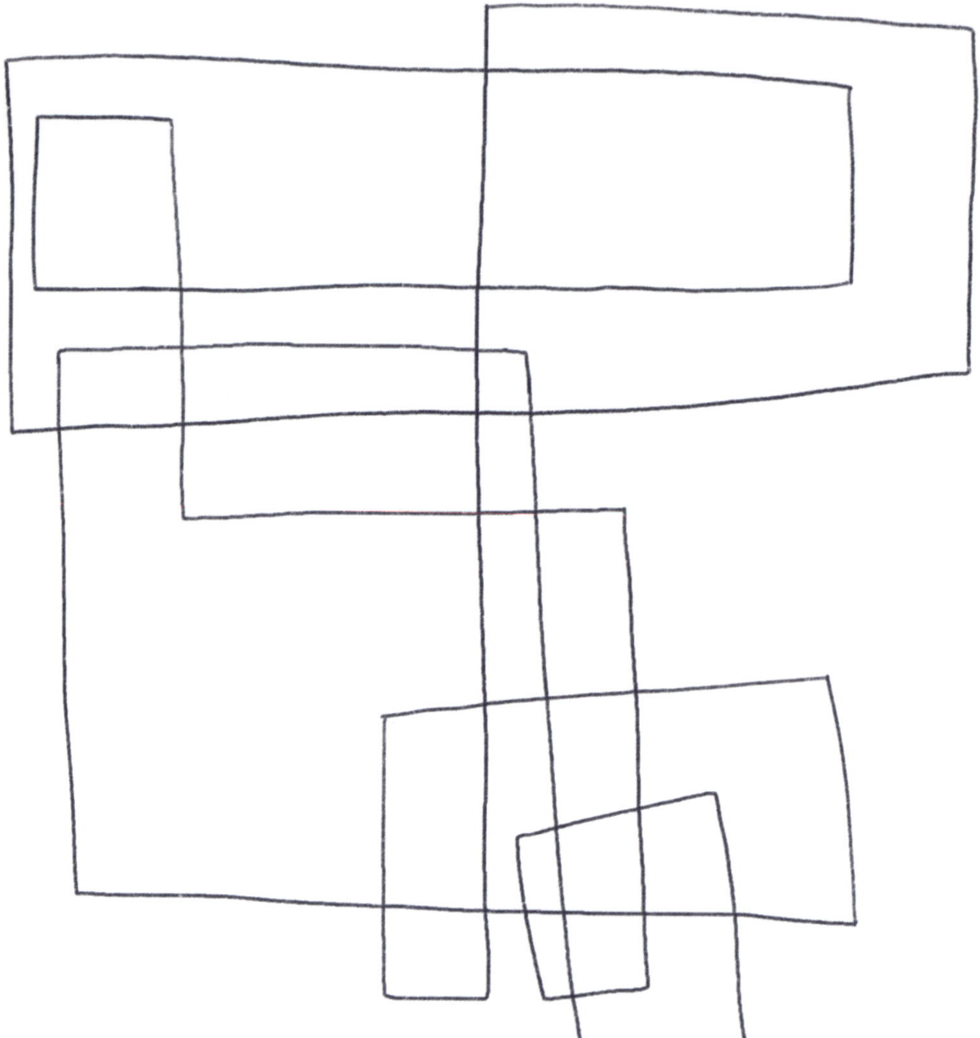

We can use color to add tone to shapes, rather than using black or gray. First, decide which direction the light will be coming from, then use tints and shades of colors to add tone. Or you could experiment with using completely different colors to add shadow. Be playful with your choices.

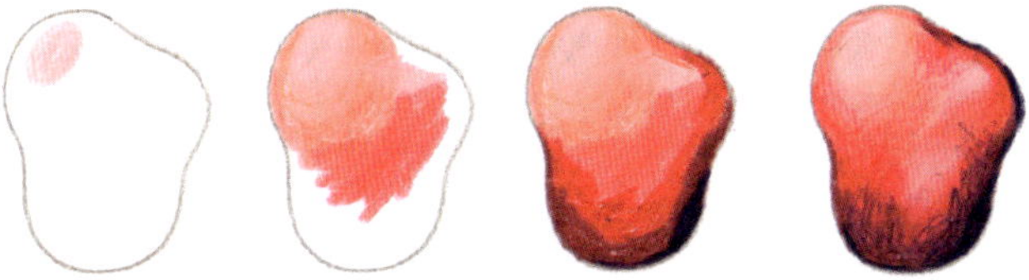

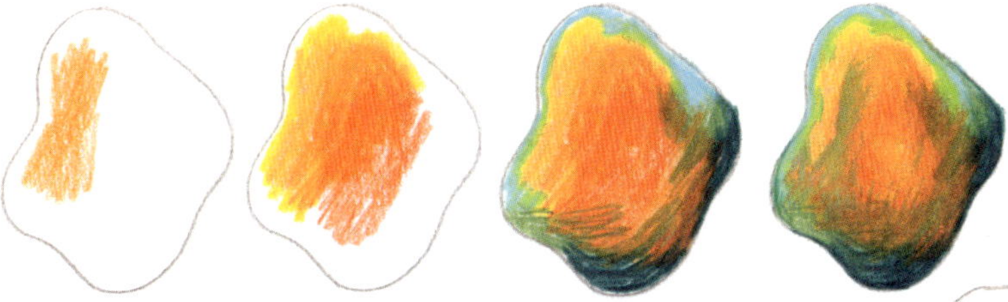

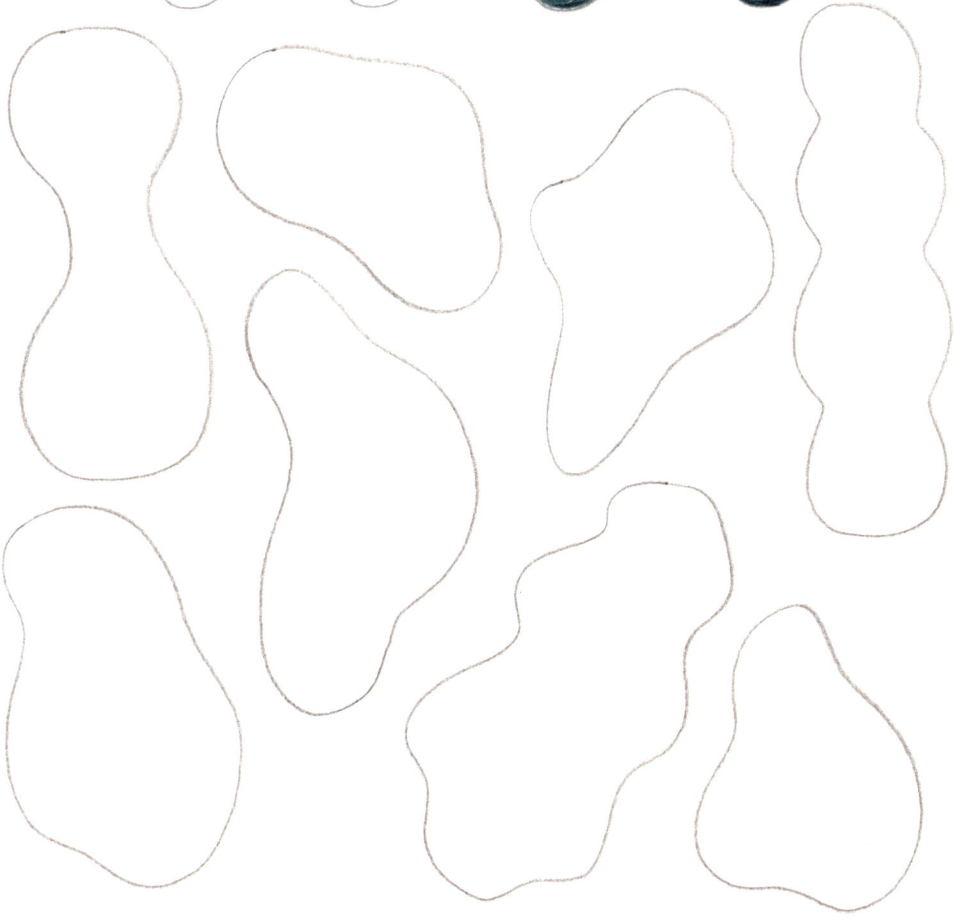

Find a grayscale photograph that you like, imagine what it might look like in color, and draw it here.

Yellow can evoke joy and be seen as a happy, friendly color. What do you think? There's no right or wrong way to feel about color—it can be subjective. Draw something yellow and consider how it makes you feel.

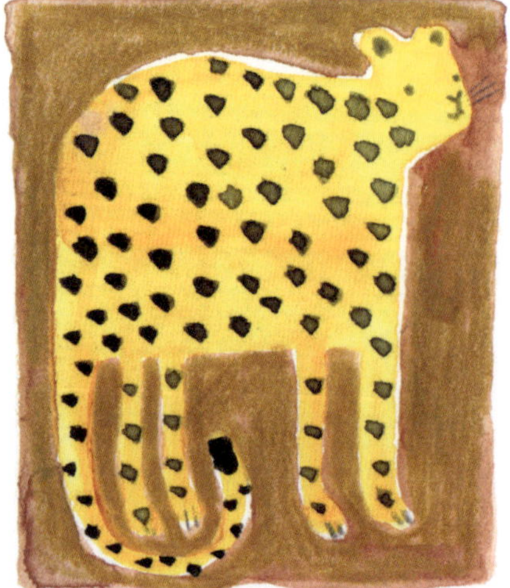

It can be tricky to make the leap to using non-realistic colors in your art. Have a play here, coloring each leaf in colors you wouldn't expect to see in nature.

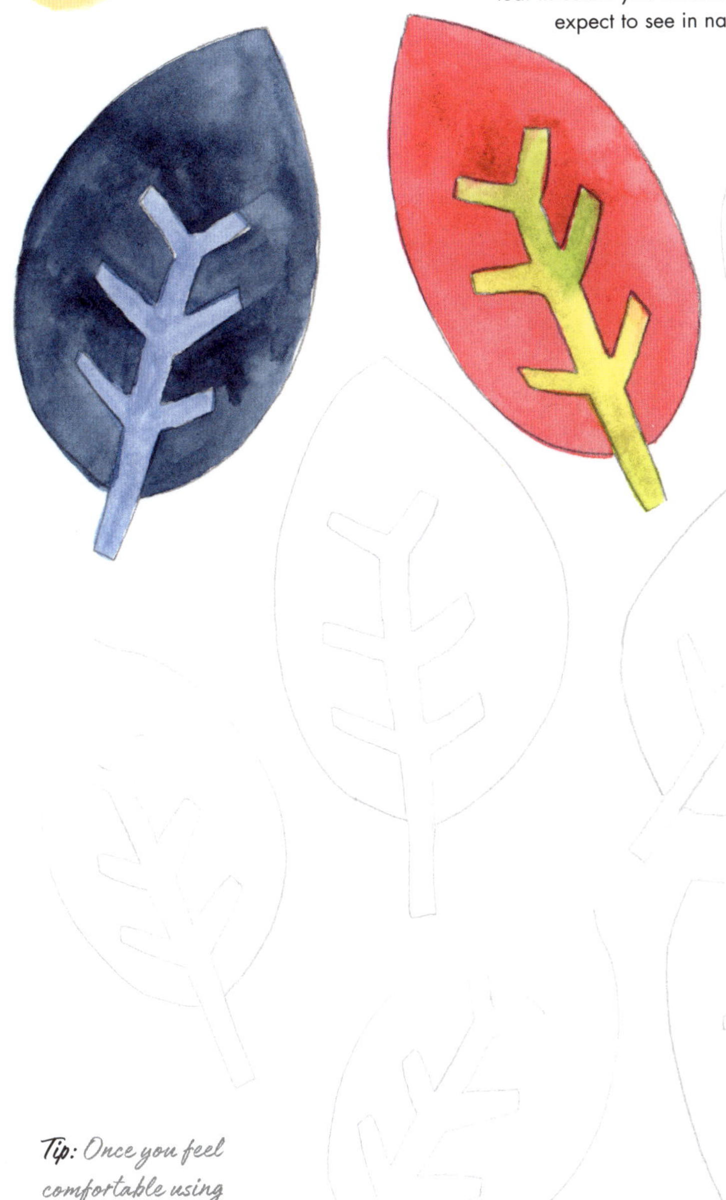

Tip: Once you feel comfortable using unexpected colors for simple forms, try it out in portraits and landscapes.

136 —— Spend time people-watching in a park or café. Draw lots of people from observation, paying particular attention to their colorful outfits. You could draw the whole scene or individual people.

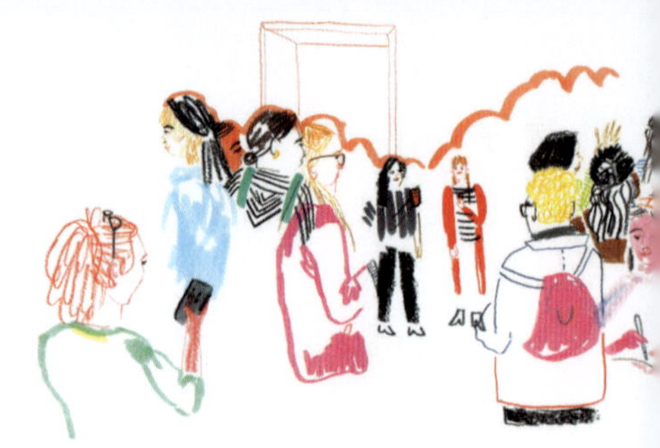

137

It can be useful to break the habit of drawing objects as blocks of a single color. Choose an object, such as a piece of fruit, and really look at all the colors you can see on its surface. Search for the colors that you wouldn't expect to see at first glance.

Tip: Perhaps start by drawing the outline of the object, then fill in the colors you see, bit by bit.

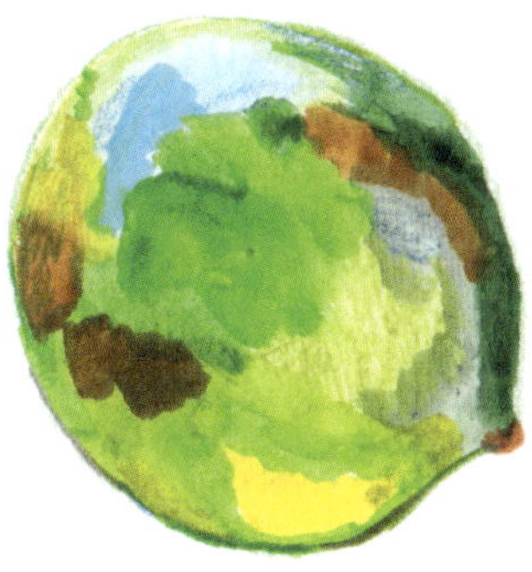

138

Paint a sweep of color and then add little details to create the silhouette of a horizon.

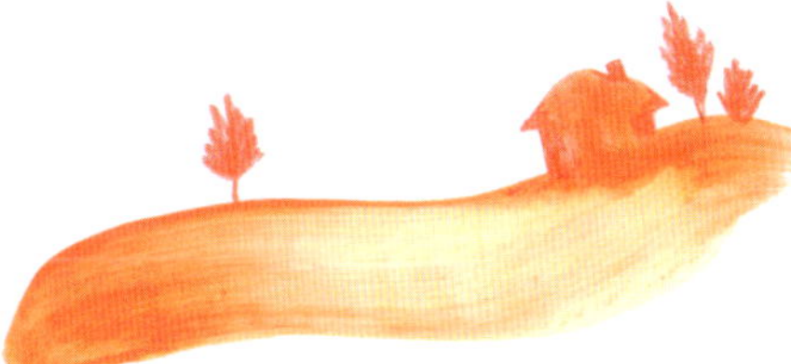

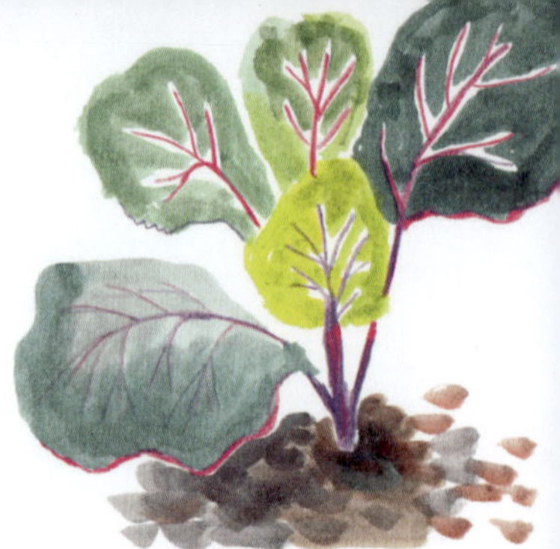

139 ——— Draw something from the natural world, paying particular attention to any vivid colors you can see.

140

When mixing primary colors together, it can be tricky to find a *pure* red, yellow, and blue paint, as they often contain a little of other primary colors. However, you can use this to your advantage and explore making even more variations in color! Choose different hues of primary colors (perhaps a sky blue and a peacock blue, for example) and mix them to make as many secondary colors as you can. Notice the slight variations you create when using different hues.

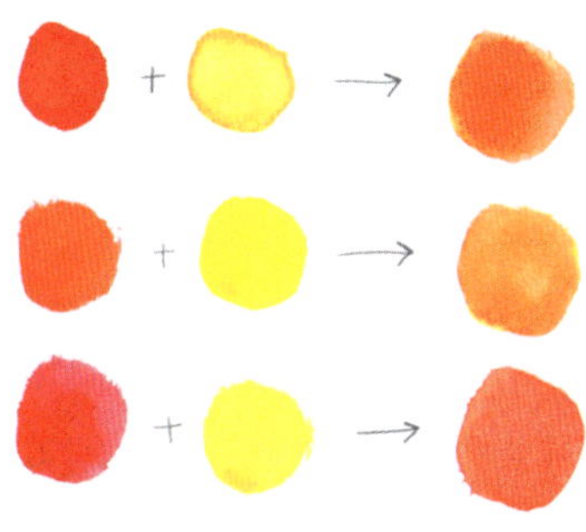

141

We can use color to show abundance, for example to depict a garden, full of life. Spend up to 20 minutes painting a scene that is bountiful. Explore layering colors on top of each other and embrace the energy of the scene by working quickly.

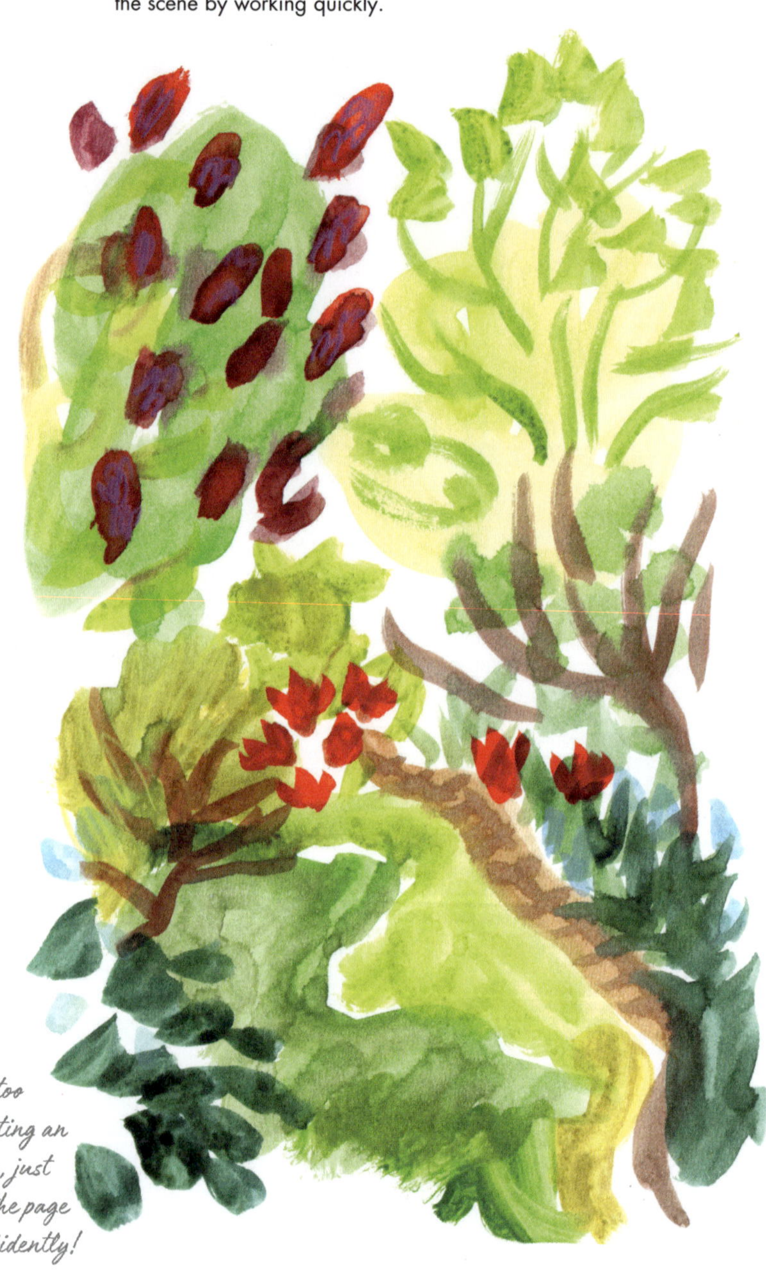

Tip: Don't worry too much about creating an accurate drawing, just get the color on the page quickly and confidently!

142 ———— By choosing a limited palette of colors—perhaps three or four— you can make an image that naturally feels cohesive. Create a pattern or design using a narrow range of colors.

143 ———— Design a flag and carefully consider the colors you use— perhaps they have a personal meaning to you.

144

Add a colorful scene to this beach. Include towels, people, parasols, and windbreakers.

145

Cut up some paper and create a colorful collage.

Tip: Don't think too much about what should go where, just cut shapes and go for it!

Use a triadic color scheme to color this pattern.
Refer to activity 94 for tips.

Create a simple, bold collage using this dark background as a starting point. Perhaps be inspired to use bright contrasting colors, or keep the whole design neutral and subdued. You could choose a subject to depict, or create an abstract piece.

Drop some blobs of watered-down paint onto the page and while it's still wet, blow it across the page using a paper straw if you have one, or just your mouth. Have fun and enjoy the unpredictability of the paint!

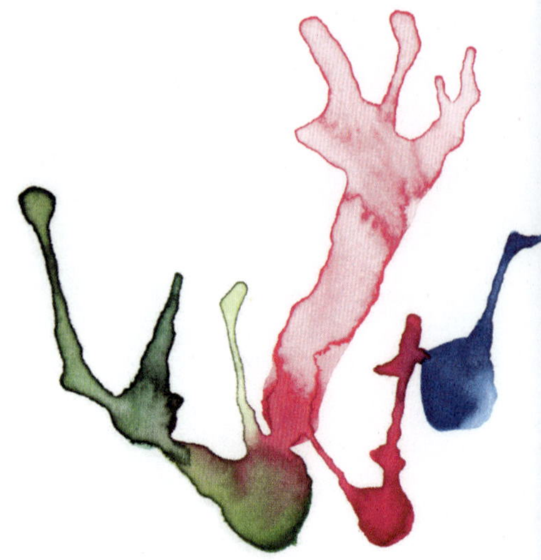

Paint or draw a piece of fruit, but use colors that you wouldn't expect, rather than making it look realistic.

150 ——————— Paint or draw a scene (indoors or outdoors) using only pastel colors. How do the colors make you feel, and what mood does this give the scene?

Add more details to the buildings then add color.

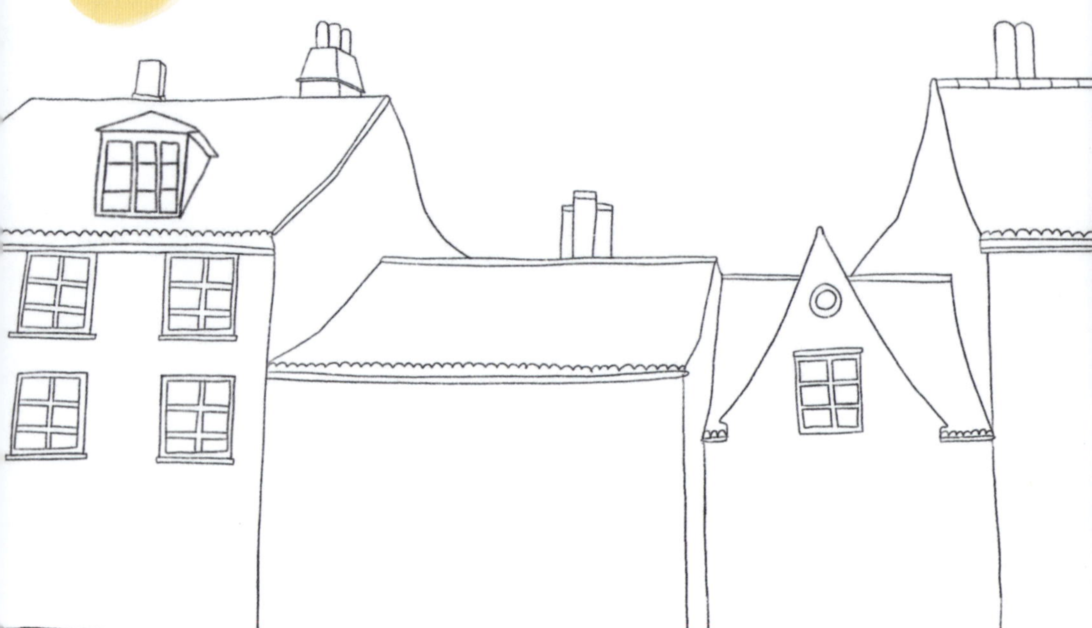

Paint a simple landscape using oranges, blues, and browns.

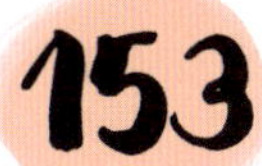

Explore how different color backgrounds can change the mood of a portrait. Draw some portraits here and consider how each makes you feel.

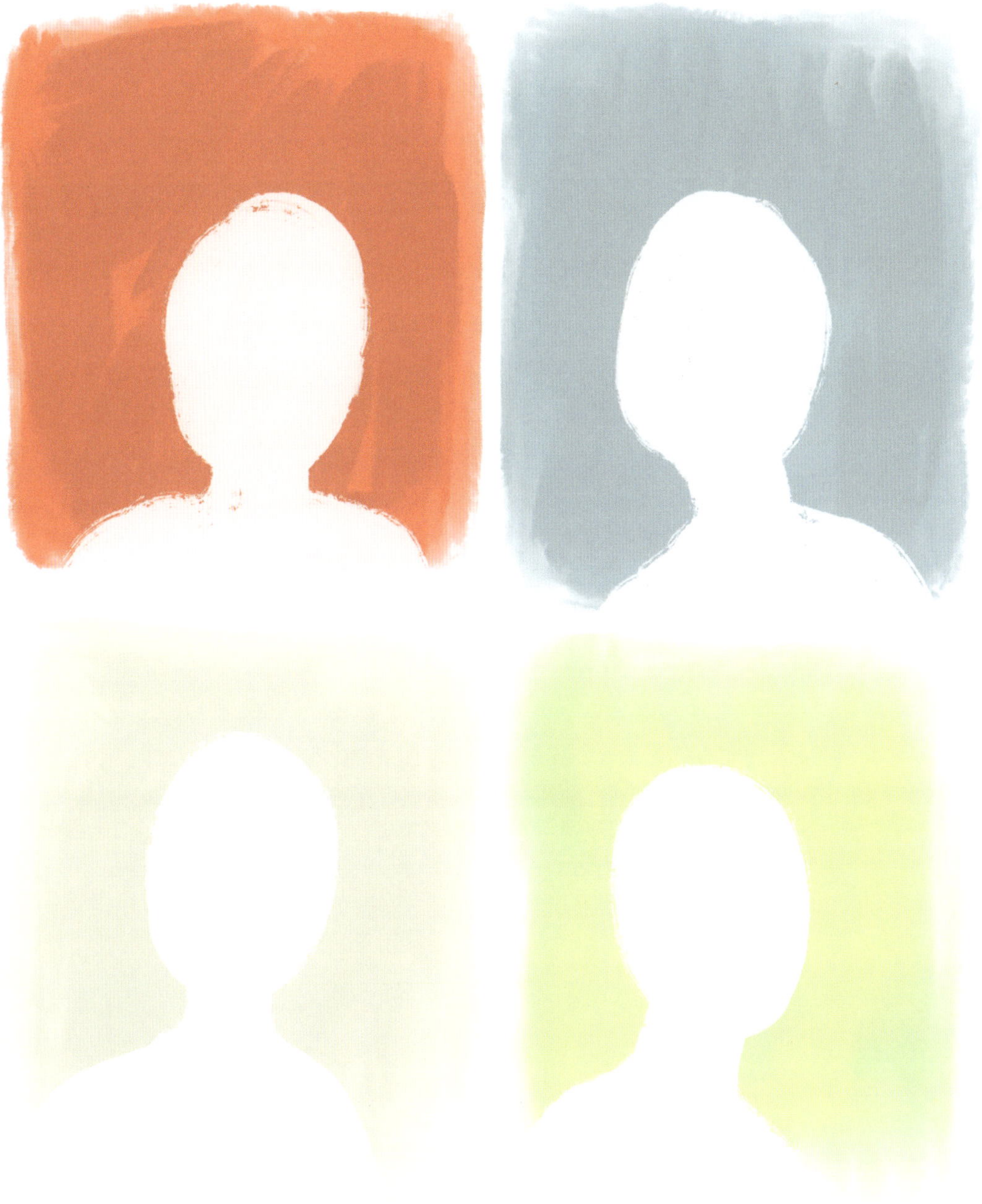

Create some mini abstract images using blocks of color in a range of different art materials.

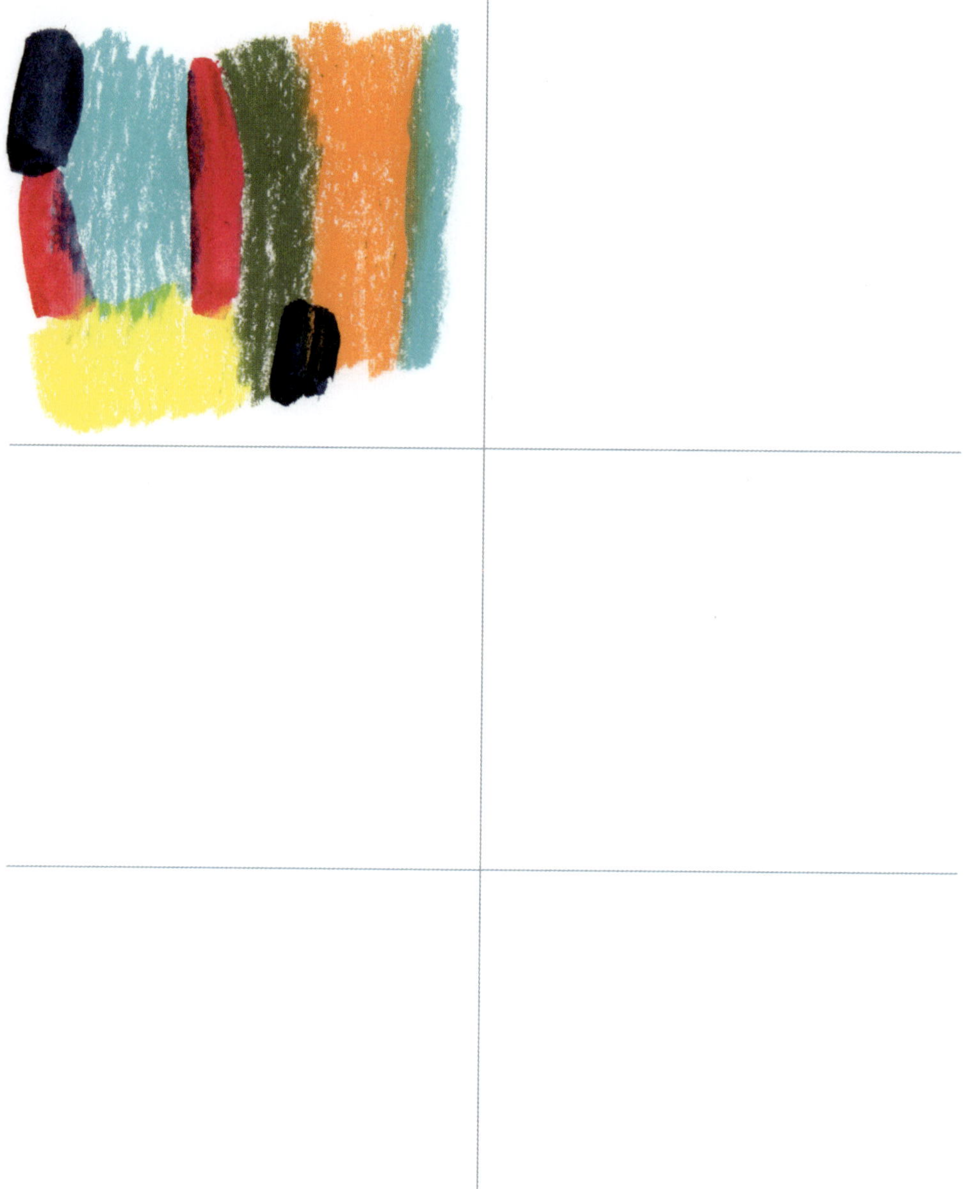

155

Make a colorful piece of art using paper. Choose a subject for your art—perhaps a vase, some fruit, or something from your kitchen. Cut shapes based on what you see in front of you.

Tip: You may want to arrange your composition first, before you use glue to fix it down. Or just glue as you go and let your piece evolve naturally.

Monochromatic color schemes are where variations of only one color are used. This can be a useful way to create a powerful atmosphere in a piece of art. Choose one color and create a piece of art using only variations of this color. Consider the mood of the piece once you've finished.

Tip: You could use tints and shades of one color, or slightly different versions—for example a teal blue and a sky blue.

157 ———— Create a collage using primary colors.

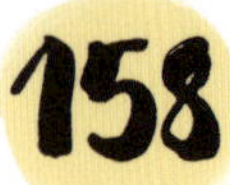

Fill the page with watercolor paint and watch as the colors blend into each other. Once the paint is dry, add a drawing on top using dark coloring pencils.

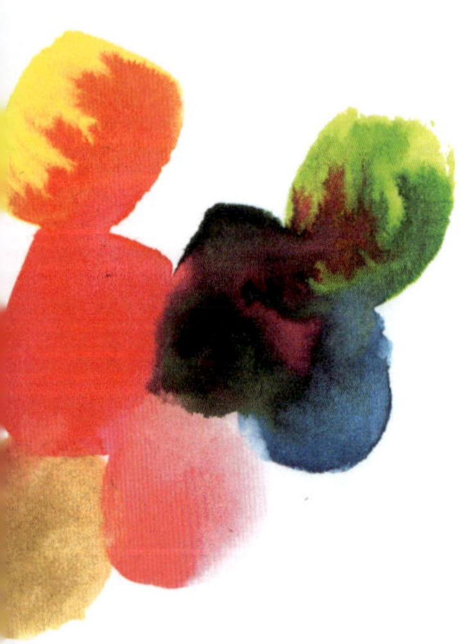

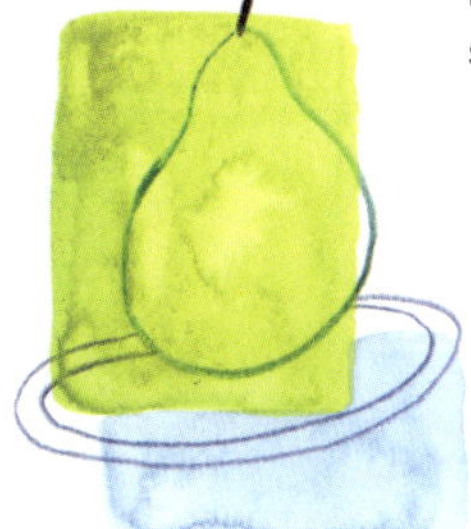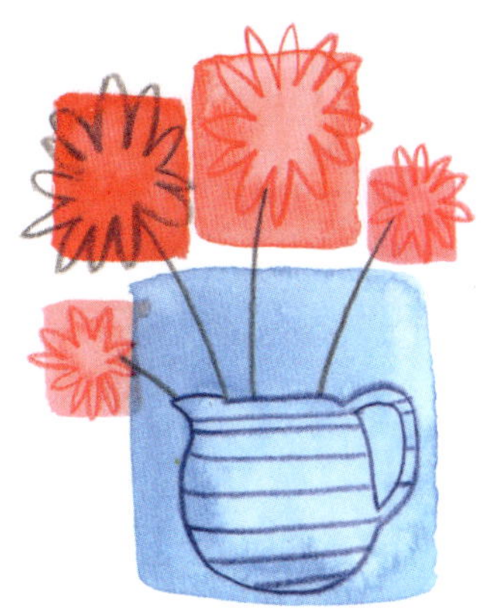

Color can be used in a simple way and still be effective. Have a look at some objects around your home and paint blocks of color to represent them. Then draw the objects in their simplest forms on top.

Track your mood throughout the day using color. When you notice a feeling, draw a segment below and add a color to represent your mood.

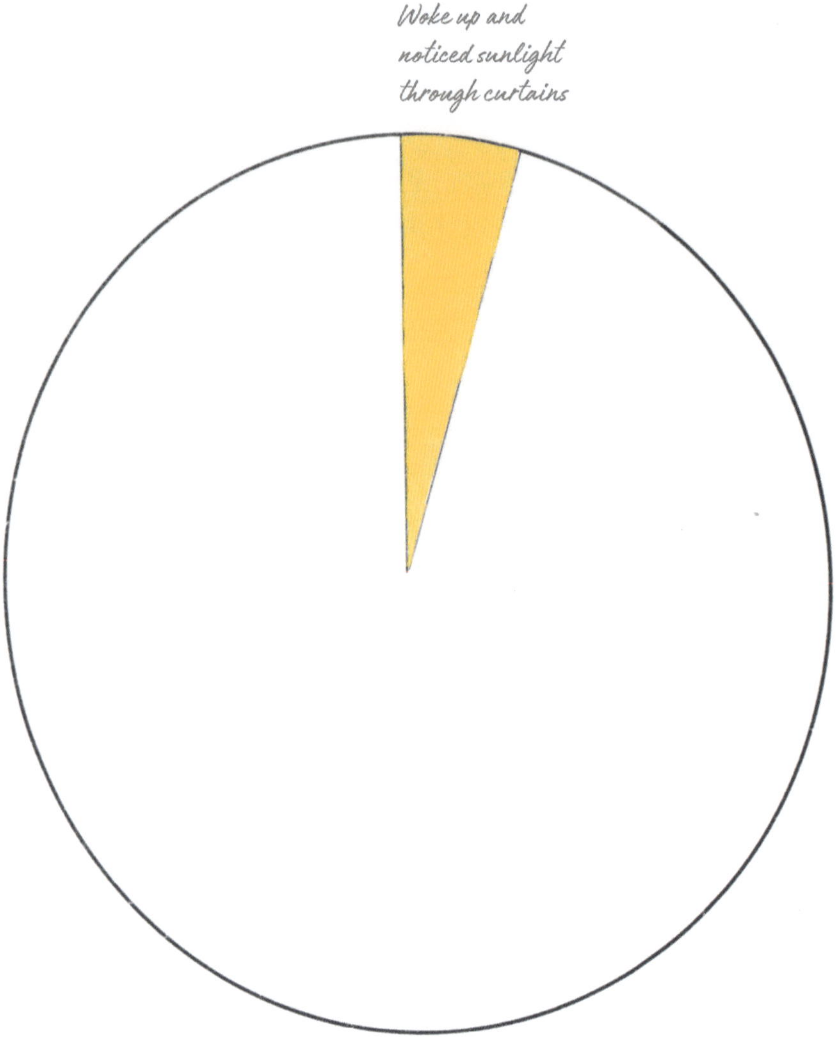

Create an observational drawing of someone you love using color.

Add bright, colorful leaves to these tree trunks.

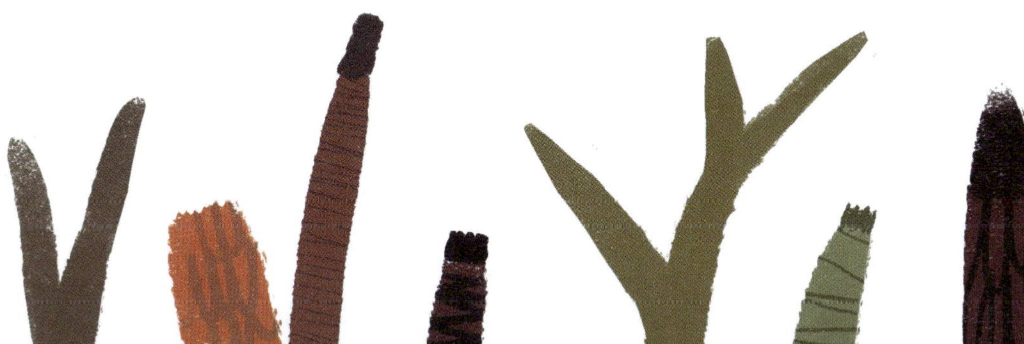

163 Green can suggest nature, life, freshness, and new things. How does green make *you* feel? Use those feelings and this shape as a starting point for an image.

164 Create a design for a deck of cards.

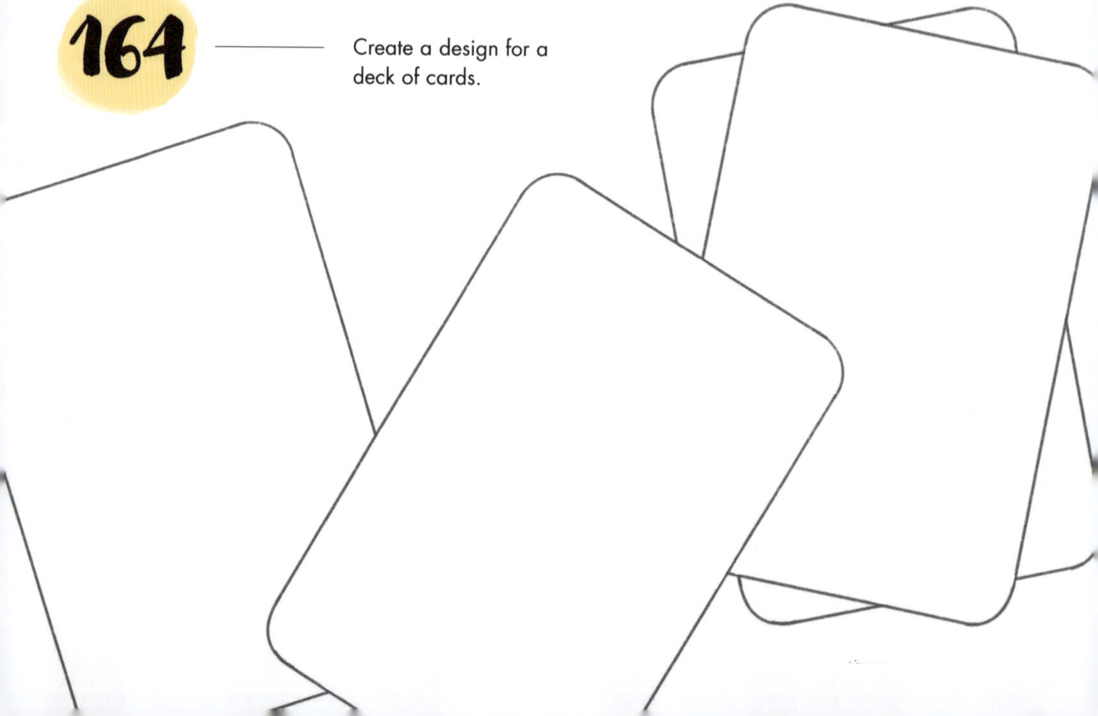

Challenge yourself to make an observational sketch in under 25 minutes. Before you begin, paint a brightly colored background and allow it to dry. This will add even more energy and life to your image.

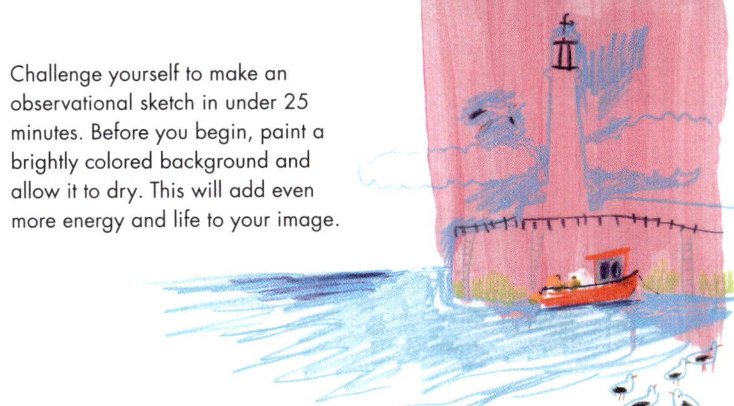

166 —————— Create a note of all the colors you'd like to use more in your art. Engage with the emotions the colors make you feel and give each color swatch a name of your own invention.

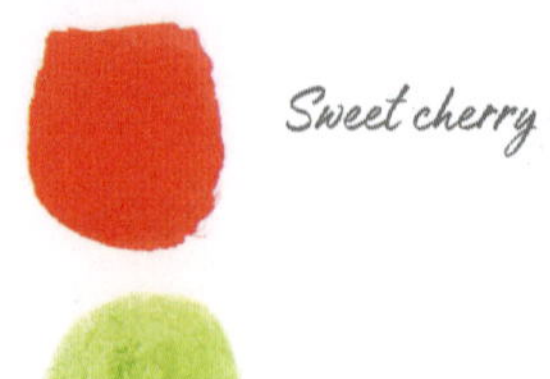

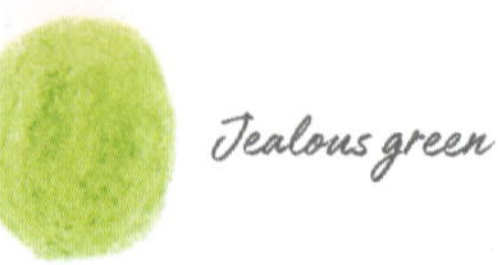

Draw as many purple things as you can think of.

168 —————— Sketch a scene, object, or person in pencil using only outlines. Then add color to your drawing using any material you like.

169 —————— Some individual hues and groups of colors can remind us of particular locations. Think about a place that you love—it could be a room, a town, or a holiday location—and create a palette below that conjures up the feelings of that place.

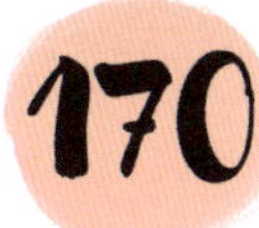

Color this drawing using only neutrals to create a serene image.

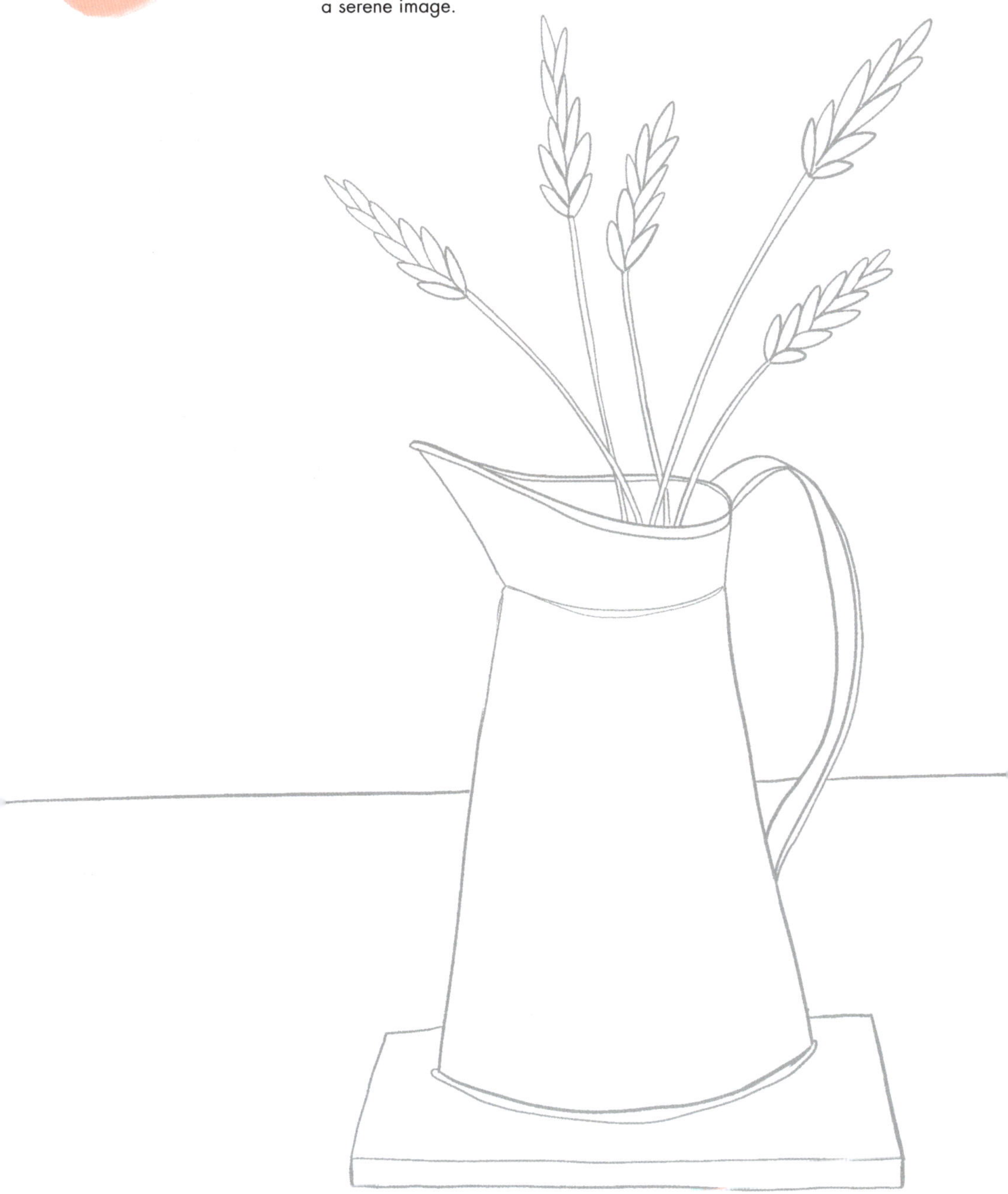

171

Make a piece of art using bright colors against muted or dark background colors. Choose a subject where you can see a strong contrast, and use any material you feel like.

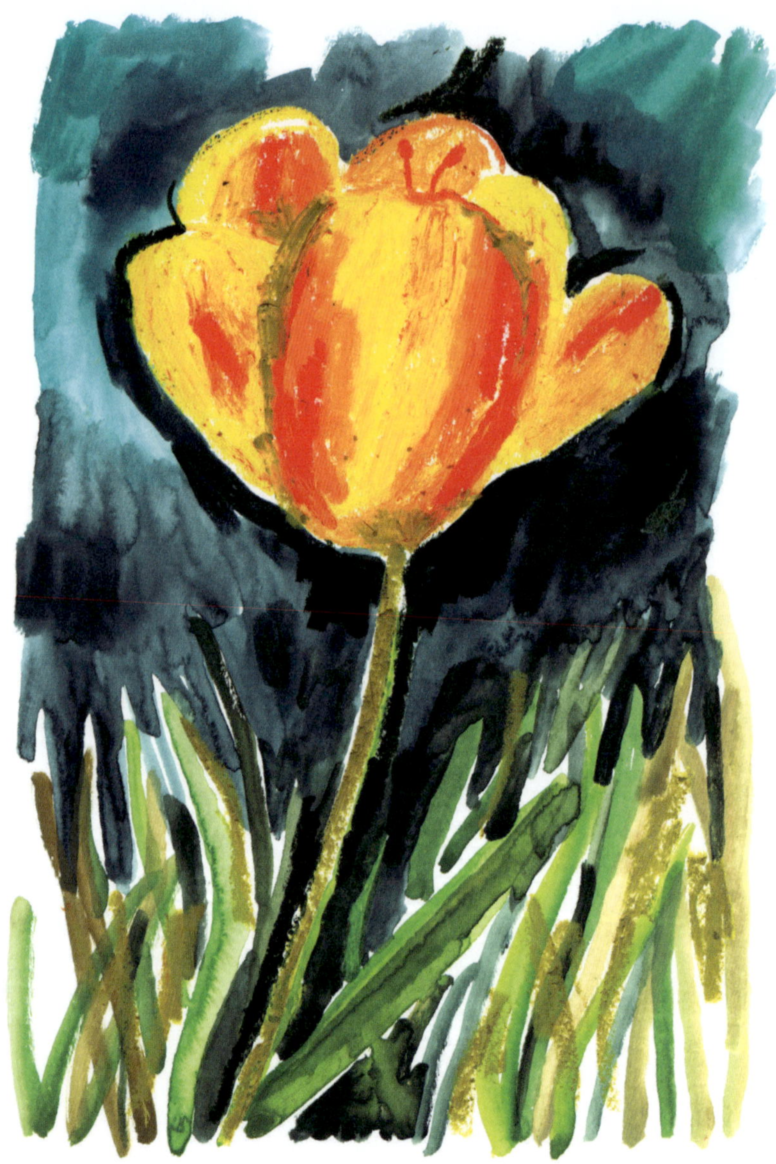

Tip: You may want to draw the light, bright elements first, then add the darker background around them … but there is no right or wrong way to approach this! Consider what you've learnt about your materials in earlier activities.

Continue adding to the design, exploring different art materials.

 ——————— Draw some fish in colors that you find harmonious.

The sea can appear one color one day, and another the next. Using these backgrounds as starting points, create four depictions of the sea.

175 —————— Paint an object or view using broad, confident brush strokes. Use color to sculpt your image, rather than an outline. You could layer colors on top of each other to add depth and energy to your image.

Tip: If you are unsure how to begin, paint the background a bright color—it's far less daunting than a white space!

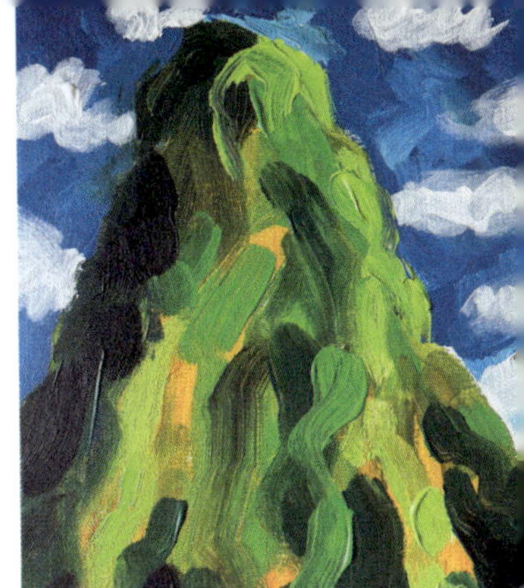

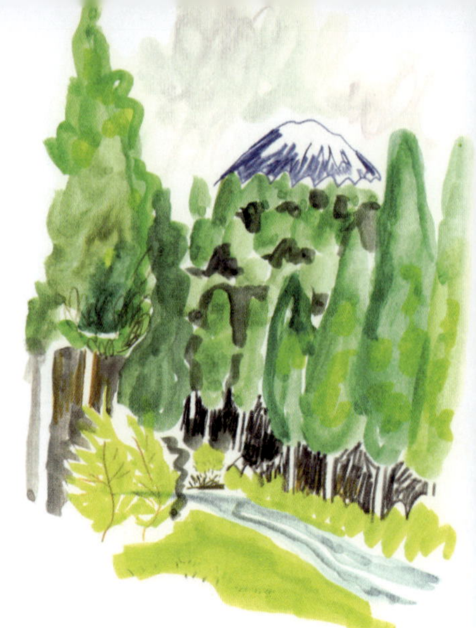

176

Warm colors tend to jump forward in a piece of art, whereas cool colors tend to recede and so can be used to suggest something is in the distance. Draw a landscape and use cool colors like blue to depict elements that are far away, such as mountains or distant buildings.

Tip: To add further depth to your image, you could include a warm colored element in the foreground—a red sign, for example.

Add color to the pattern to create a tartan.

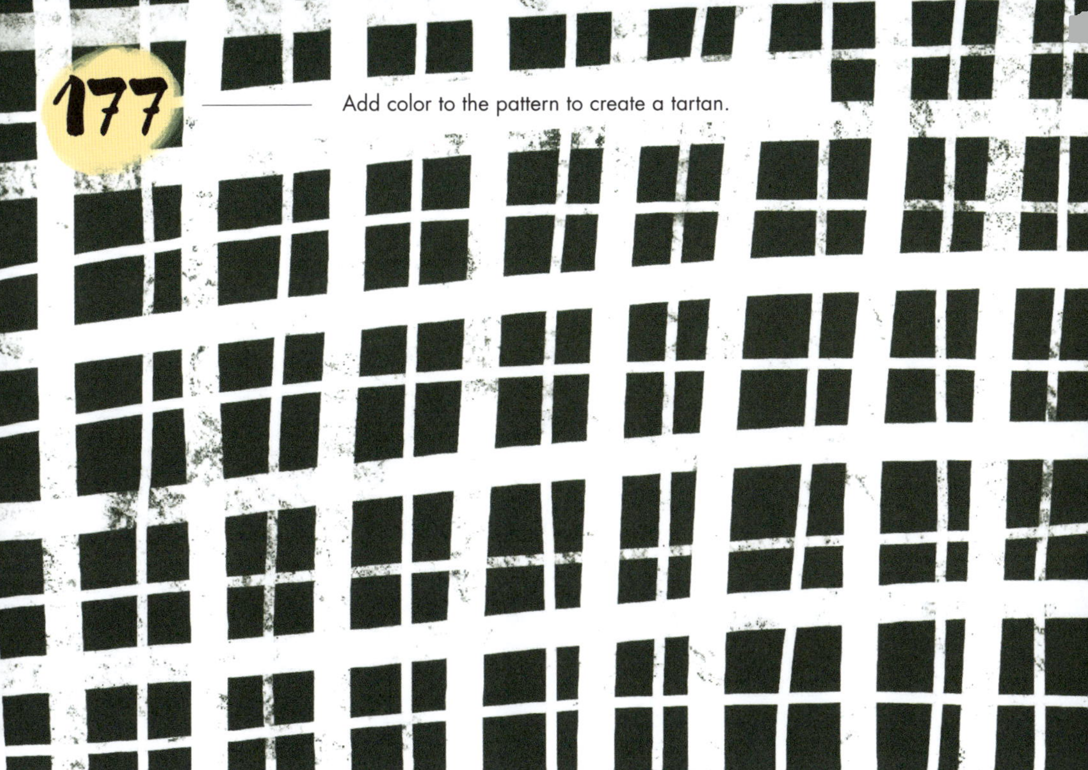

Draw a tempest using colors that evoke tumultuous feelings.

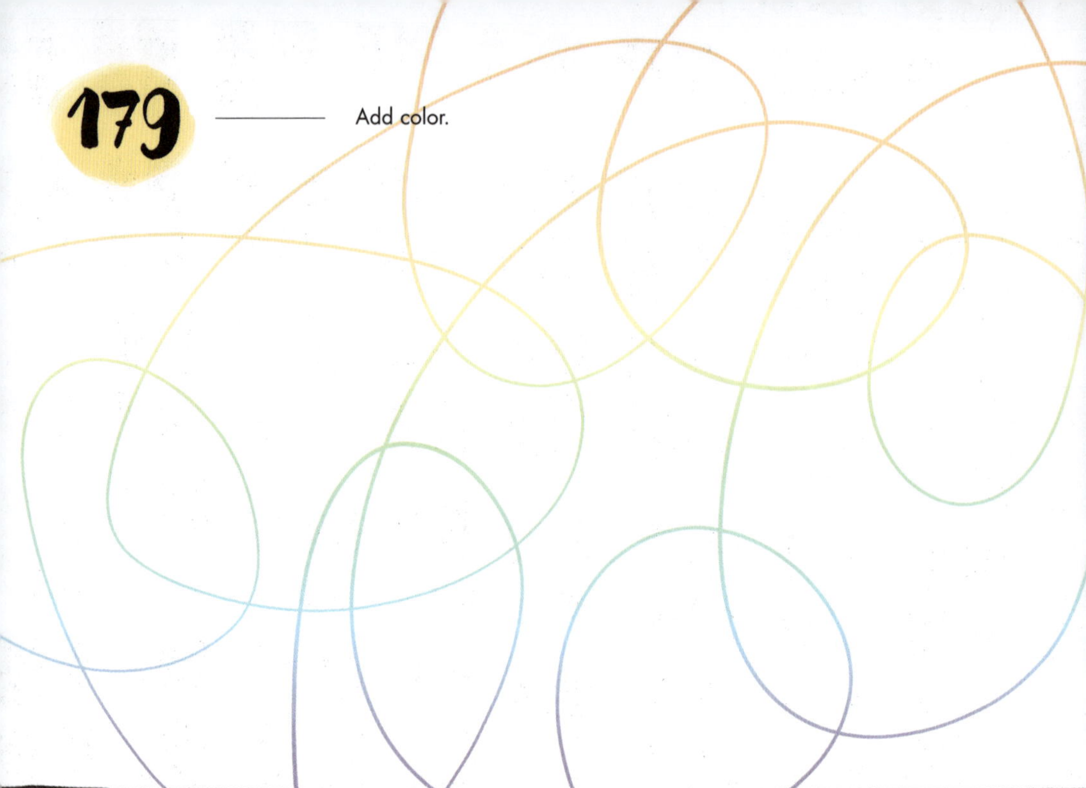

179 ———— Add color.

180 ———— Fill the page with the color green—how does it make you feel?

181

You can use a pattern to surround a white image so that the busy 'negative space' makes the clean, white object become the focus. Use a bold pattern to frame a white object.

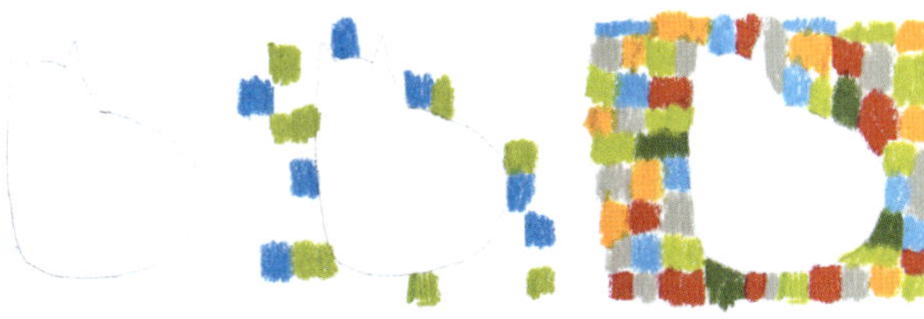

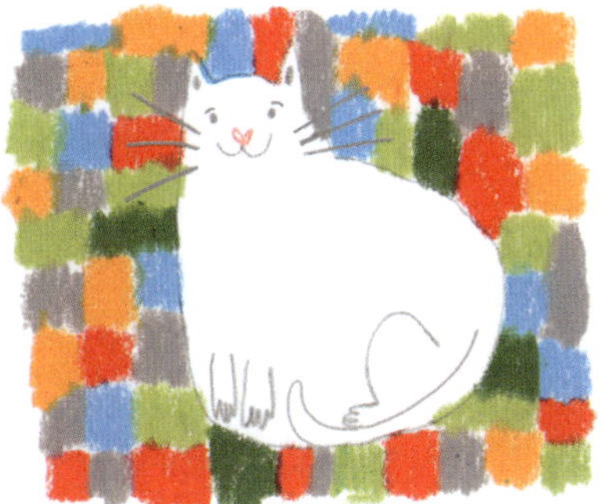

Create a faint outline of your object, then fill the surrounding area with a colorful pattern. Then add details to your object but keep lots of the paper white so that it stands out.

Using a limited palette of three to five colors, draw a landscape or object. Use wax pastels if you have some, or colored pencils.

Tip: Look carefully at your scene before starting. Which colors could you choose? Perhaps there is a tree trunk that is almost the same tone as some purple leaves, so you choose a purple to represent both. Maybe the palest green leaves you see are a similar tone to the pale sky, so you use a soft green for both.

183 ———————

Cut lots of shapes out of colored paper, then create a series of compositions, using the pieces. Work quickly— spend around 10 minutes on each design.

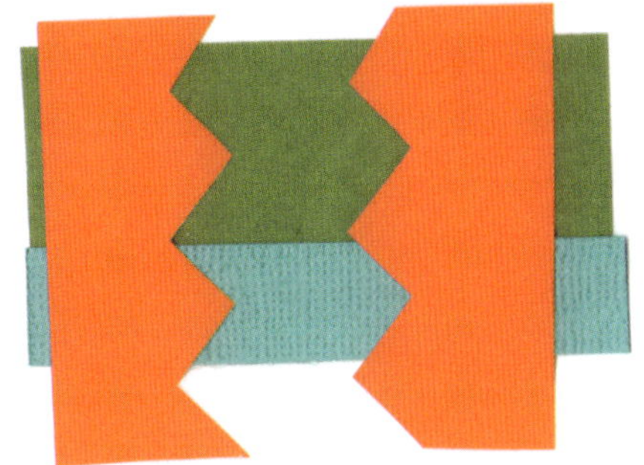

Tip: Working quickly will encourage you to make instinctual decisions— don't worry if your compositions look 'right' or 'wrong' just enjoy the process of choosing shapes and being playful.

184

Using blues, create graphic representations of tranquillity and water.

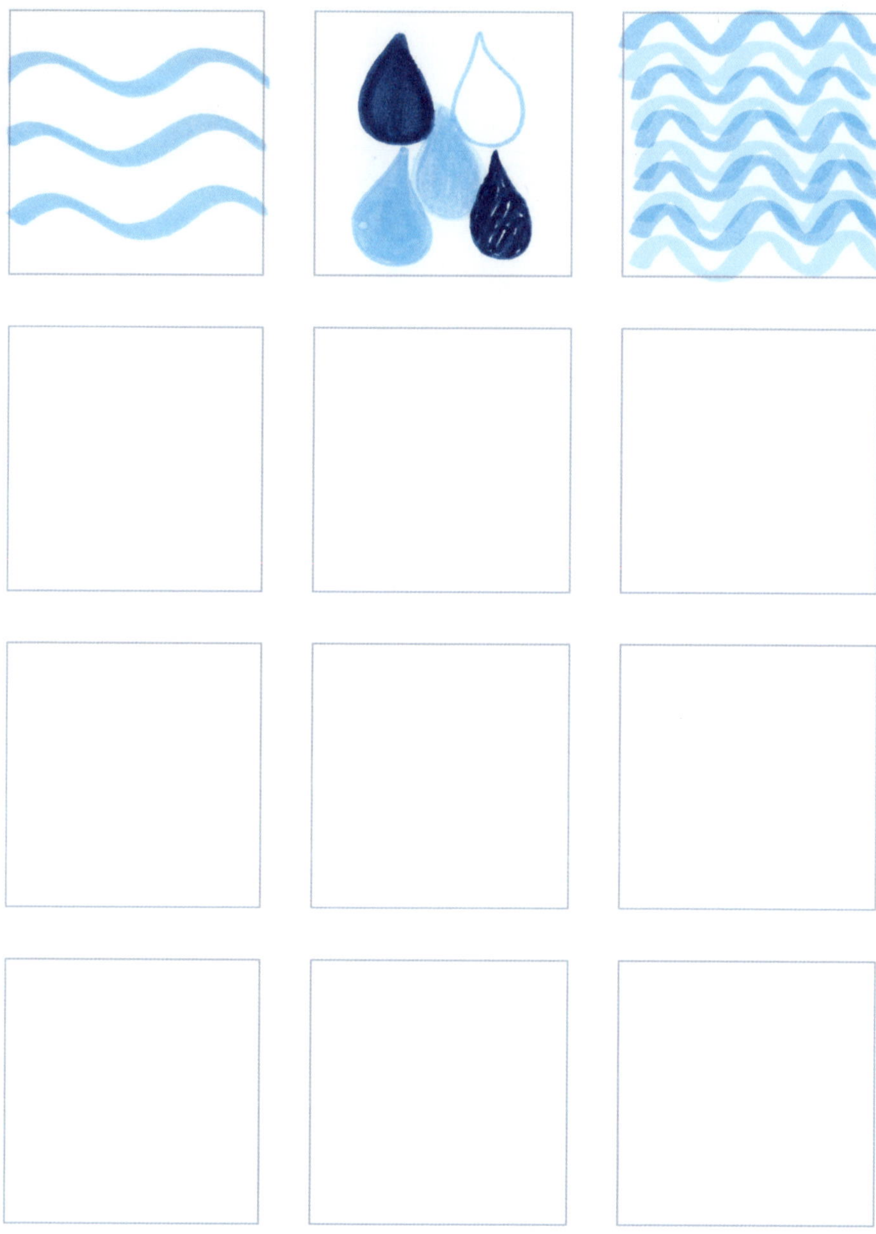

Color in these pencils.

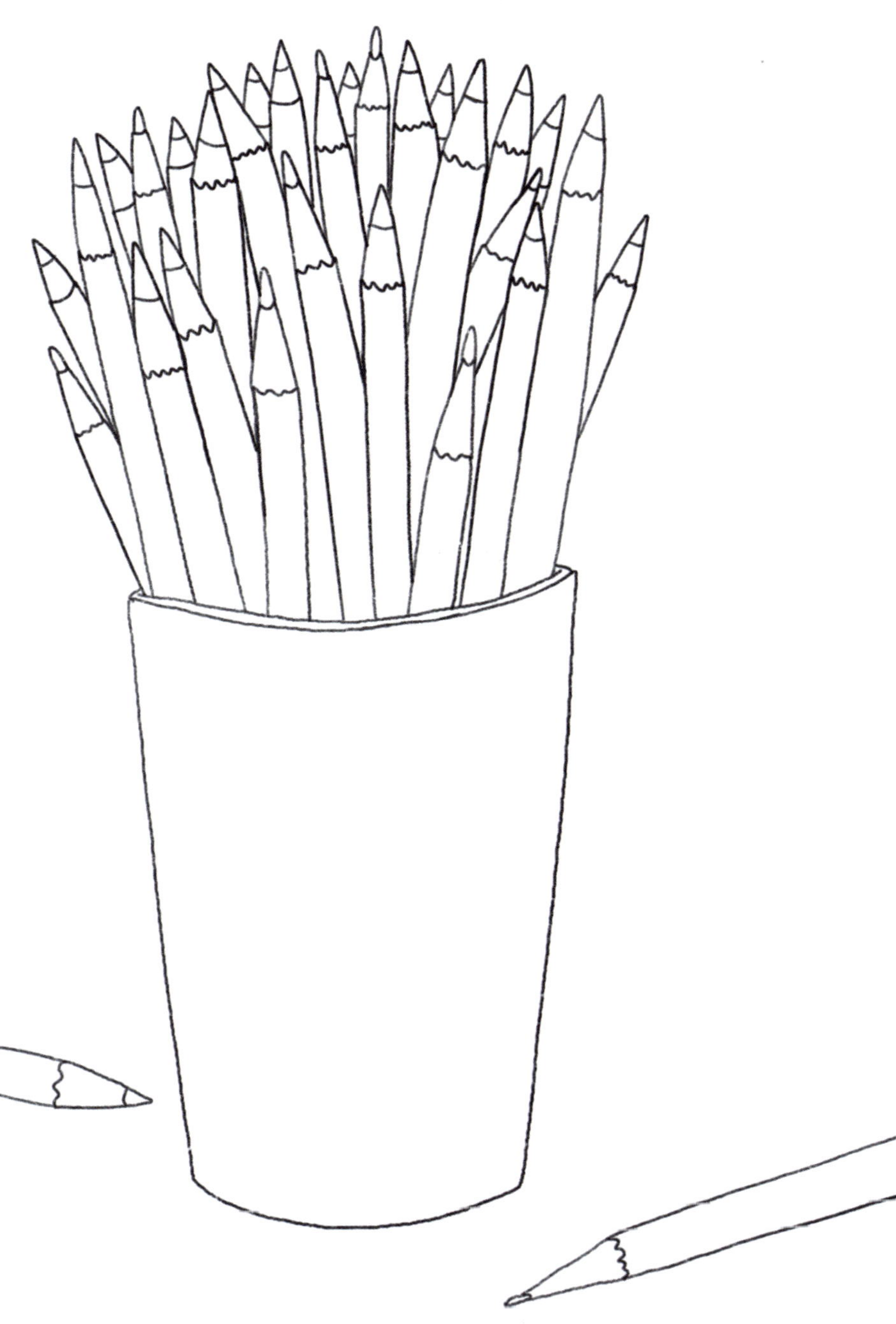

Add color to this design, taking inspiration from the element of either fire or water.

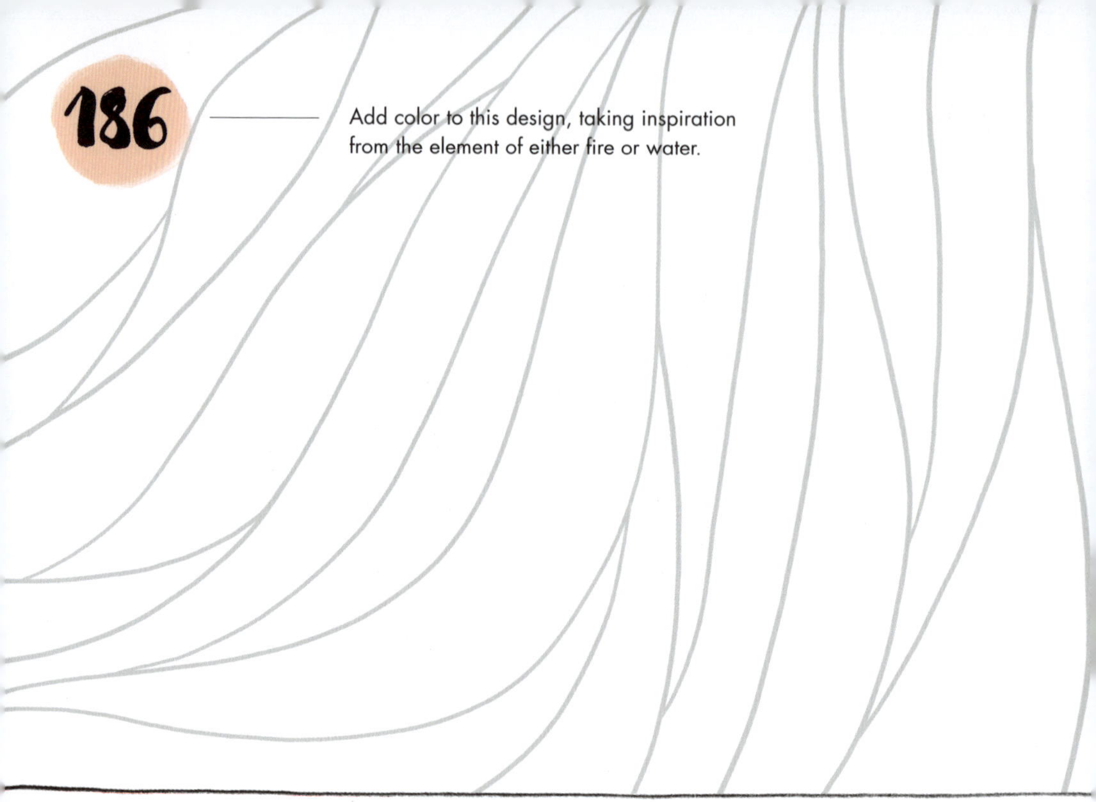

Continue adding lines of color to fill the space.

188 —————— Spend some time observing the shadow on objects and surfaces, noticing all the different colors you see. Look carefully. Draw some simple objects and then paint their shadows as accurately as possible.

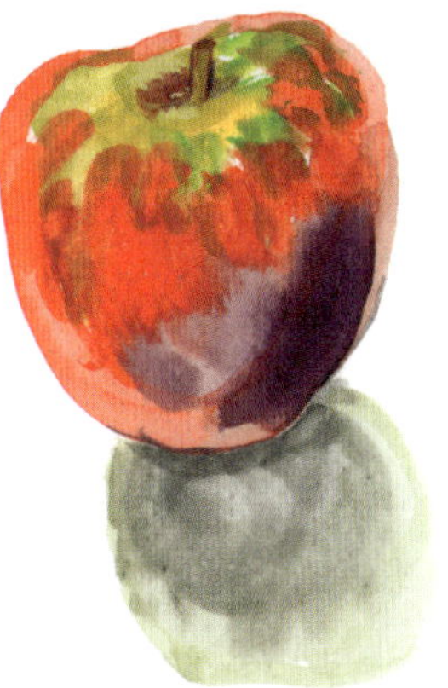

Build scenes with color. Choose three landscapes (from photos, what you see in front of you, or even Google Maps) and paint them using blocks of color to represent what you see. You don't need the hues to match perfectly—in fact, it can be really fun to overemphasise the colors to make your painting vivid and striking. The boxes are small to encourage you to use fearless marks and not too much detail.

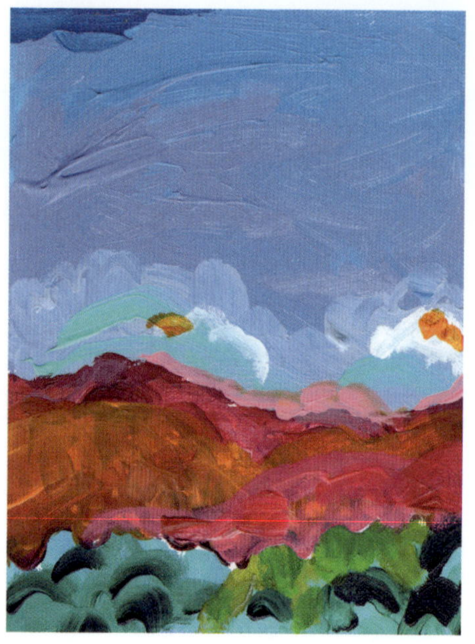

190 ——————— Fill the page with
colorful birds.

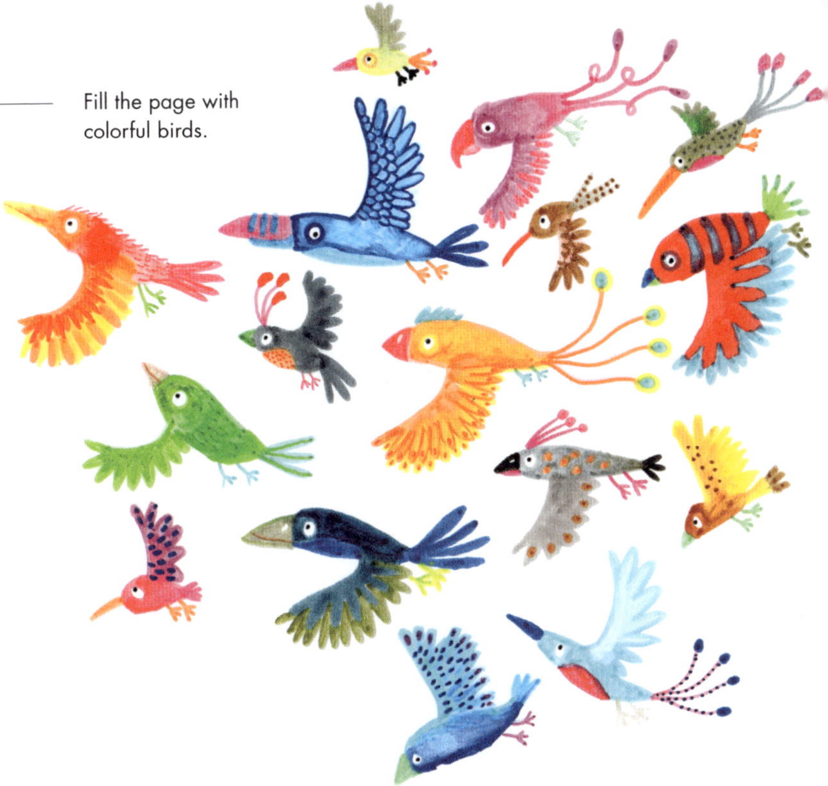

191 ———— Draw a family tree or a tree to depict friendships.
Consider using color to represent the people.

192

Add watercolor shapes and allow the colors to bleed into each other. Then add bold patterns to the shapes in contrasting colors.

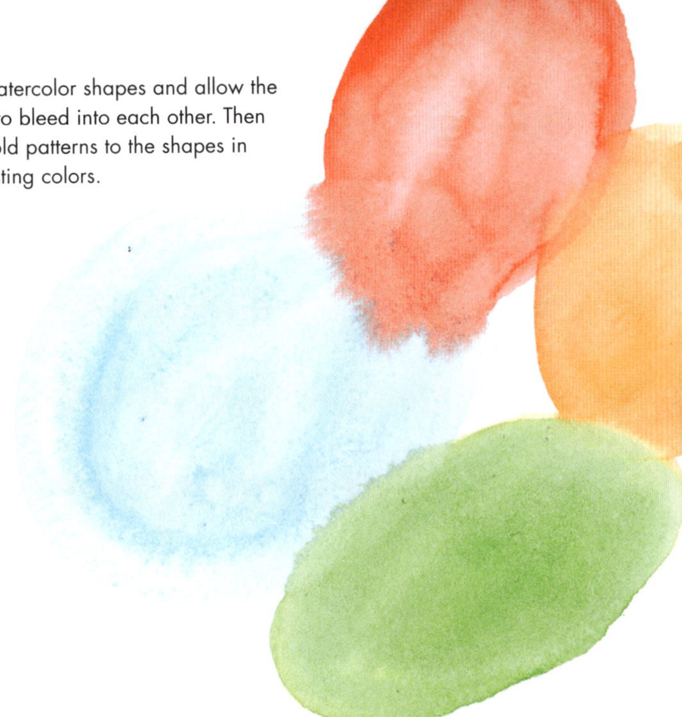

Draw the same object twice, when you are experiencing two different emotions. Note down the mood you are feeling, and notice how the colors you naturally gravitate towards vary.

Mood:

Mood:

Continue the squiggle using a variety of colors.

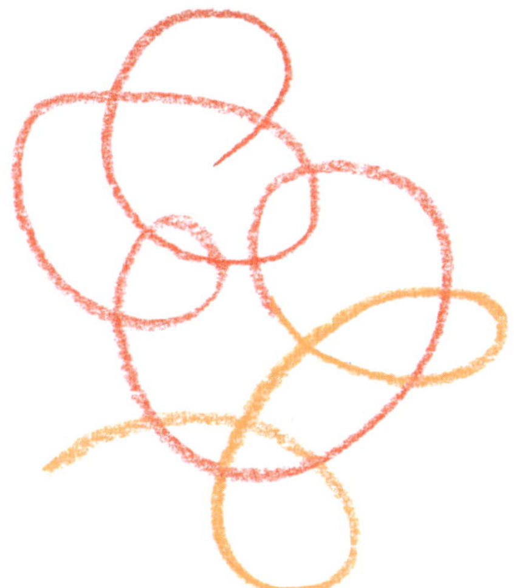

Refer to activity 17 to paint a cube using a tint and shade of a color in order to give it a 3-D effect.

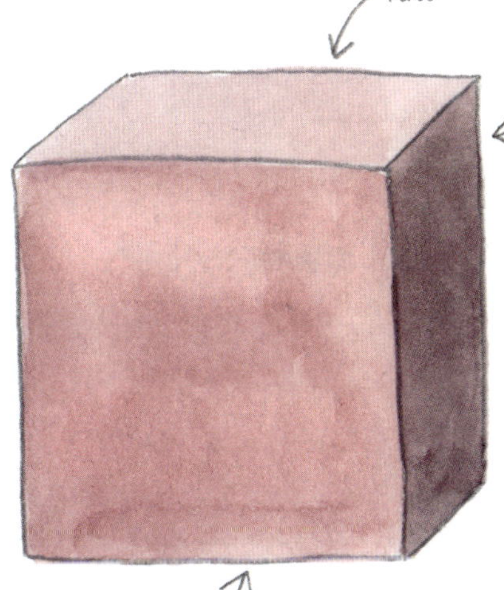

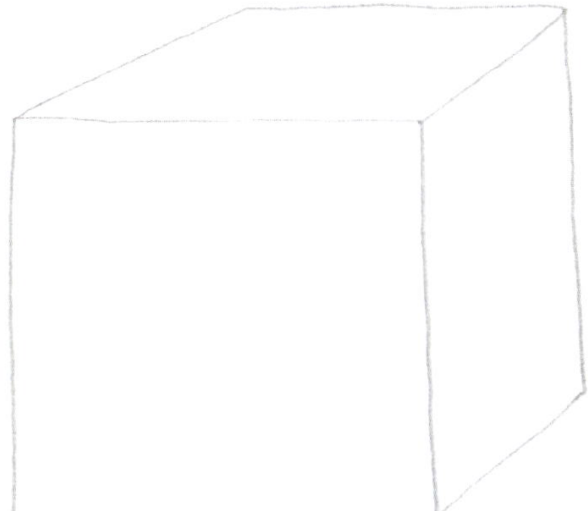

Add cheerful flowers to this vase. Create an arrangement that brings you joy.

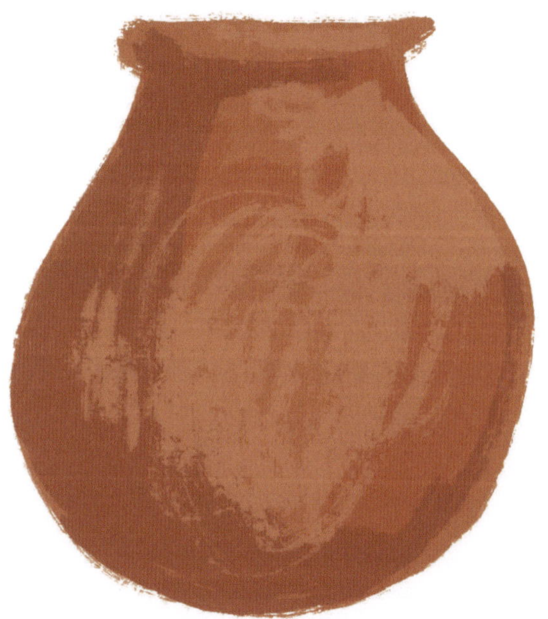

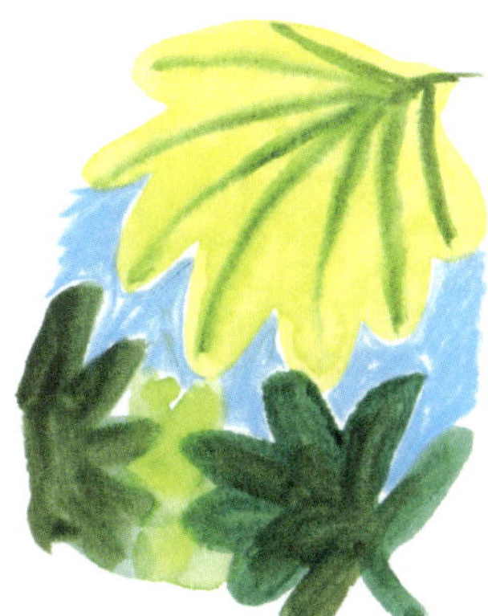

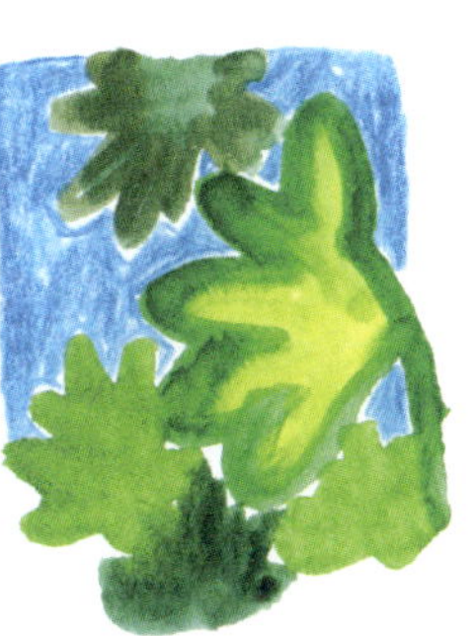

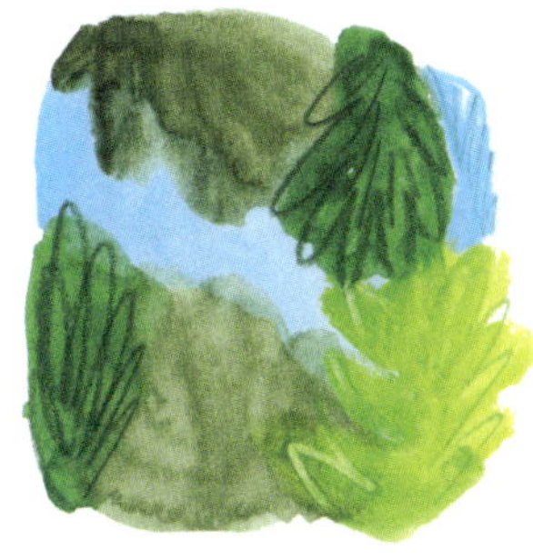

197

Analogous colors produce calm, harmonious palettes. Create some thumbnail sketches in color for possible paintings using analogous colors. Refer back to your color wheel and choose three or four colors that are next to each other on the wheel—this will be your palette!

You can combine materials within your art, and be led by which color you'd like to use rather than restricting yourself to one material. Use any art tools you like to create a landscape. Perhaps start by laying out a selection of materials in front of you—paints, pastels, coloring pencils, and pens—and choosing from them as you go along.

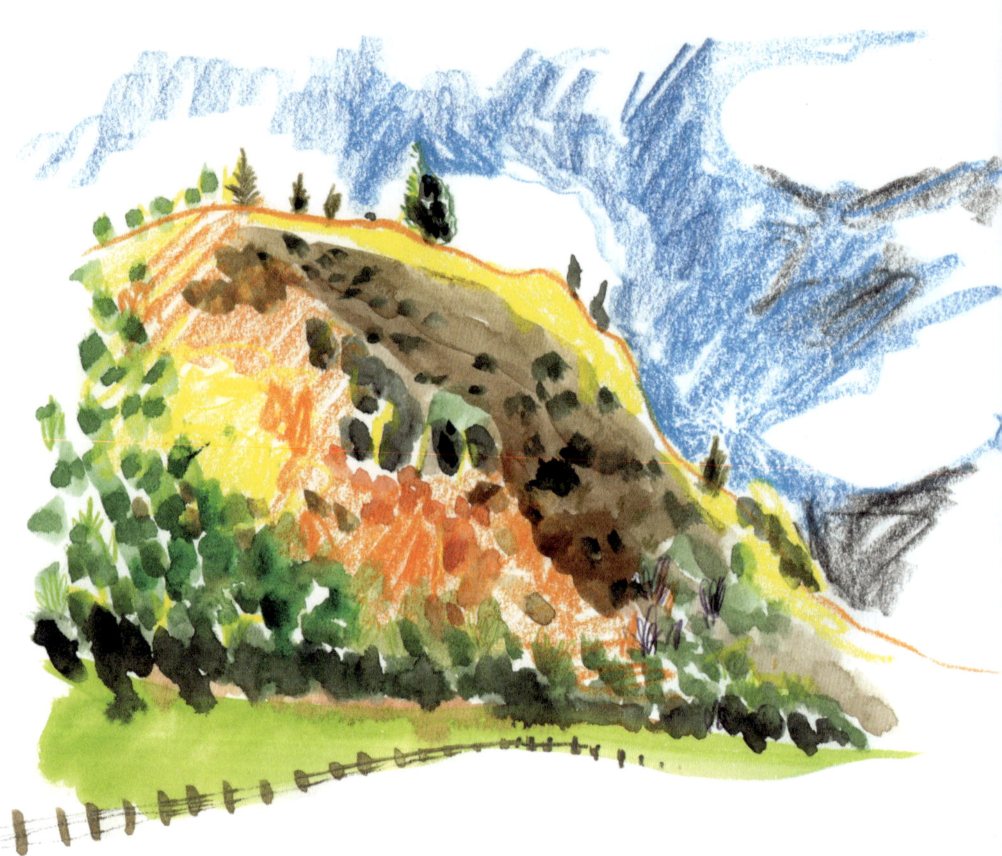

Tip: You can also use the white of the paper as a material—rather than filling the whole page, try leaving some areas of white paper showing through to represent light areas.

Use a limited range of colors to create some abstract compositions. Think about what colors could go in each section below to make the piece feel balanced. Then choose your own colors and create your own sections.

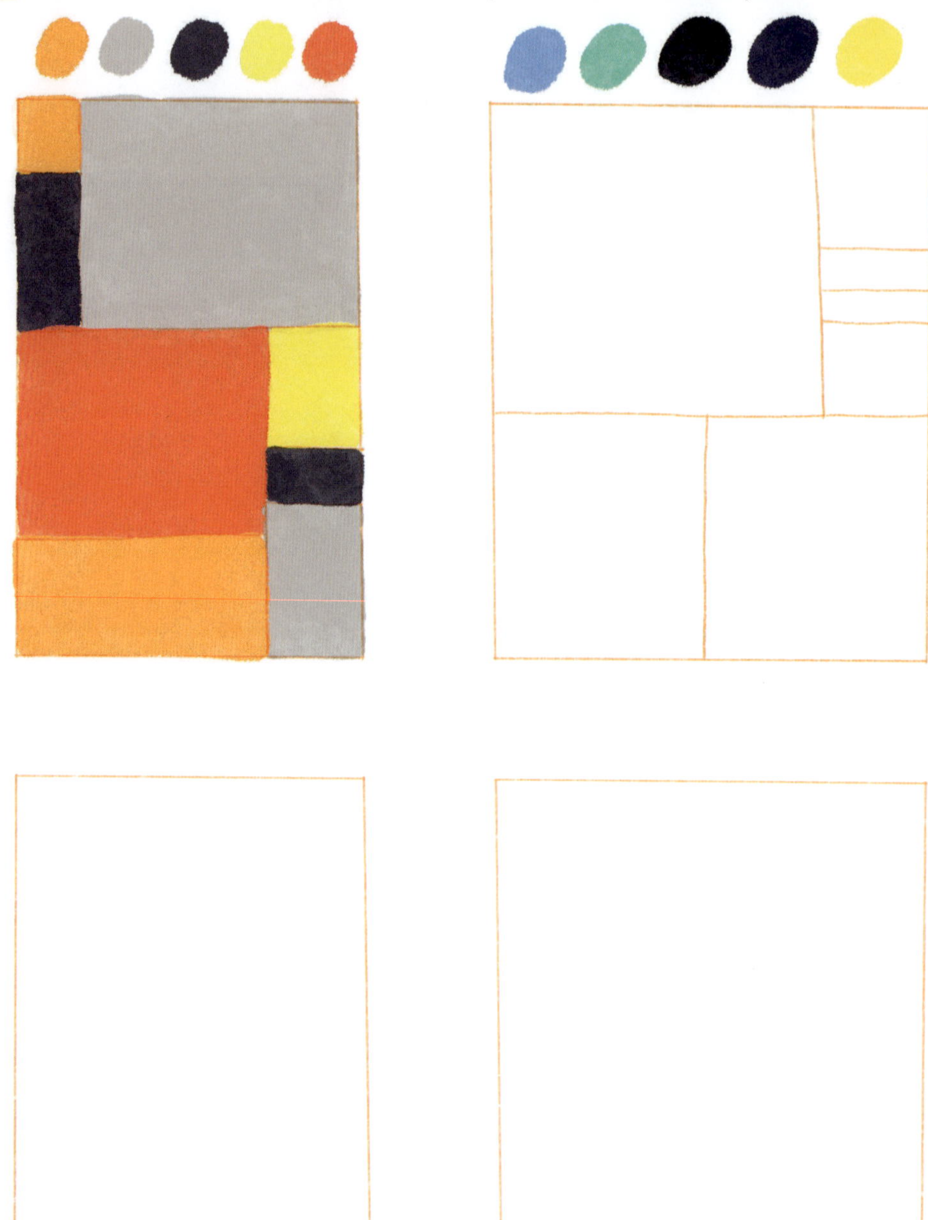

Tip: Small amounts of bright colors can have a big impact among less saturated colors.

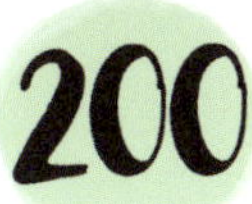

200 ——————— Create color palettes that represent things you can see around you.

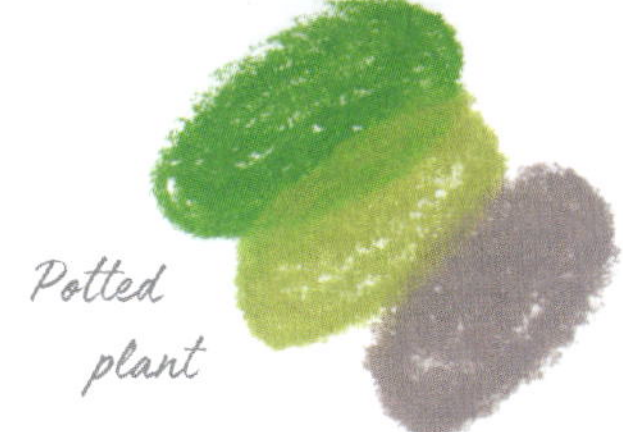

201 ——————— Design a pattern using only green triangles.

202

It can be useful to note down colors, even when you are just making a pencil sketch. Draw some people, based on a photo or real life. Jot down anything you observe about the colors—ideas about which colors could go where, or colors you'd like to test out.

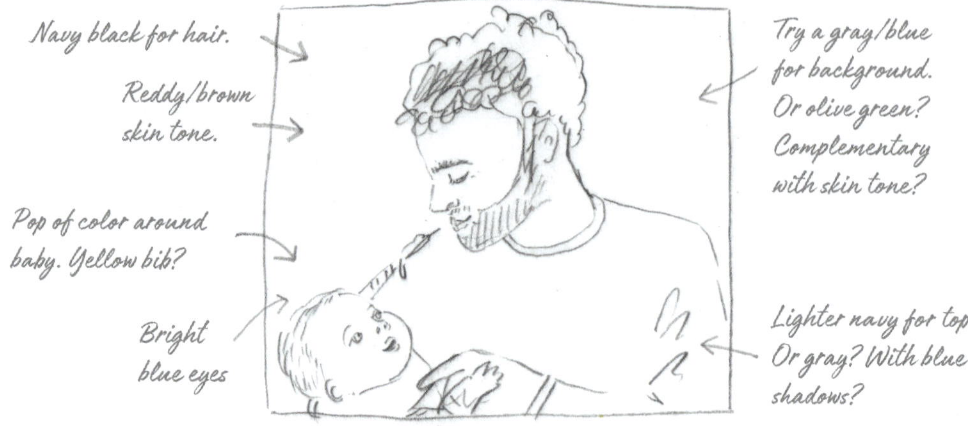

203

Make an image based on this springtime palette. Be inspired by how the colors make you feel.

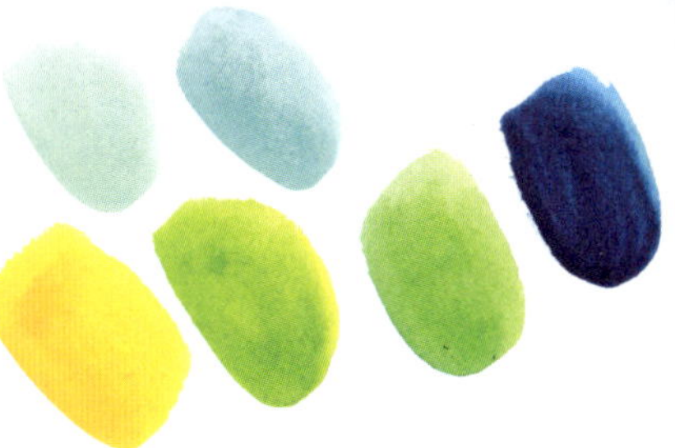

Draw a rainbow of food—portray a different food for every color.

Add flowers and plants to the vases. Perhaps some of the leaves could be purple, or red.

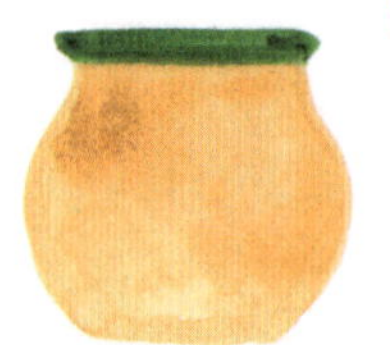 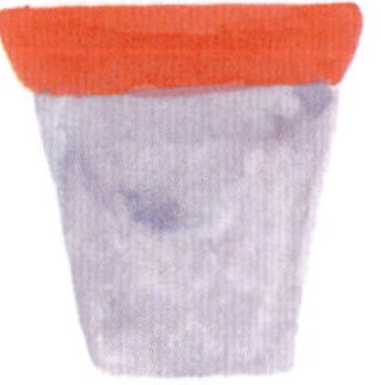 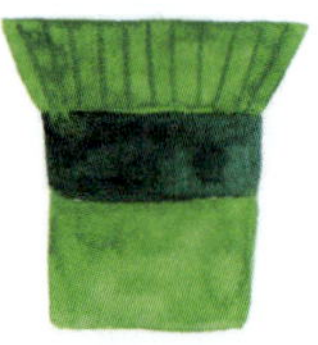 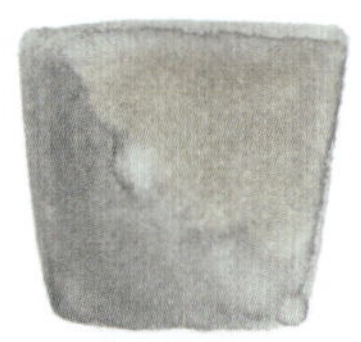 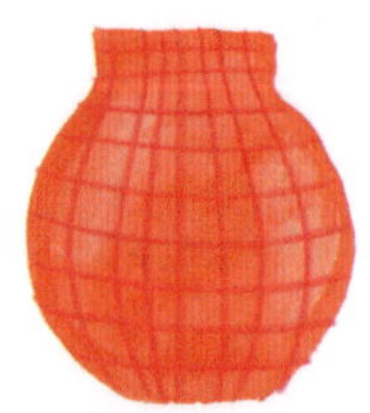

206

Add calm colors to these shapes.

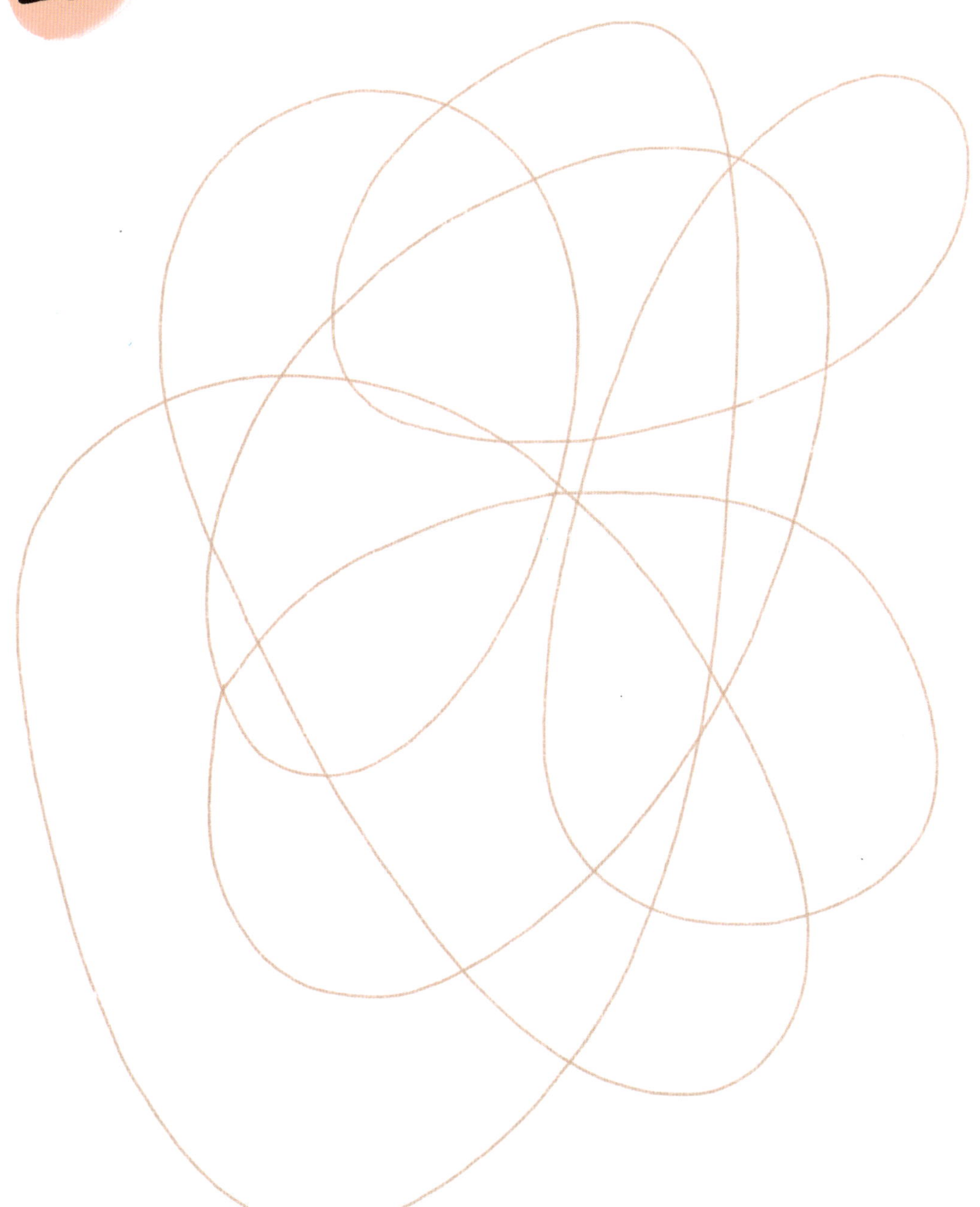

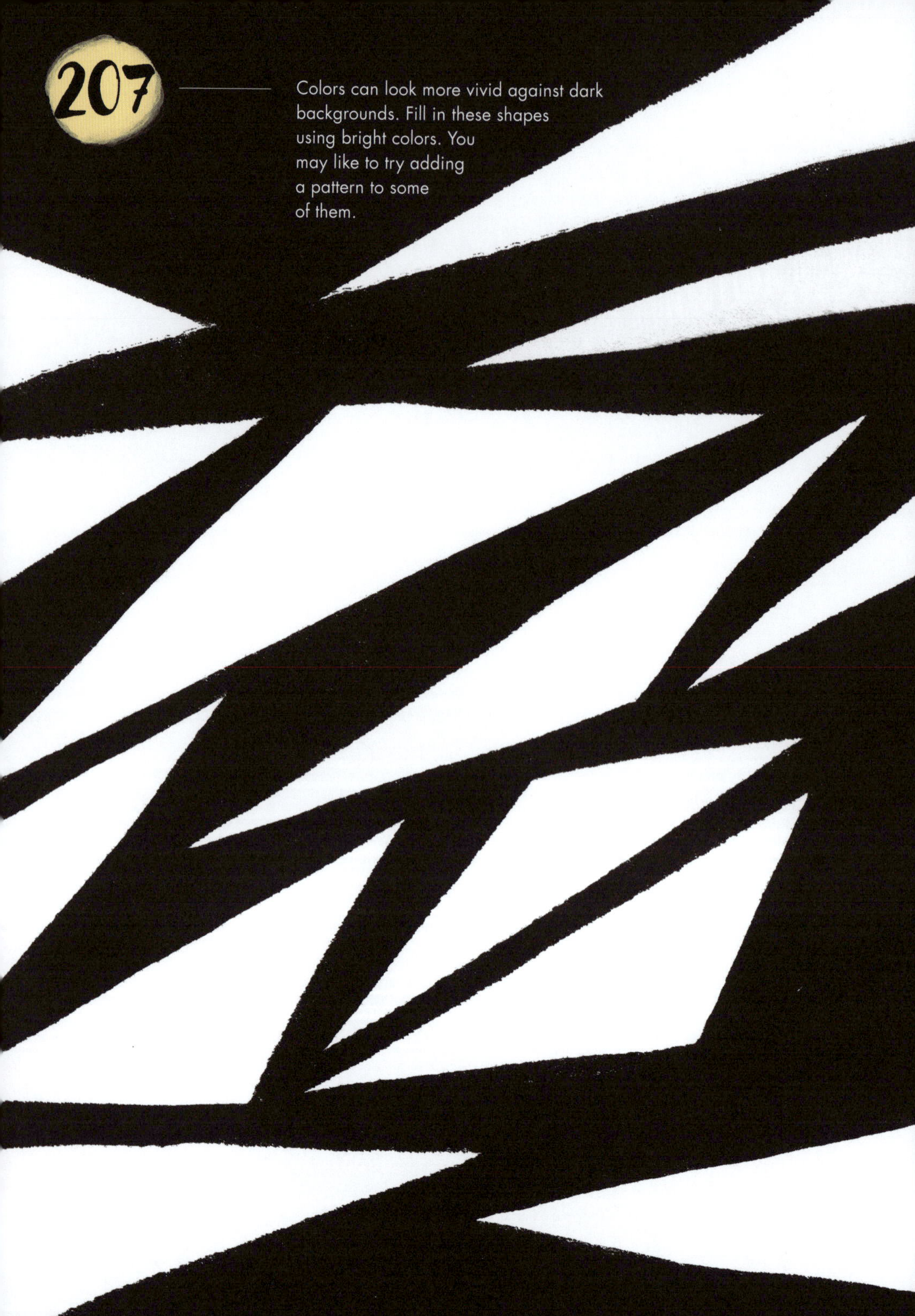

207
Colors can look more vivid against dark
backgrounds. Fill in these shapes
using bright colors. You
may like to try adding
a pattern to some
of them.

The way we use color can add depth to artwork. Closer objects appear more saturated than those in the distance. Explore this by coloring a forest. As it recedes, colors should become less saturated.

Pink can suggest fun, humor, and playfulness. Be inspired by how pink makes *you* feel and turn this shape into an image.

210 ———— Draw as many yellow things as you can think of.

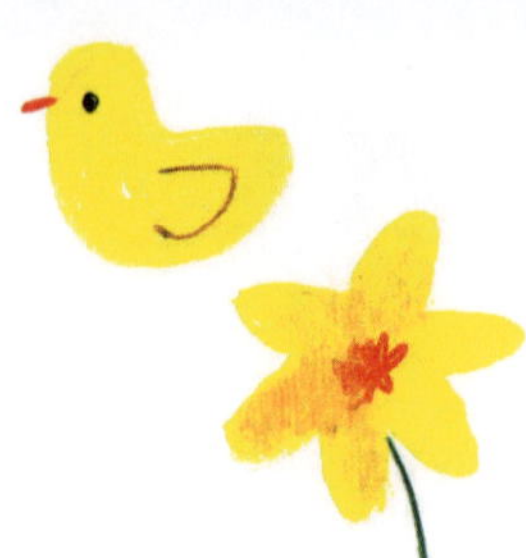

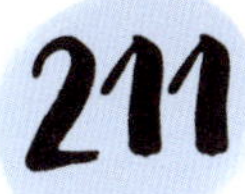

211

Color using primary colors, plus black if you'd like to. Notice how bold and striking the image is when you use these hues.

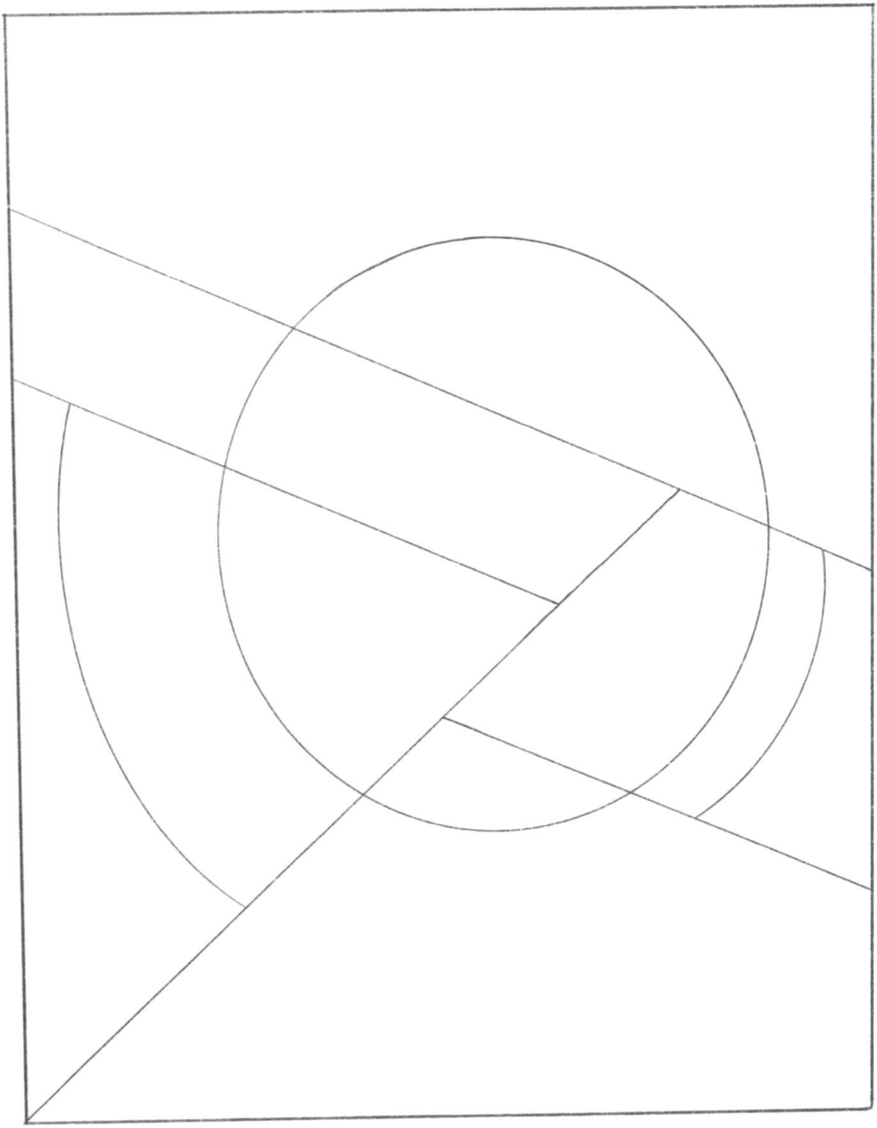

It can be useful to use dark colors in your art, and there are lots of ways of creating a black by mixing colors of paint. Using a pure black from a tube can deaden an image, whereas a black or dark color that is mixed by you can feel more cohesive. This is especially true if your black or dark color is mixed using colors from the rest of your palette. Explore mixing your own black from a palette of colors, then paint an object using this palette.

Tip: Mixing green, magenta, and yellow will make a black, as will blue, magenta, and yellow. Have a go at mixing these and other colors together to make dark colors. Try ultramarine blue and burnt sienna, or perhaps a crimson, blue, and a brown.

Use color to express your feelings today.

214

Create a landscape using blocks of
color. You could use torn paper.

Add a stormy sky.

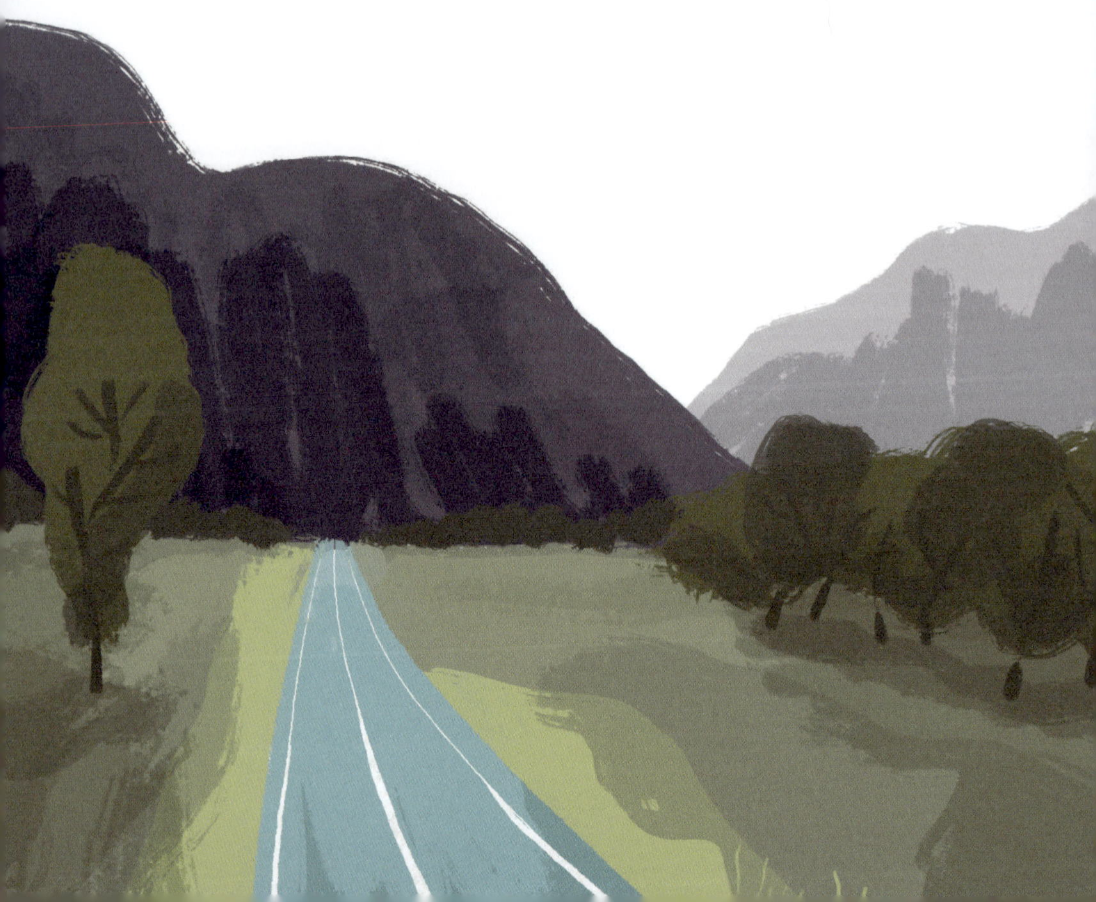

Choose five colors and create abstract thumbnail compositions.

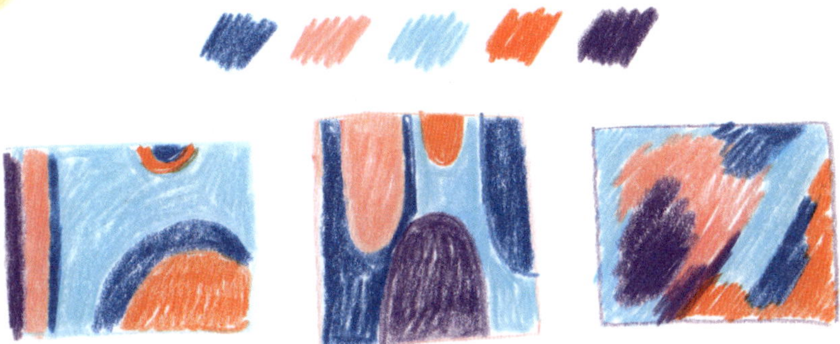

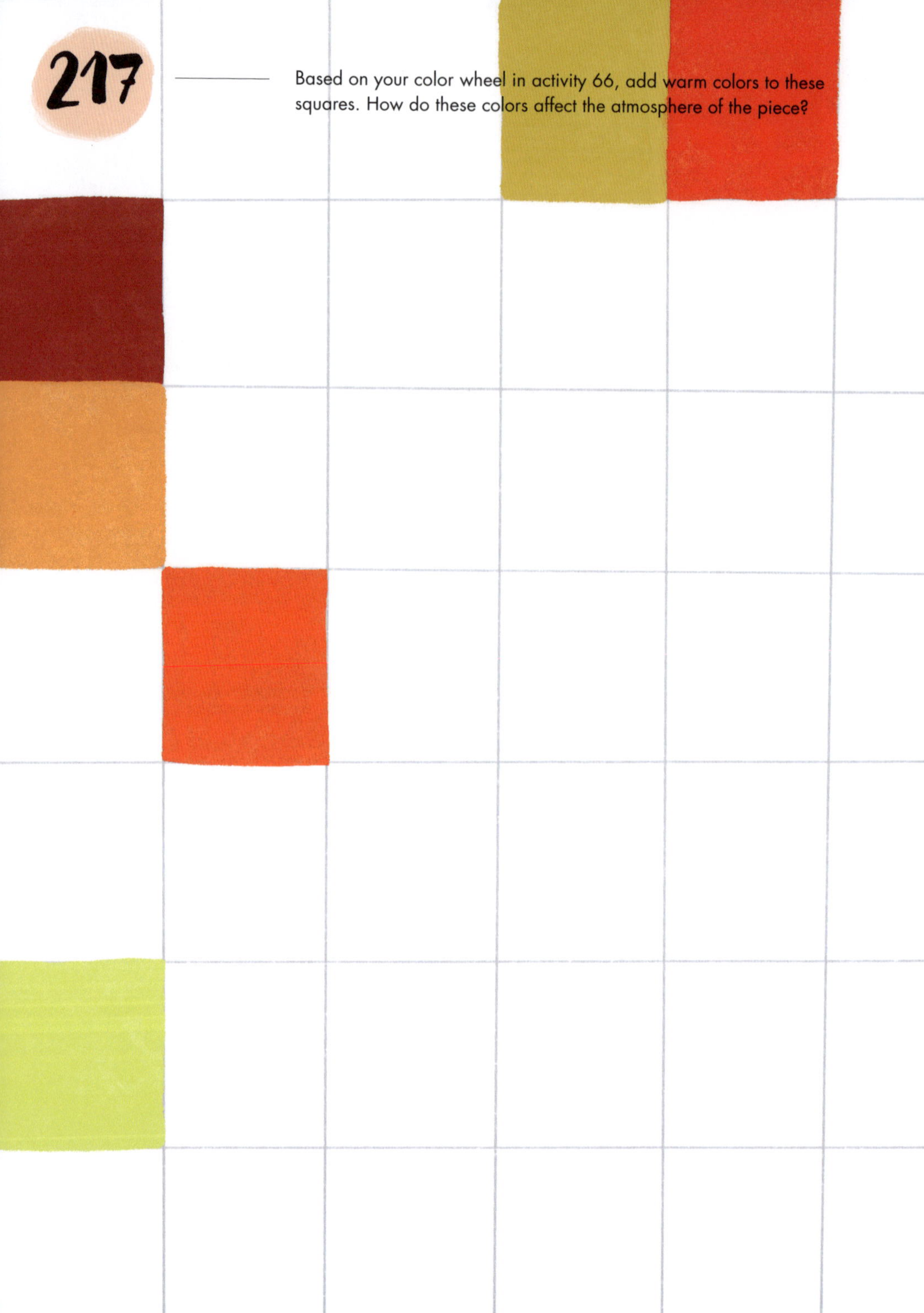

Based on your color wheel in activity 66, add warm colors to these squares. How do these colors affect the atmosphere of the piece?

Continue this colorful beach scene.

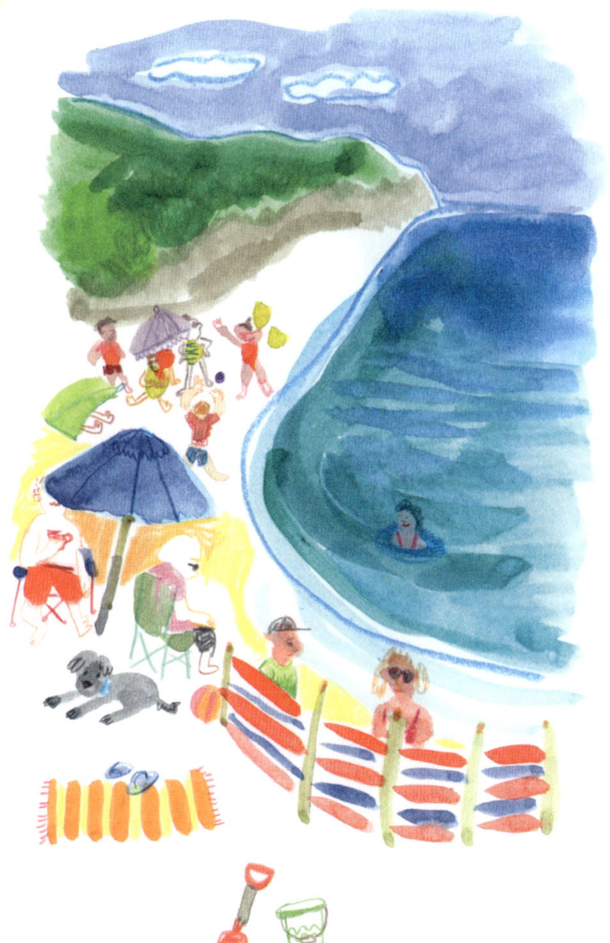

Draw the view out of a window today.

Add color.

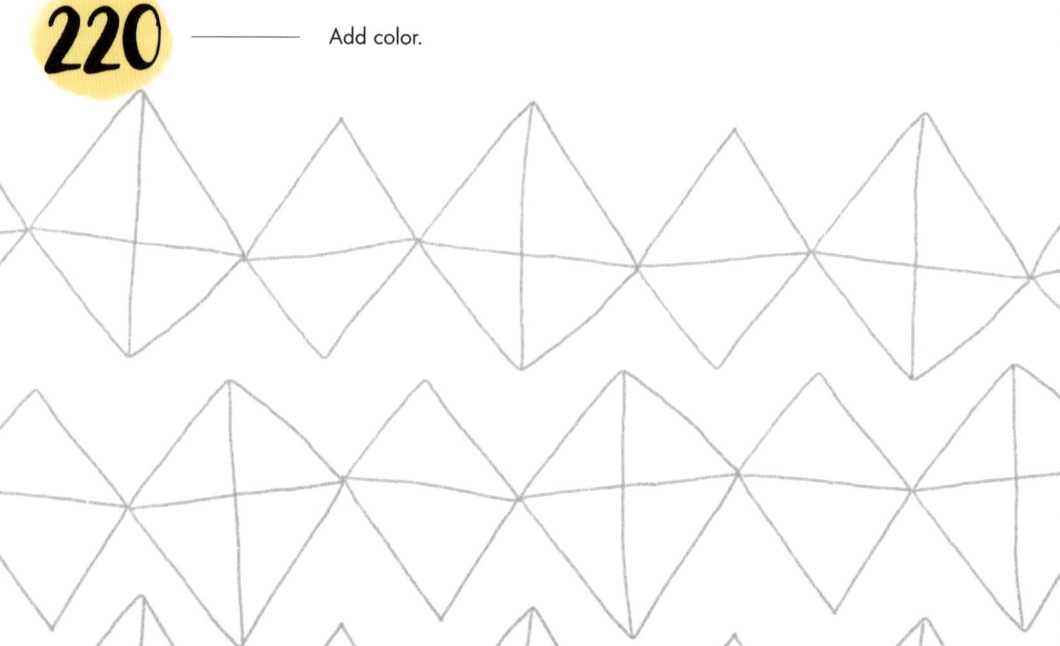

221

Use complementary colors to create an eye-catching graphic image. Your subject could be an everyday household object. Half of the image should show one combination of colors, and the other half should show the same image, but with the colors inverted.

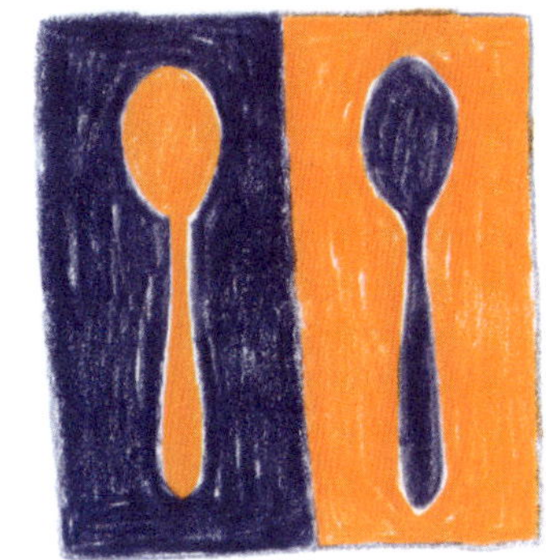

222

When used in an image, primary colors will automatically jump out, so you can use them intentionally in your art. If the main subject of your painting is a primary color (whether that's something abstract or an object) the eye will be drawn to it. Create a drawing where the focal point is in a primary color. For example, you could draw a red apple in a bowl of oranges and grapes, or a person wearing a bright yellow top.

223

Turn these splodges into objects, characters, or mini scenes. Let your imagination run wild!

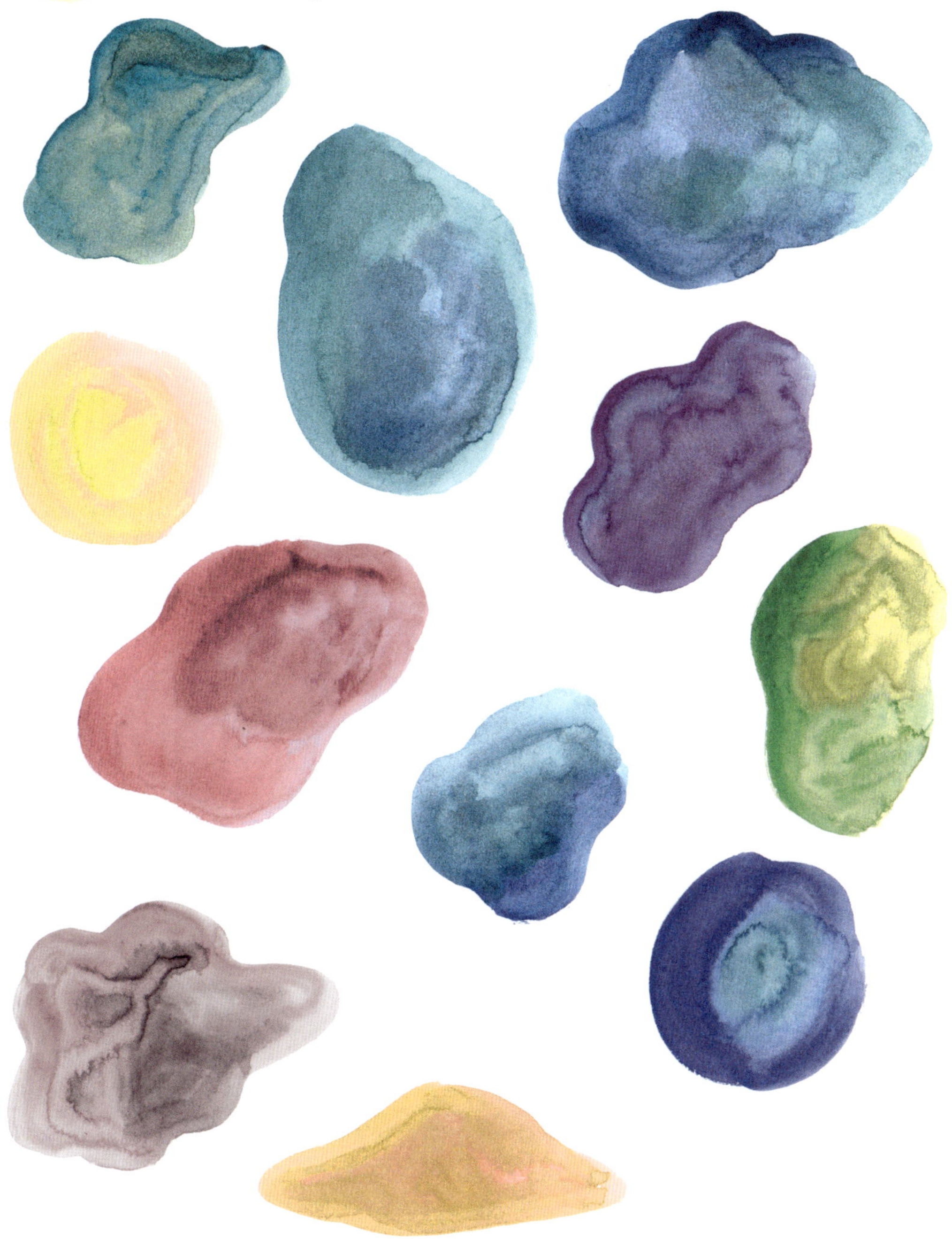

Draw a scene using only blues and greens. You could use a variety of materials. What atmosphere does your artwork evoke?

225 ———————— Find a photograph you like, stick it down and then add colors around it to represent your feelings when looking at the image.

---

226 ———————— Fill the page with balloons.

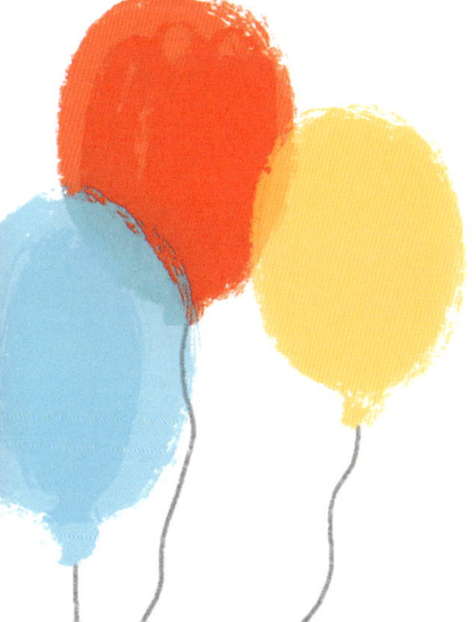

227

Refer to your clean and dirty colors in activity 75. Choose some items from around your home and set up a still life, being sure to include objects that have dirty colors (muted, murky) as well as clean colors (bright, pure).

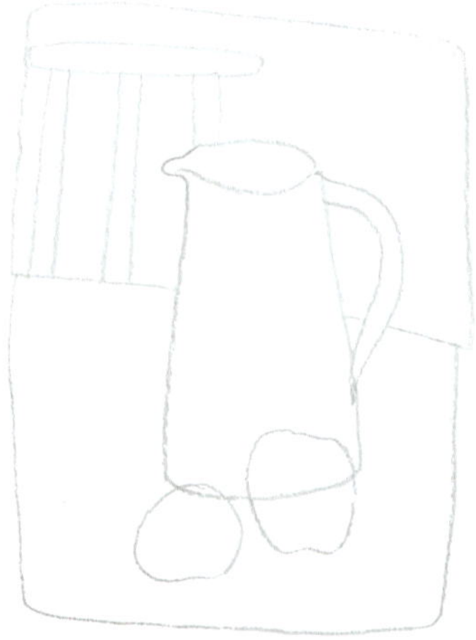

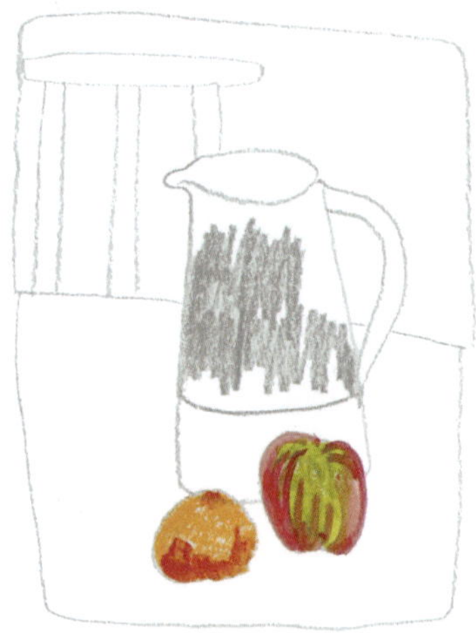

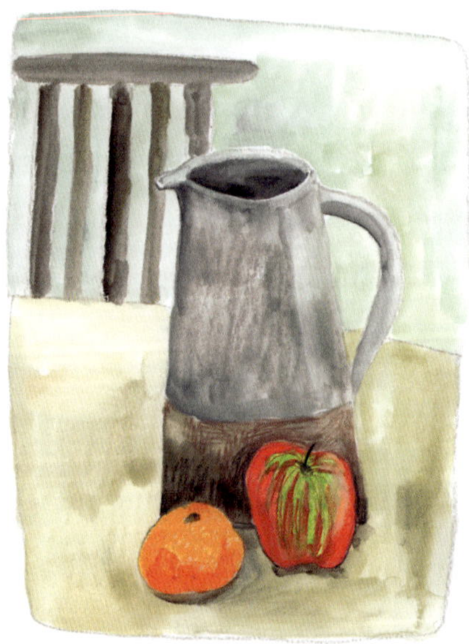

Begin by making a simple sketch of the scene. Map out the prominent elements and consider the composition—where could you place the objects on the page?

Choose your palette and materials and add blocks of color to your sketch. Work into these, adding tone, detail, and texture. Perhaps consider adding more detail to the areas you want to highlight, and keep background elements looser.

Notice how using the clean and dirty colors together can create a harmonious image. The more muted areas of the image offer a place for the eye to rest, and the clean colors become the focus.

Draw your hand and then add color. Pay particular attention to the exact colors you see in your skin tone. Hands can be tricky to draw. Take your time and don't worry if it doesn't look quite right—this exercise is about studying the colors rather than capturing accurate proportions.

Tip: You may like to create some swatches of the colors you see in your skin tone before starting.

Color in the rock pool.

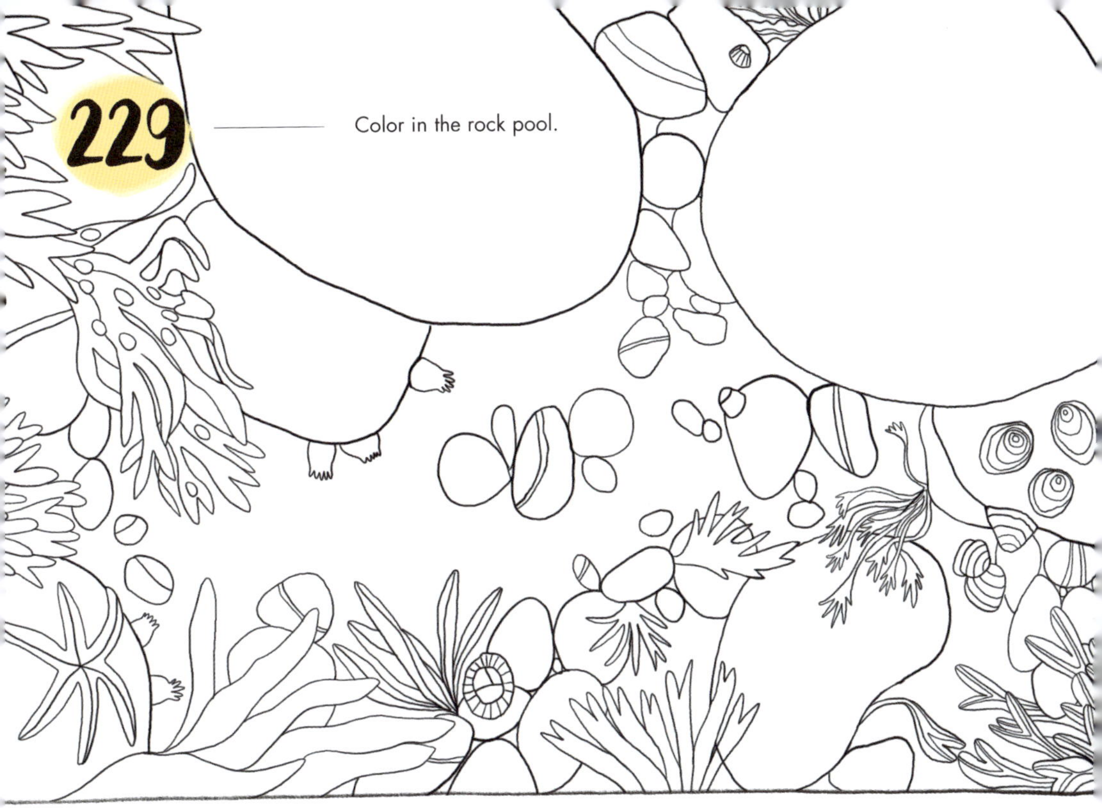

Blues can be used to create a peaceful mood as they can evoke water, the sea, and a day clear of clouds. You may feel like blues evoke different emotions. Use blues to fill the circle and consider what the colors make you feel.

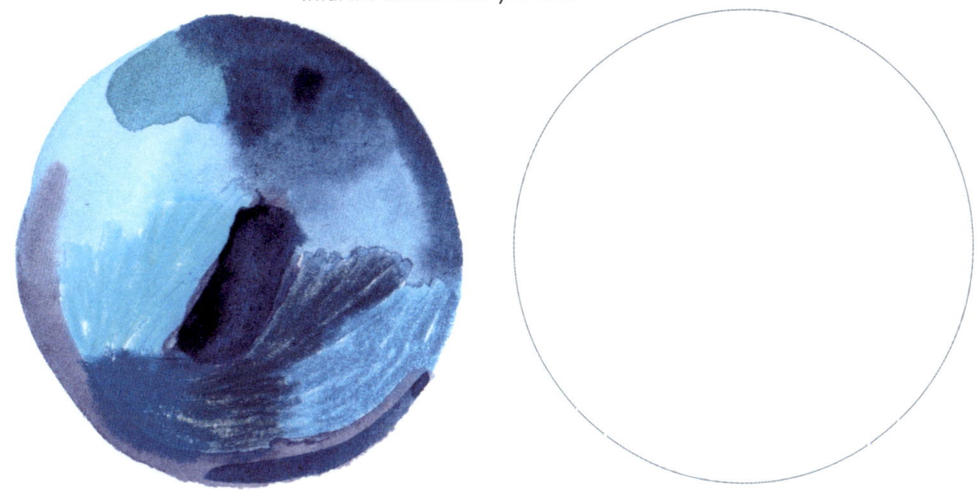

231

Set up some items for a mini still life and make color studies of what you see. These can be a quick, handy way to test various color combinations, and also to try some bold ideas that you wouldn't initially think to use.
It can be useful to create a palette of color options first, and then paint lots of quick versions of the same scene. Try lots of different versions, keeping the images very simple and rough, without detail.

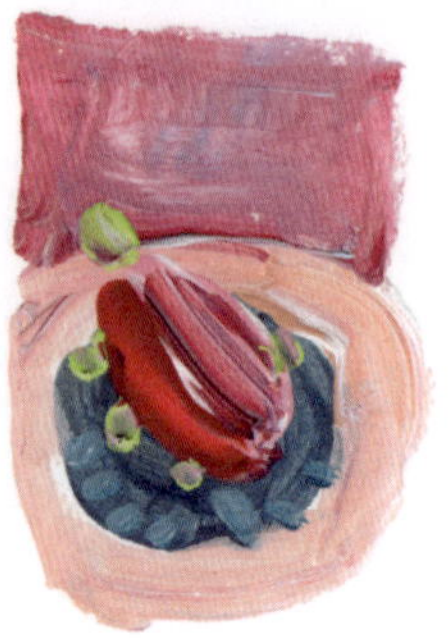 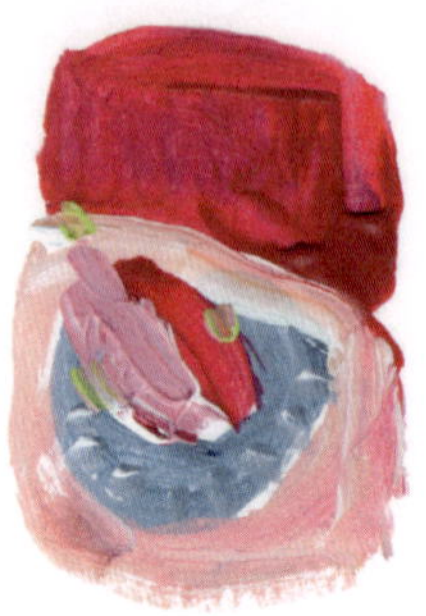 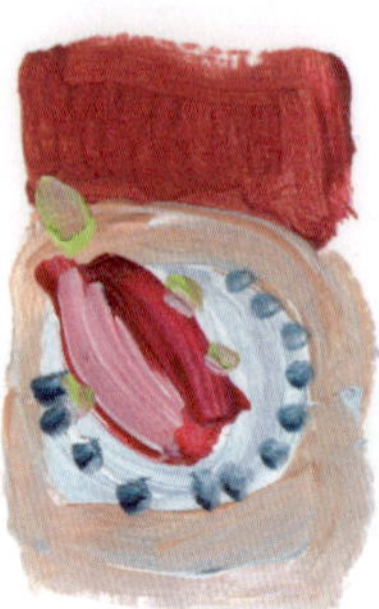

Tip: Perhaps do a few with unusual color choices—what have you got to lose?!

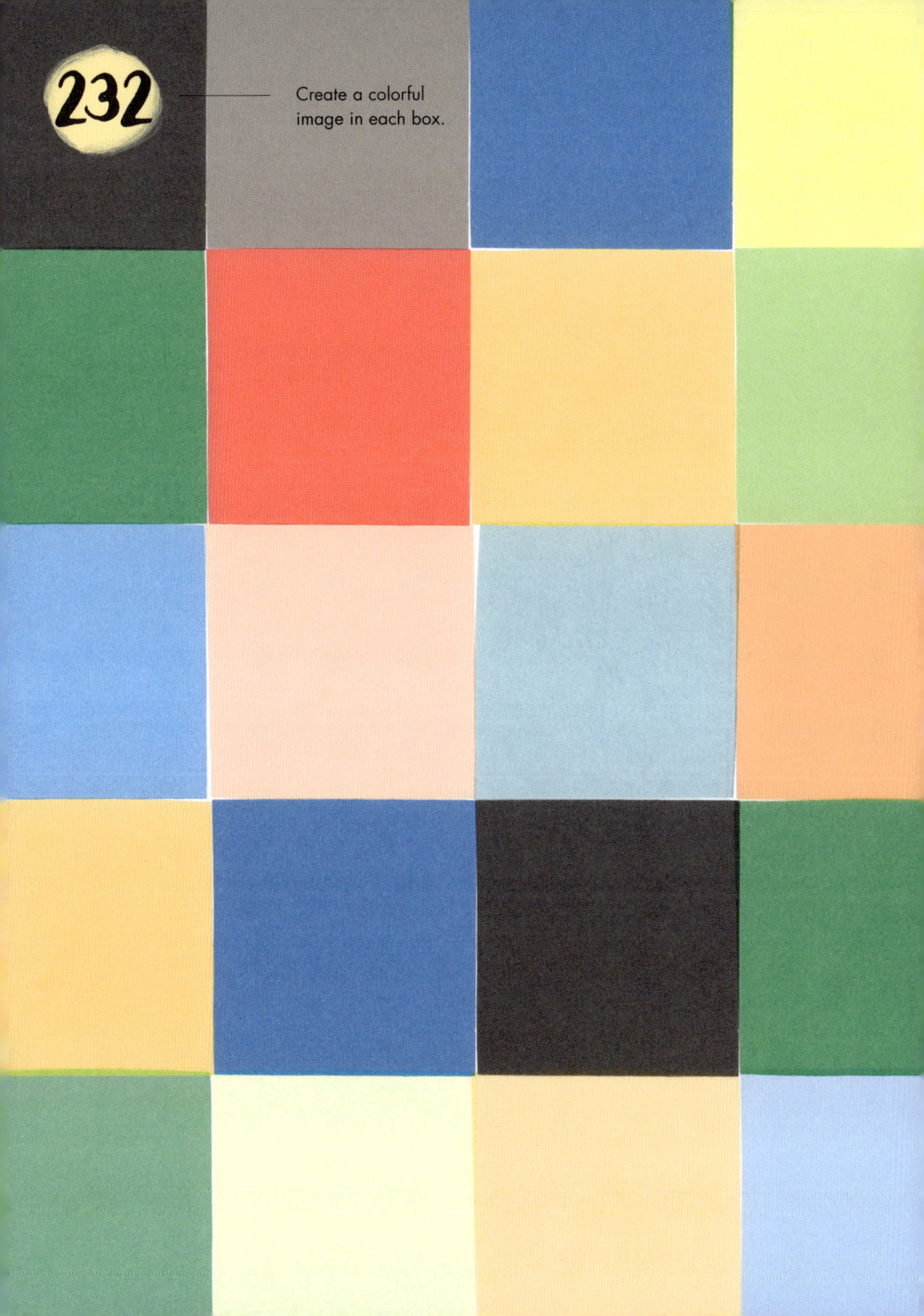
232
Create a colorful
image in each box.

Doodle using colored pastels. Try holding two at the same time and moving them across the page together.

Blend coloring pencils to add color to these hearts.

There are so many tones in our skin. Create swatches or mini drawings of all the colors you can see in your skin and the skin of your friends and family.

236

Turn these marks into a scene.

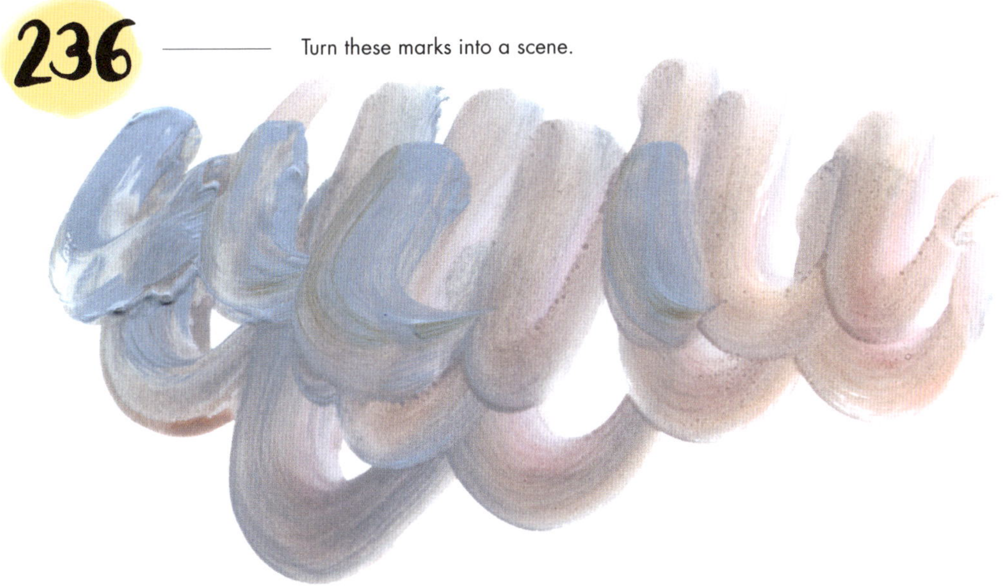

237

What colors and imagery suggest strength and bravery?
Make an image here based on those emotions.

238 ————————— Draw a portrait of someone using only cool colors. How does the image make you feel? What mood does it evoke?

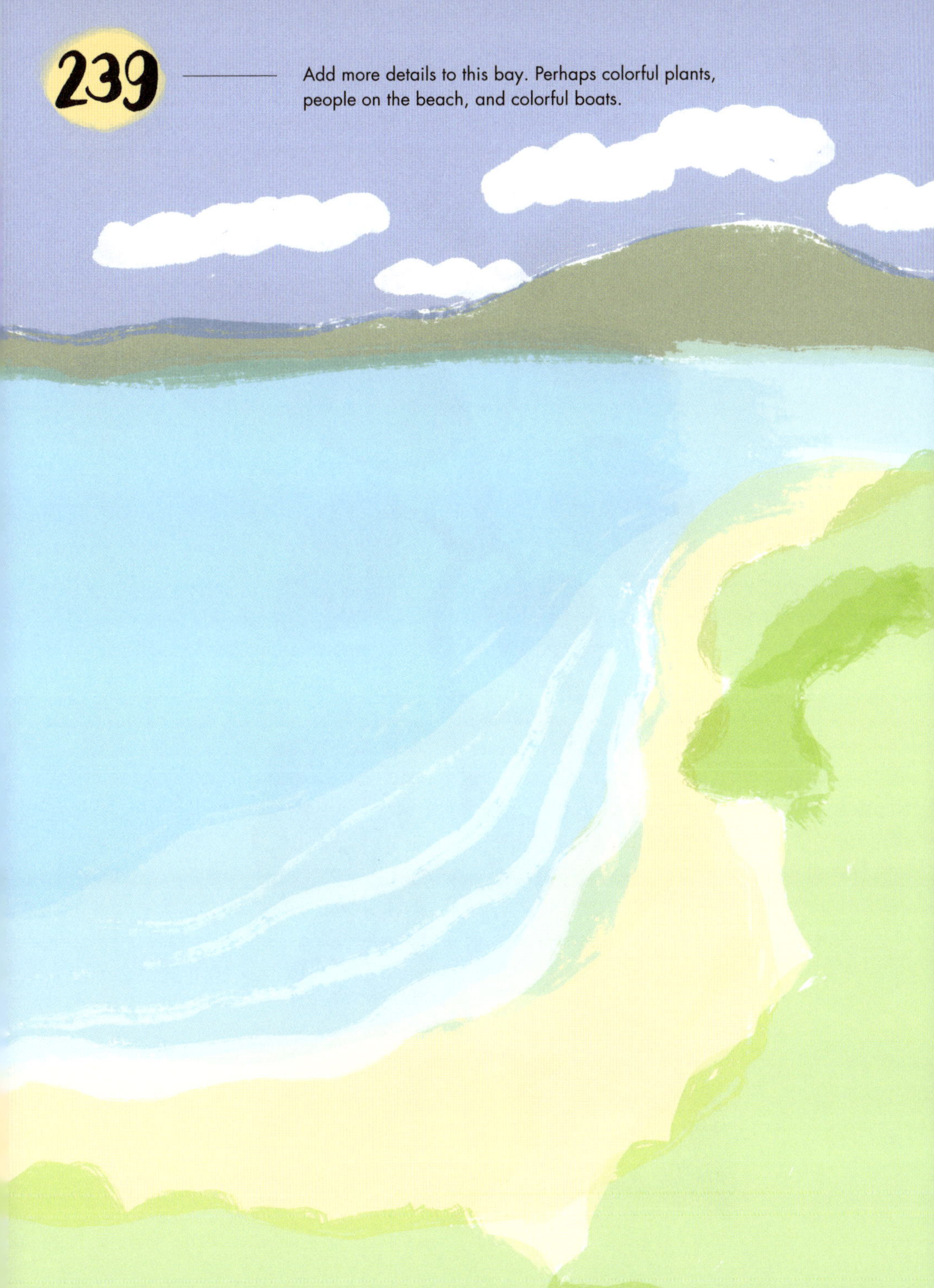

239
Add more details to this bay. Perhaps colorful plants, people on the beach, and colorful boats.

You can use dark shades to create bold, contrasting images, especially against white. Draw or paint an image using only dark shades. Don't worry about what should look dark and what should look light, just have fun with the dark tones to create a graphic drawing.

Tip: You could mix your dark shades before starting, or use them straight from the palette. It doesn't matter which colors you use, focus on enjoying shape and contrast instead.

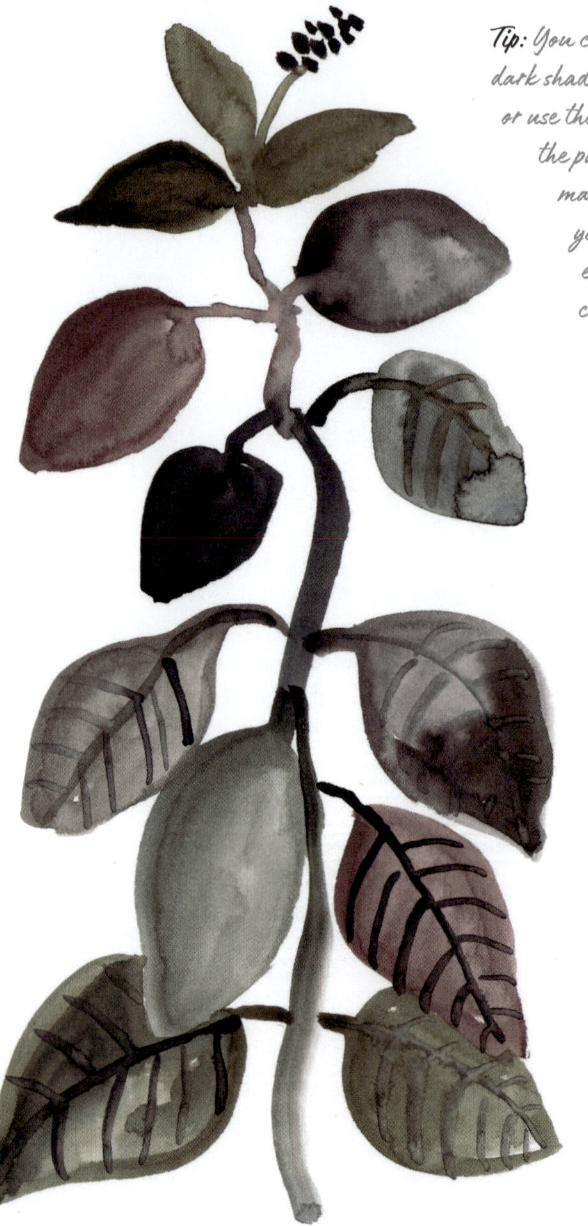

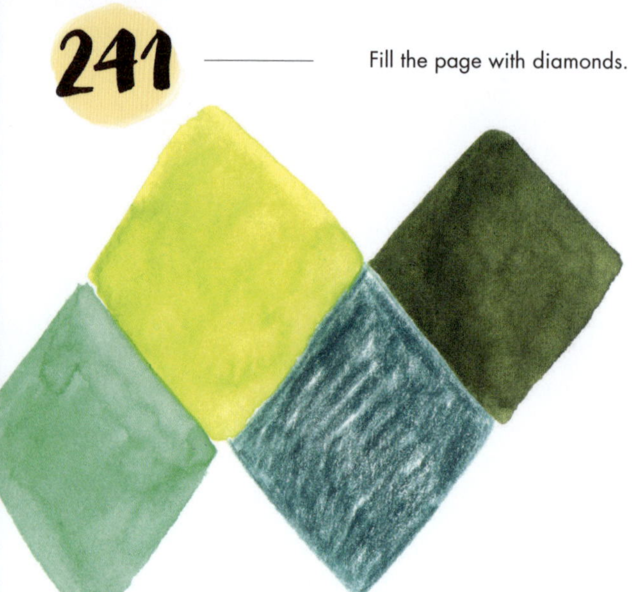

241 — Fill the page with diamonds.

242 ———— Look at an artist's work that you like—in a book or gallery.
Notice which colors you are drawn to, and draw your own
version of little areas that you particularly like in the artworks.

243 ———— Draw ripples on a swimming pool. What colors do you notice?

What colors and shapes evoke joy for you?
Make an image here in response to those emotions.

Design a mobile using
bold shapes.

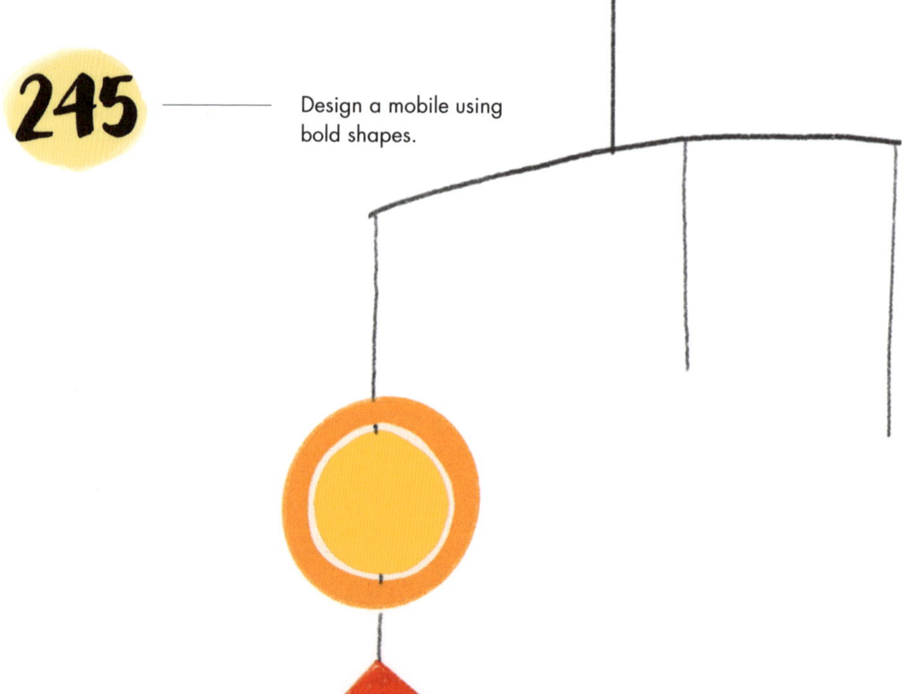

Mix or blend colors together to match these
colors as closely as possible.

Tip: Look at the color and think about what colors might have been used to make it.
Perhaps the green looks slightly yellowy so there may be a lot of yellow and just a tiny
amount of blue. This can take time! It's no problem at all if you aren't able to get
close to matching the colors—it's a skill that takes practice and a lot of trial and error
too! Don't be afraid to try many combinations.

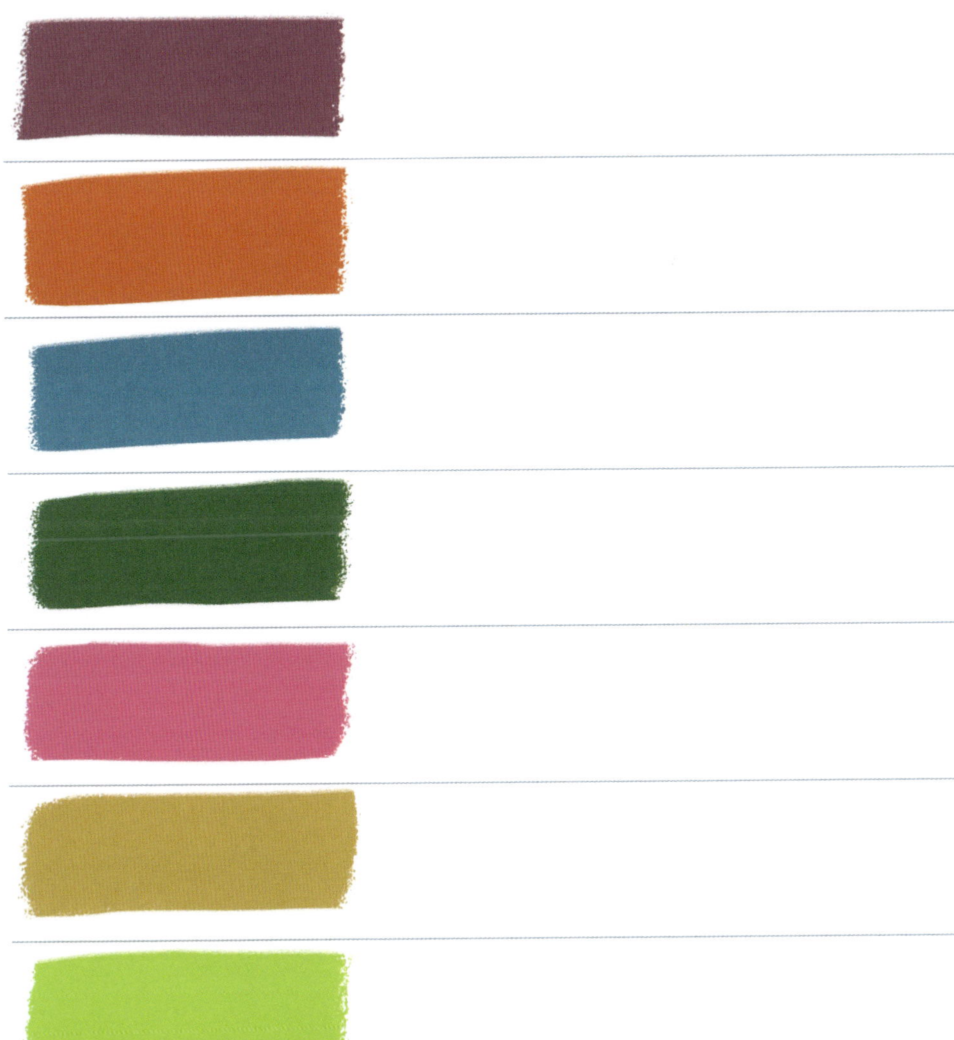

247
Create a pastel flower pattern.

Paint an everyday scene with bold colors. Use any that inspire you. Start with big colored shapes and then add detail, keeping the image loose and free to give it lots of energy.

Draw a colorful animal from observation.
Perhaps look at images in a book or online.

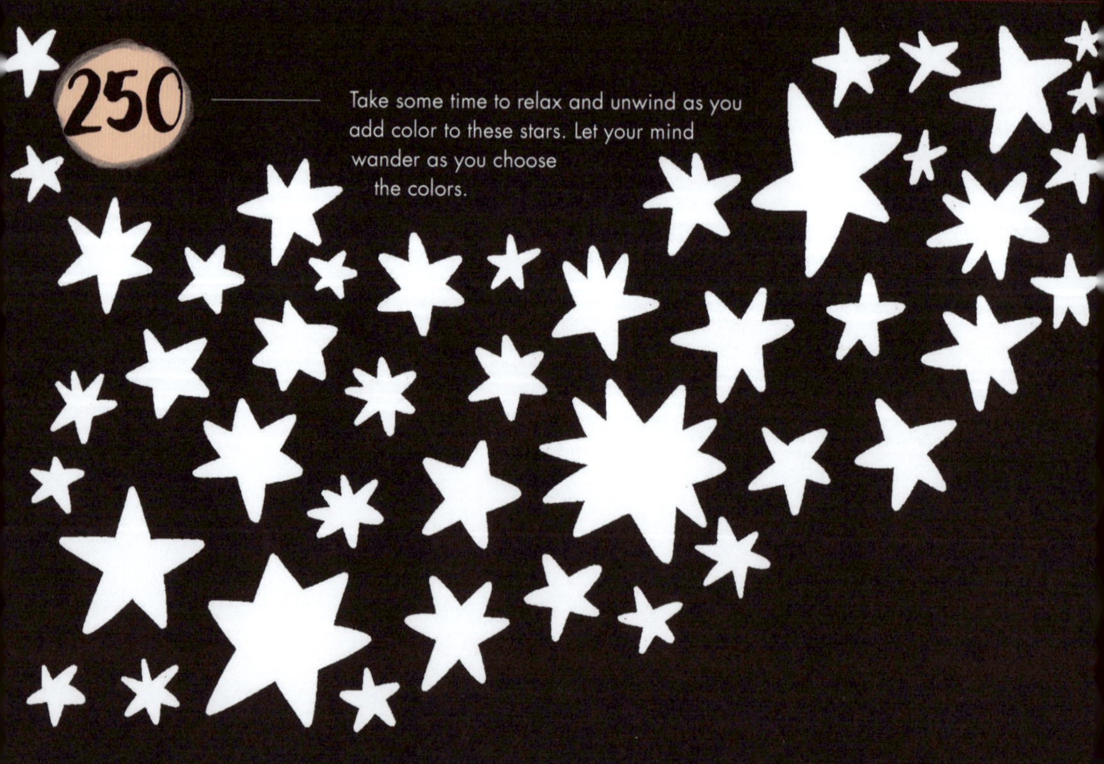

Take some time to relax and unwind as you add color to these stars. Let your mind wander as you choose the colors.

Create an image using only secondary and primary colors. You can use as few or as many as you like.

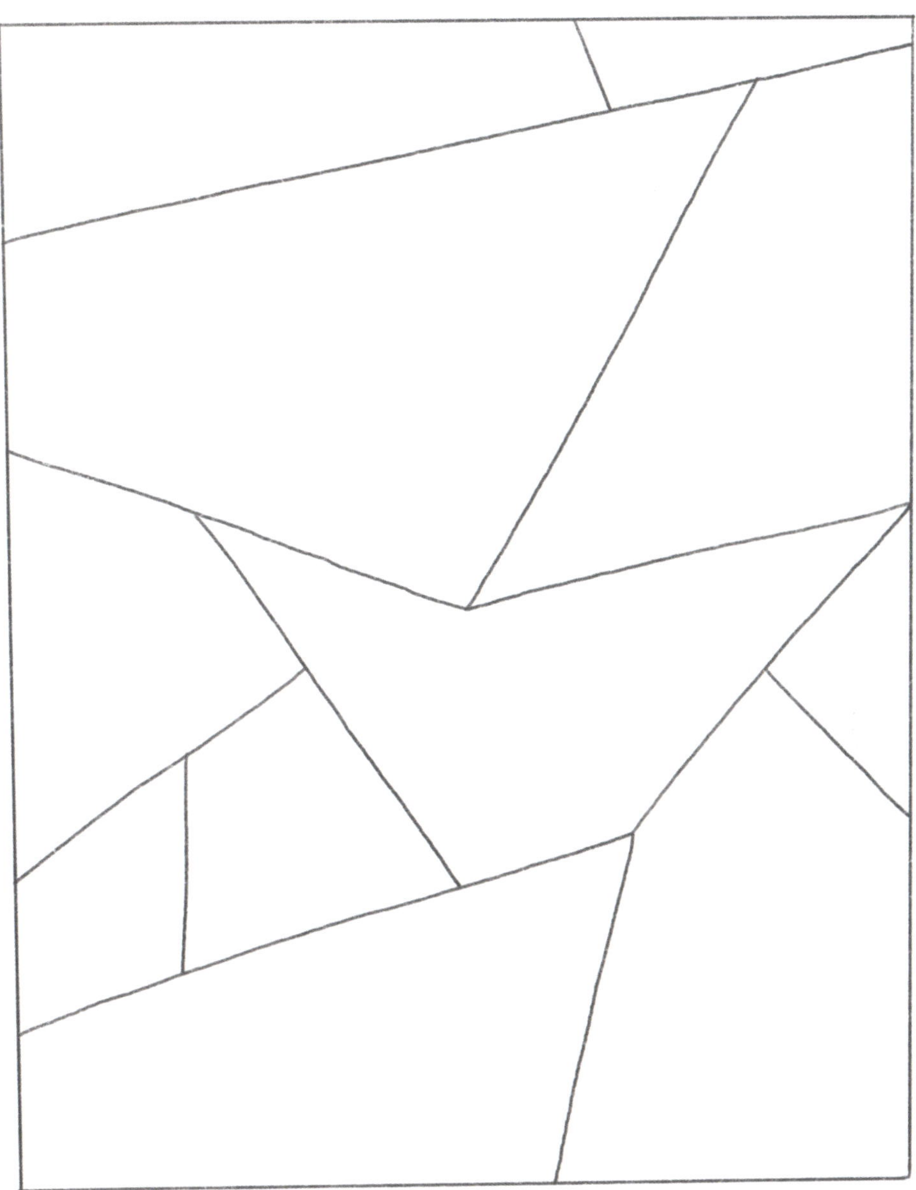

Tip: Primary colors are red, blue, and yellow. Secondary colors are made by mixing the primary colors to get violet, orange, and green.

Turn these simple blocks of color into objects.

Draw a shell. Look carefully at the colors you see, especially the areas of light and dark.

Including a small amount of a clean, bright color against neutrals can make it appear eye-catching and jewel-like. Draw some abstract designs where there is just a pop of bright color among muted tones.

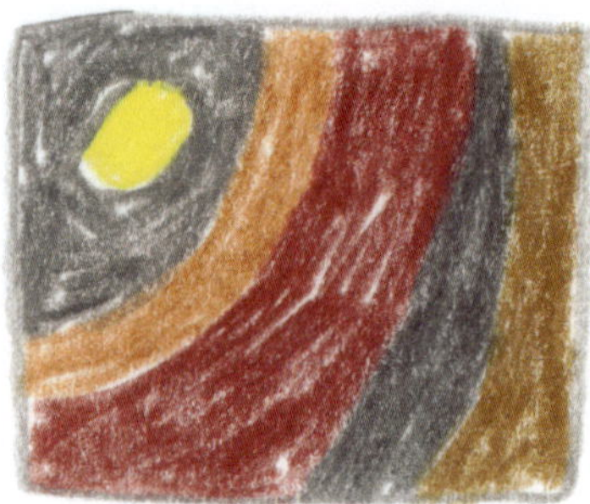

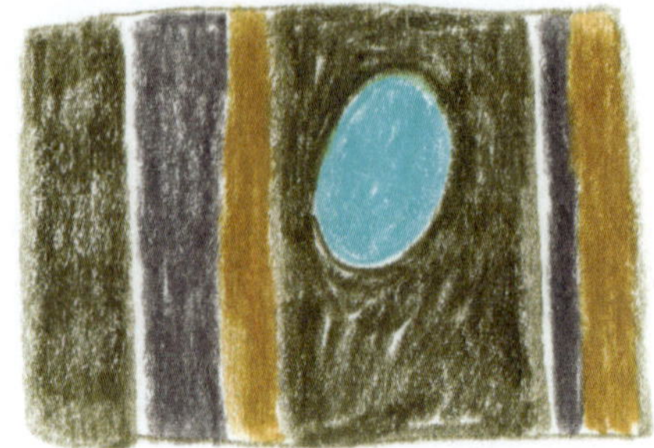

Fill the page with colorful squiggles.

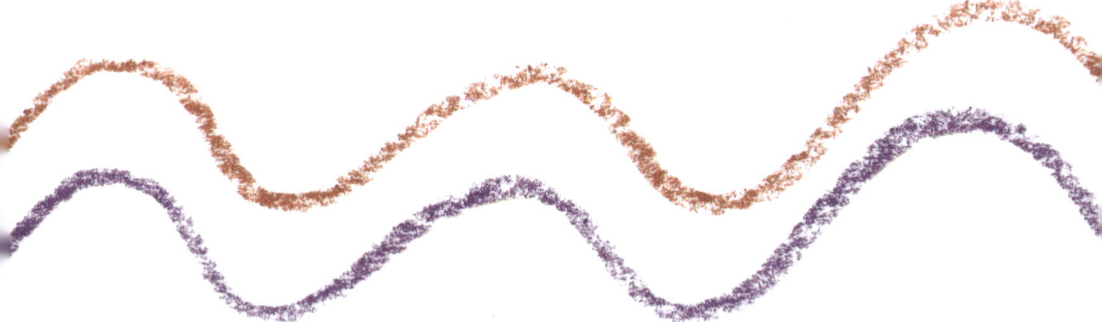

Take some time to make a sustained, detailed color study. Choose your subject and look carefully at what colors you can see before starting. In a green plant, for example, you will be able to see many hues of green and perhaps yellows, purples, browns, and others. Gather the appropriate materials and add specific colors deliberately, rather than rushing.

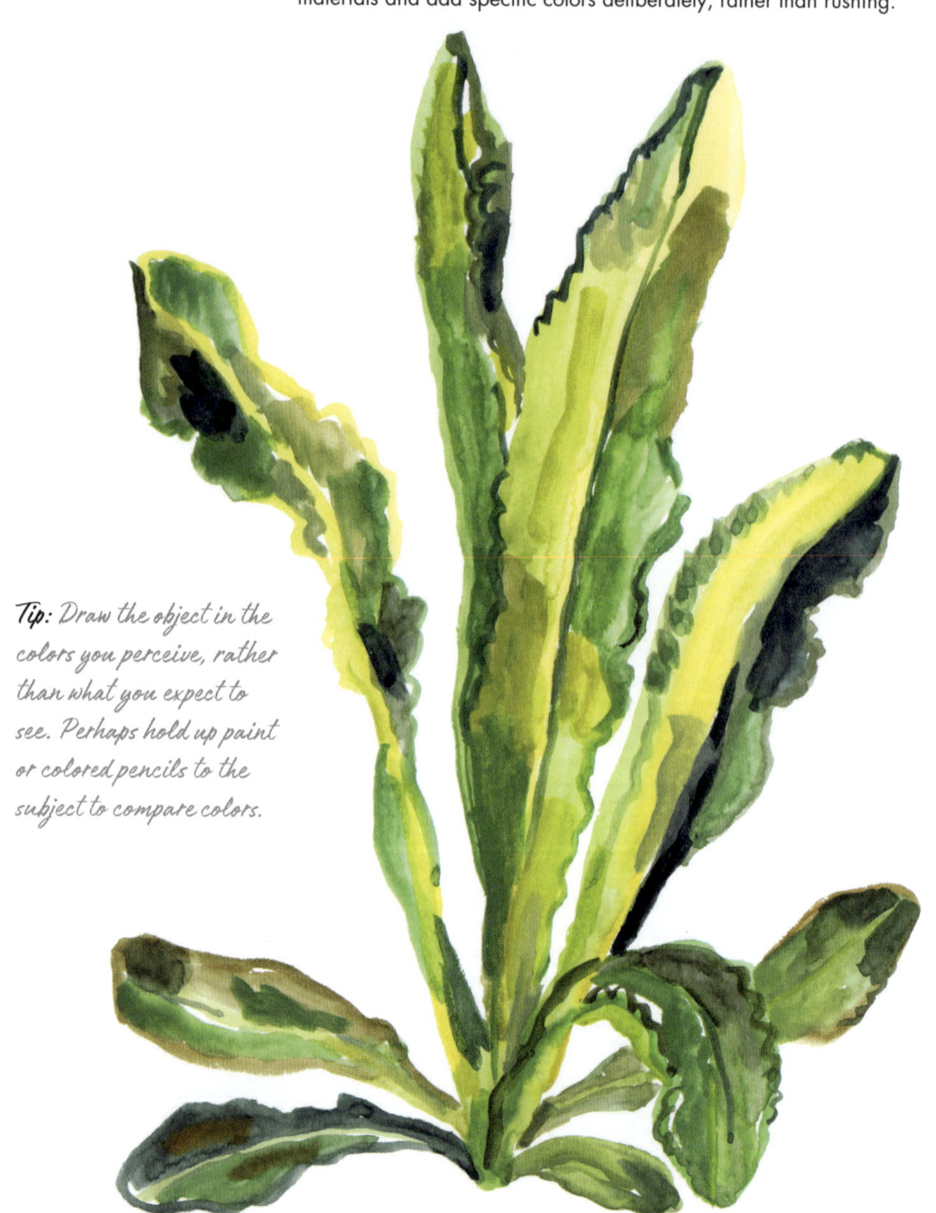

Tip: Draw the object in the colors you perceive, rather than what you expect to see. Perhaps hold up paint or colored pencils to the subject to compare colors.

257

Groups of gourds and pumpkins create a pleasing autumnal palette, perhaps because the color palette is often analogous (these colors are found alongside each other on the color wheel). Paint some vibrant gourds.

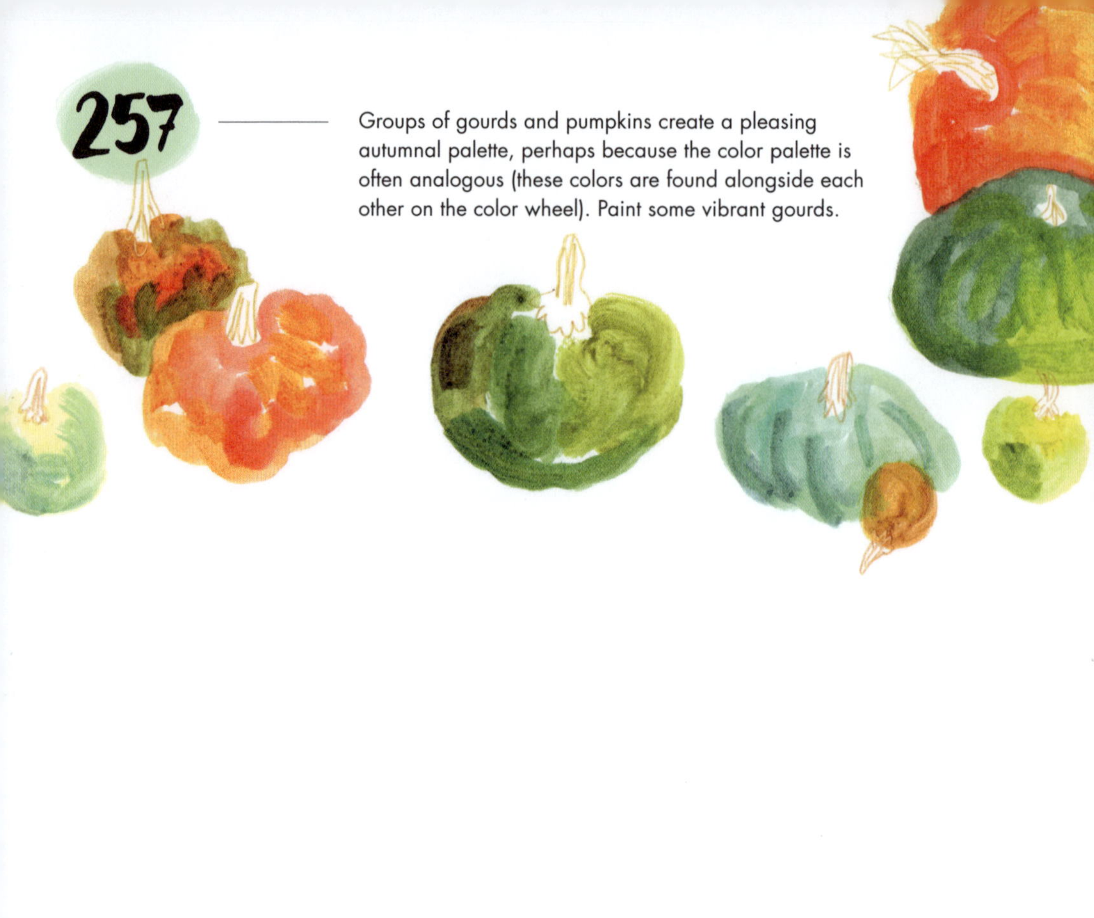

258

Match these flavours to colors. Fill in each shape using one color you'd use to describe the flavour that comes to mind.

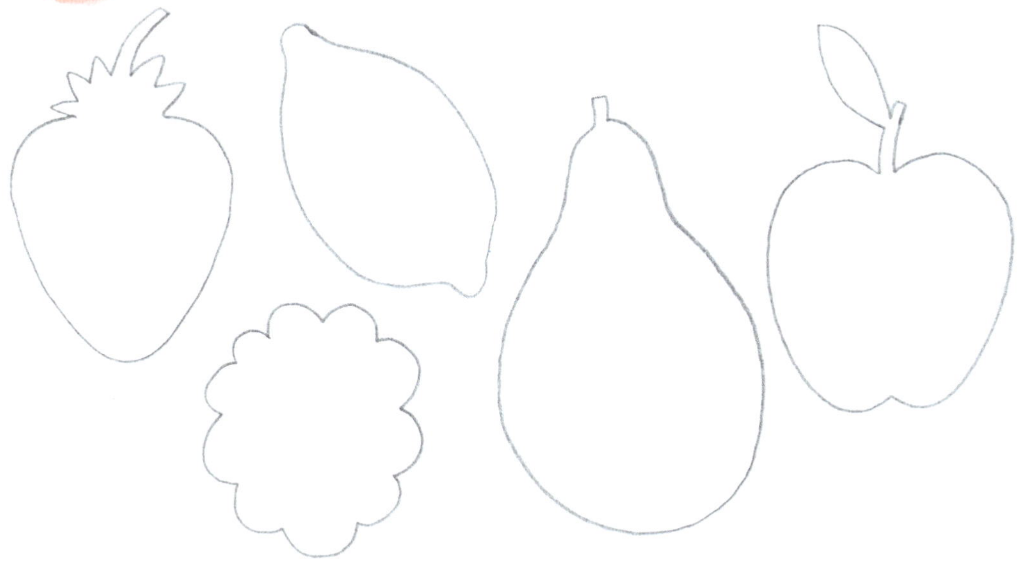

259

Put on some lively music and draw!

260 — How does the color violet make you feel? Create a pattern using violet. Perhaps use it alongside small amounts of yellow to explore the effect of working with these complementary colors.

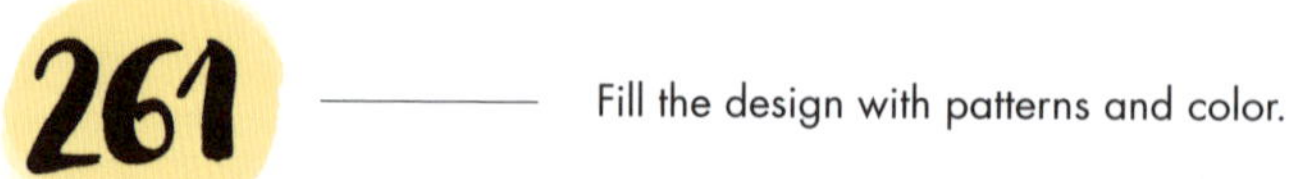

261 — Fill the design with patterns and color.

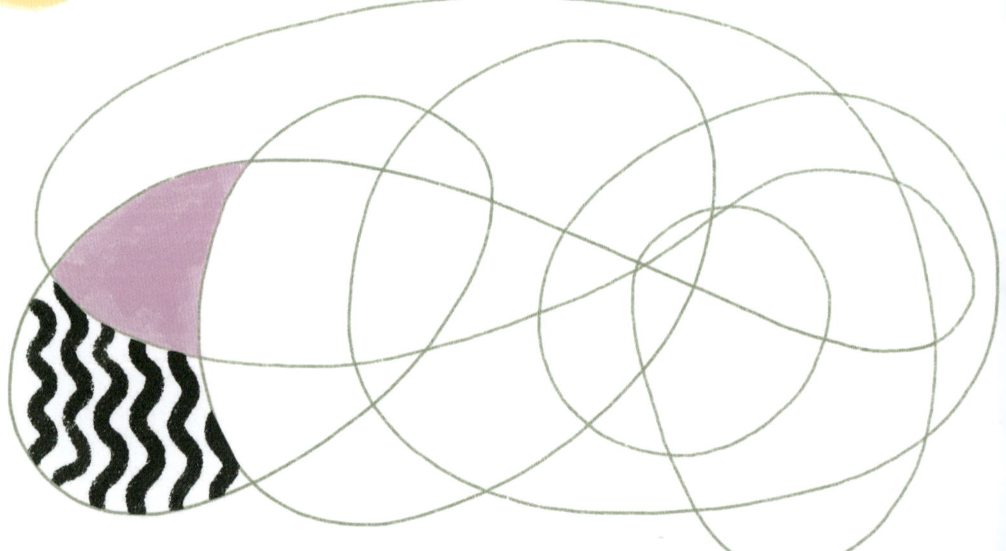

262 ———— Paint a sky on a day where you can see many different colors.

263 ———— Warm, dark colors like burgundy, deep oranges, and reds can make an image feel intimate. Use these colors to depict a cozy space.

Spend just five or 10 minutes capturing a colorful still life. Choose some items from your home to draw, then select the colored materials you'd like to use. Work quickly with lots of energy to add lines and blocks of color to the page.

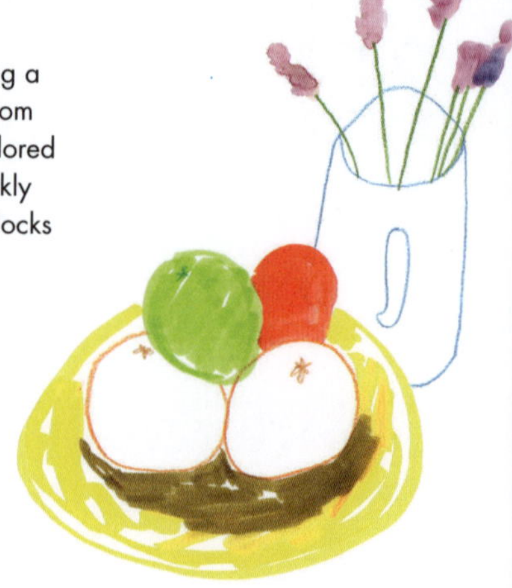

265

Add color to this design.

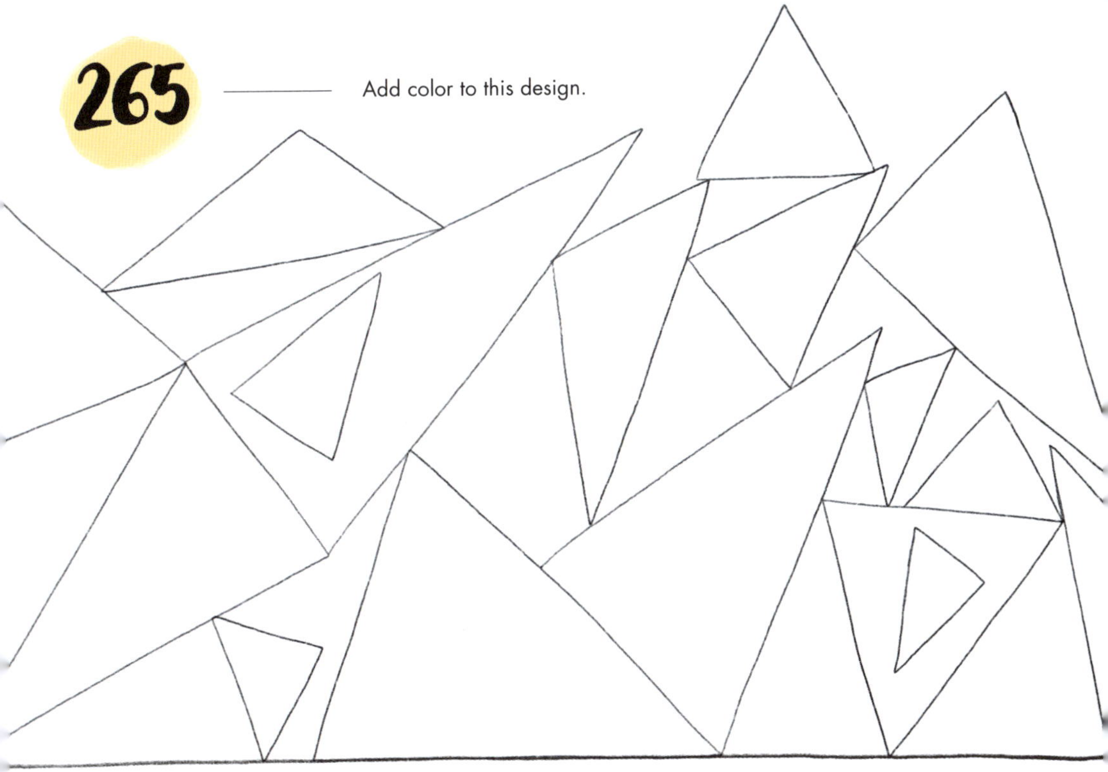

266

We can use cool and warm colors deliberately in art. Color these three subjects and backgrounds using warm and cold colors, and notice how you can achieve different effects and atmosphere.

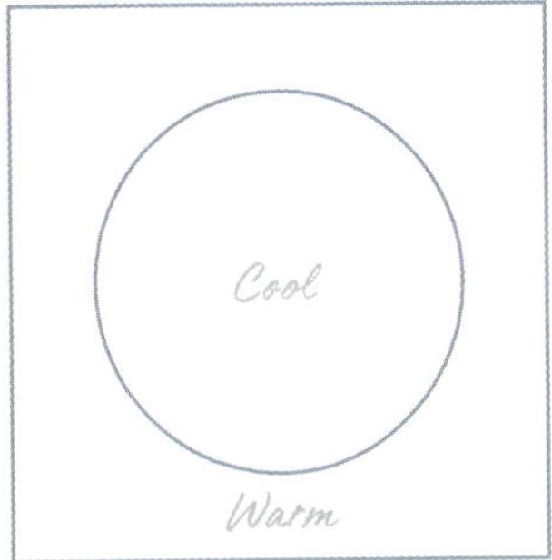

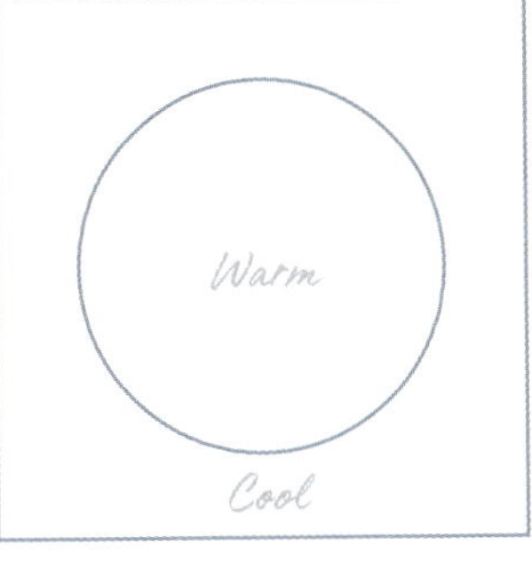

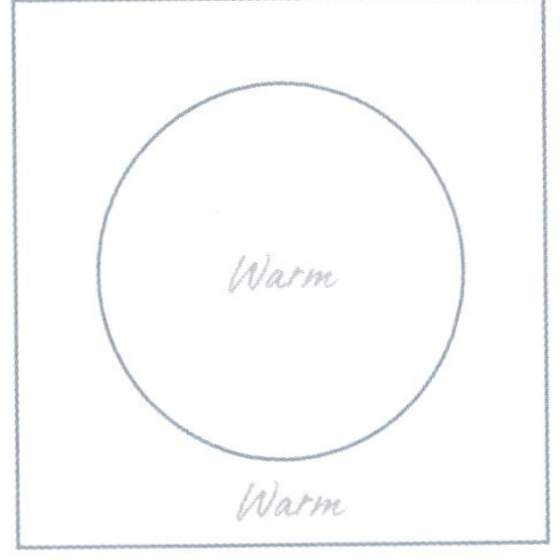

Cool colors will recede. How does a cool subject affect the mood of the image?

Warm colors will advance. How does a warm subject affect the mood?

A warm color may seem cooler when placed on an even warmer background.

267

Make a painting of your eye, focusing on all the different colors you can see in your eye and in the skin around it.

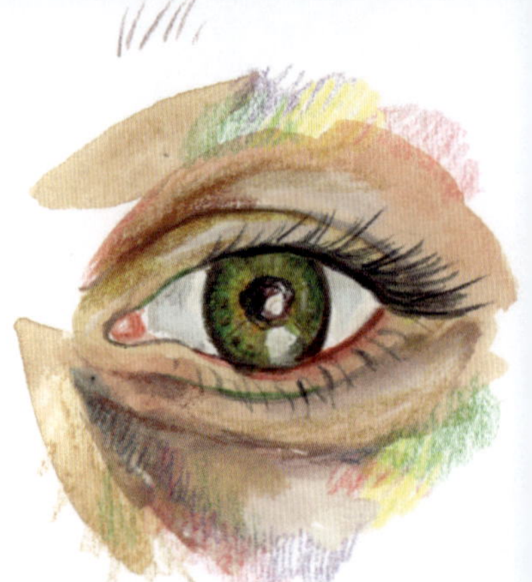

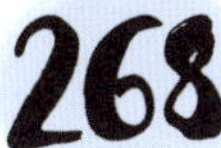

Continue adding rings of colors to fill the page, but choose a color that is analogous to the color before it.

Tip: Analogous colors are those that appear next to each other in the color wheel. So, for example, after the purple ring you could add a different purple, or a blue, or red ring.

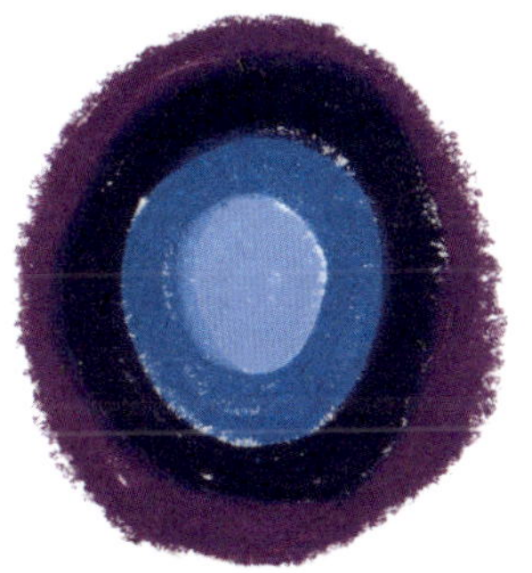

Design colorful pots and vases. Perhaps some are abstract and some have patterns.

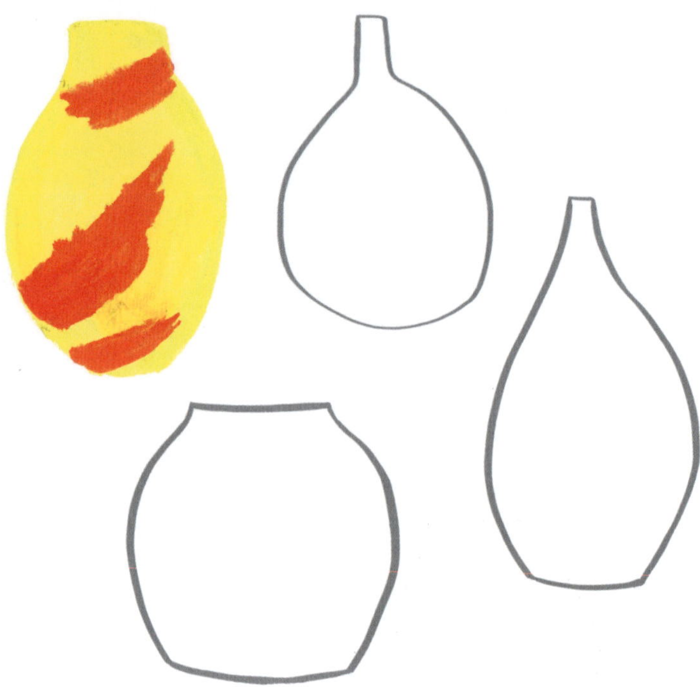

270

Consider which colors evoke feelings of happiness.
Create an image using only happy colors.

271

You can create powerful drawings with simple use of color. Choose a subject, then draw it using a restricted palette of three to five colors. Rather than creating blocks of color, focus on just rendering the outlines of the object.

Tip: You don't need to draw all the lines that you see, just choose a few to keep the drawing delicate. Stop the composition as soon as it feels balanced.

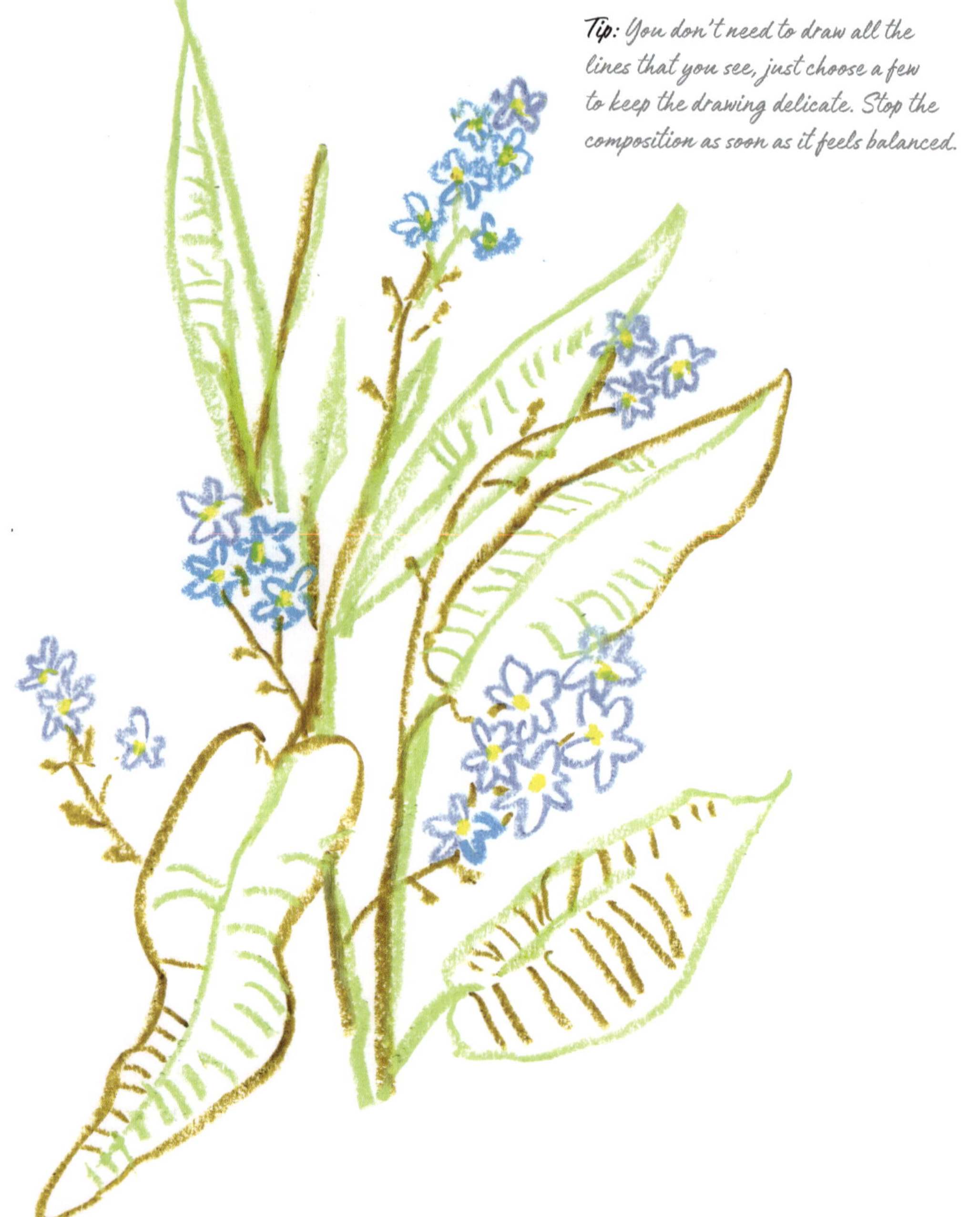

Add leaves using different colors. Notice that because the shape is recognizable, the color doesn't have to be accurate to show what it is.

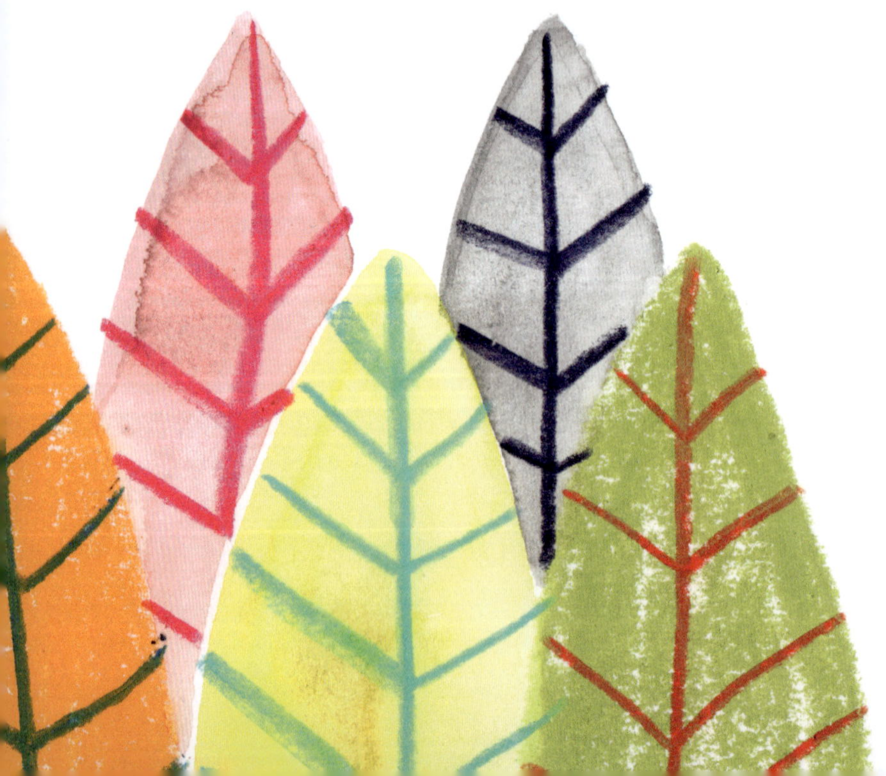

273 ———— Color the polka dots.

Different background tones can make a subject appear brighter or duller. A dark tone can make a color really pop. Choose a bright object and draw it here on a dark-toned background.

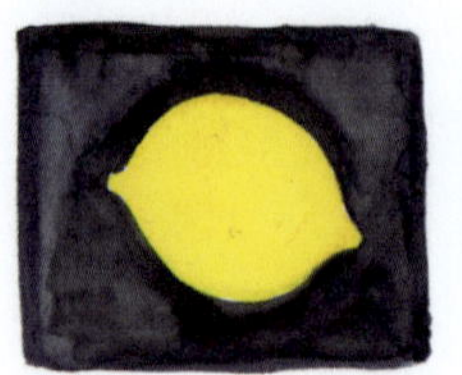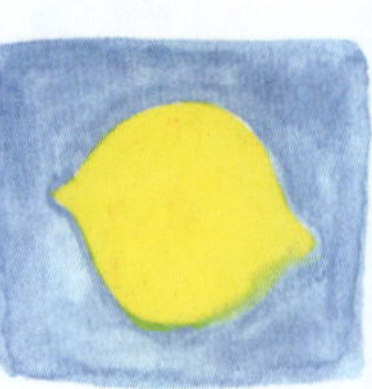

275 ———————— Draw a portrait of a friend or pet using vibrant colors.

Explore how straight, colored lines can have a powerful visual impact. Add straight lines to this grid. Try different colors.

277

You don't need to always be in a good mood to create art! Create a piece of art when you aren't quite feeling yourself. Notice which colors you reach for, and how you feel after you've been creative.

Add color to this garden. There could be leaves and flowers on the tree and in the pots. Perhaps wildlife, a pathway, some grass, and shrubs?

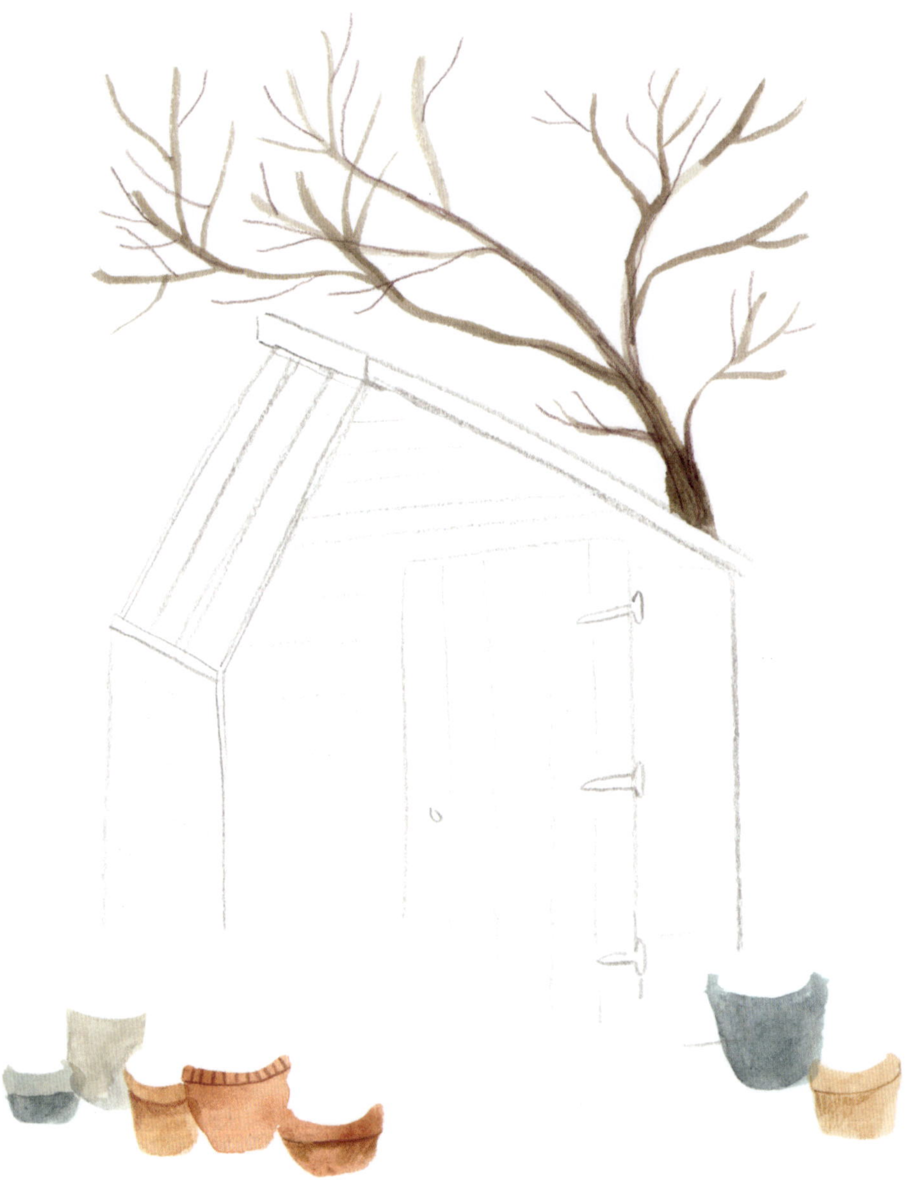

279 ——————— Create a piece of art using primary colors.

While letting your mind wander, add colorful shapes.

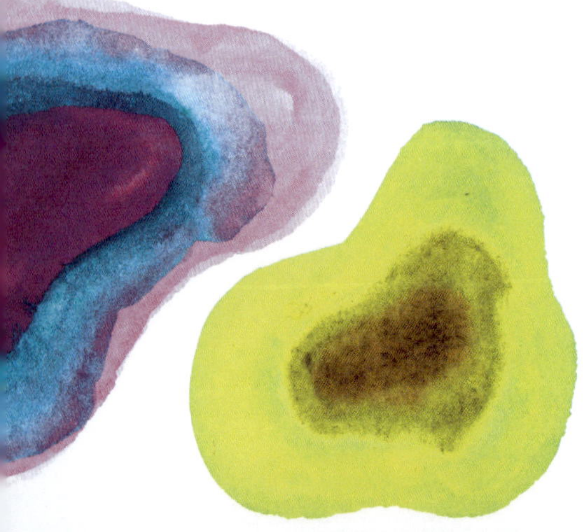

281

If you look carefully at colors that appear black, they are often not *pure* black, but dark shades of colors—very dark blues, violets, and greens, for example. Fill the page with lots of dark shades that aren't pure black.

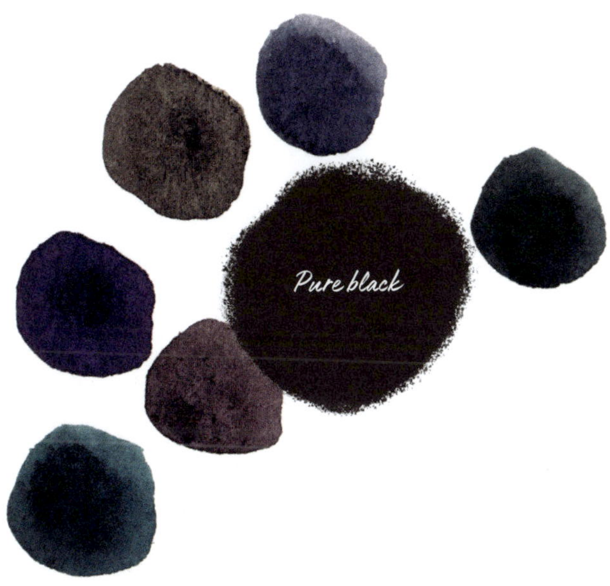

282

Design a mural for where you live.

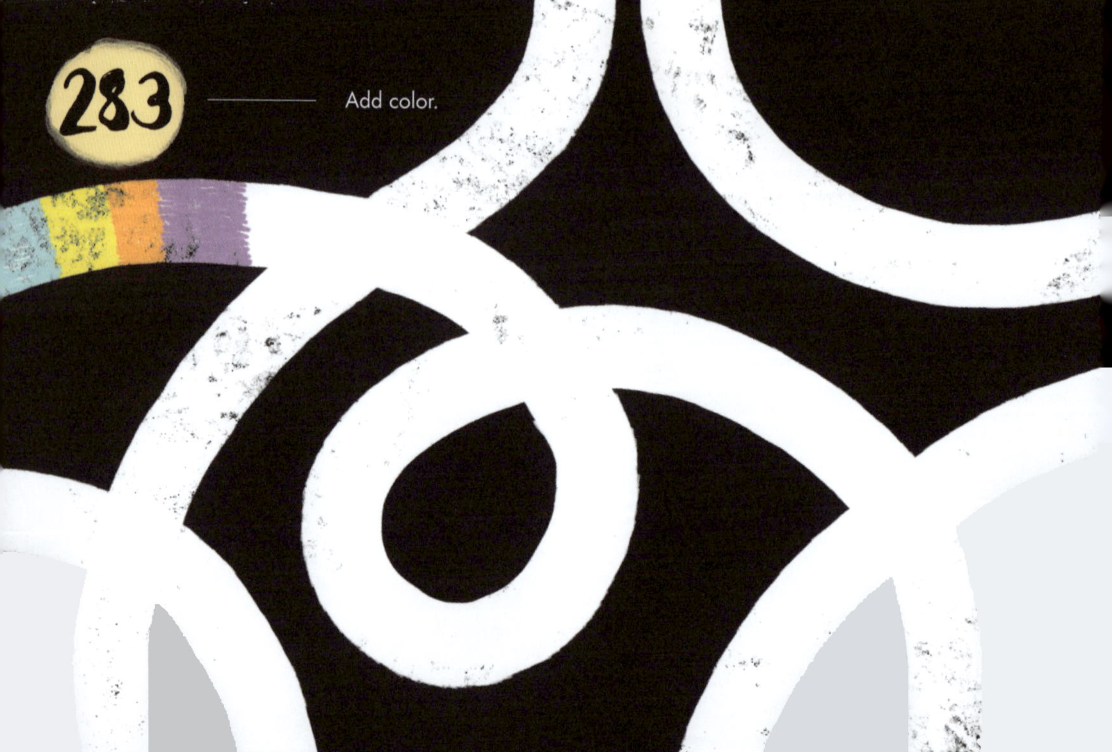

Draw two red things you can find in your home.

285

Create an image using collage and any other material you like. Explore texture—perhaps with the paper you use, how you cut or tear the paper, and the marks you make with additional materials.

Tip: You could make lots of these on a separate piece of thin card and turn your images into greetings cards!

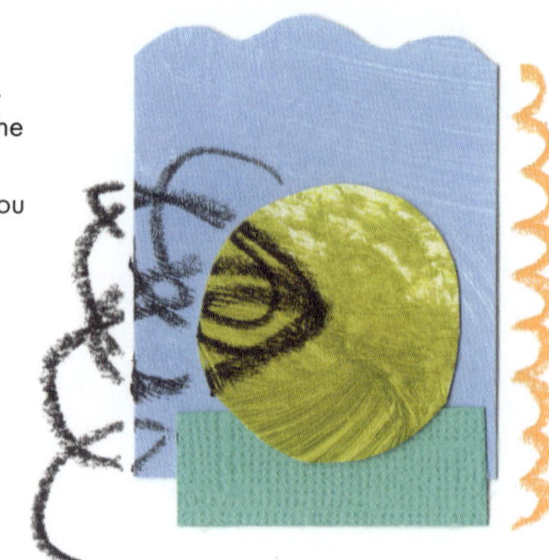

286

Using jagged shapes can bring an energetic, assertive quality to artwork. Add colors to this design to enhance the feeling of force, movement, and dynamism.

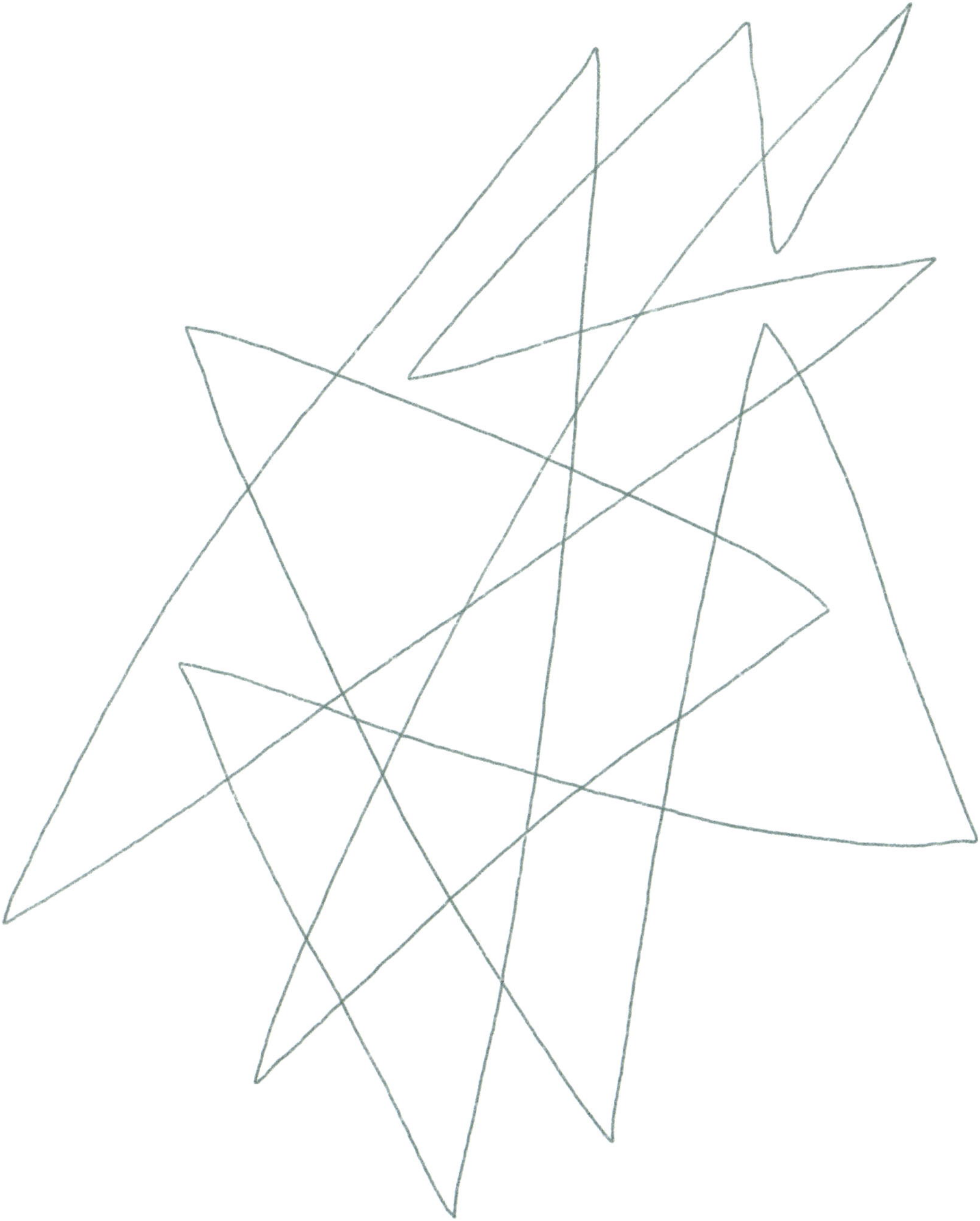

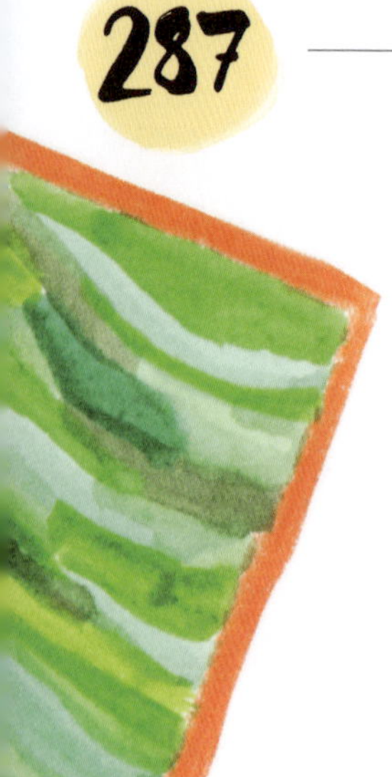

Design some colorful silk scarves.
Consider pattern and symmetry.

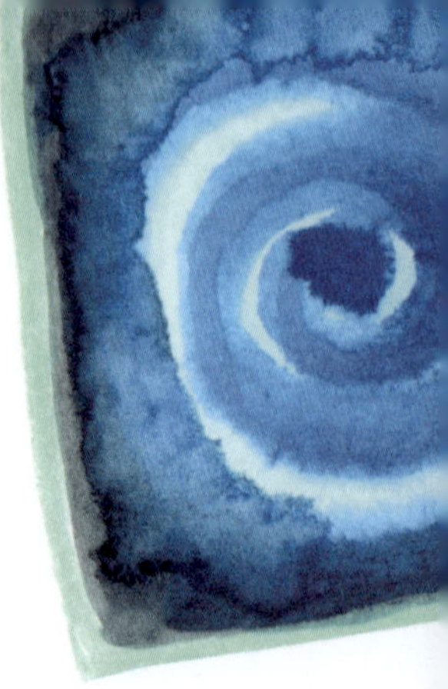

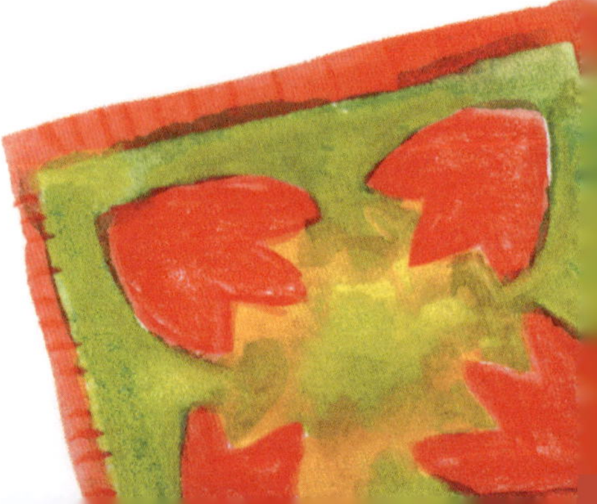

What colors would you choose to represent feeling optimistic? Design a pattern here using those colors.

Color in the rainbows.

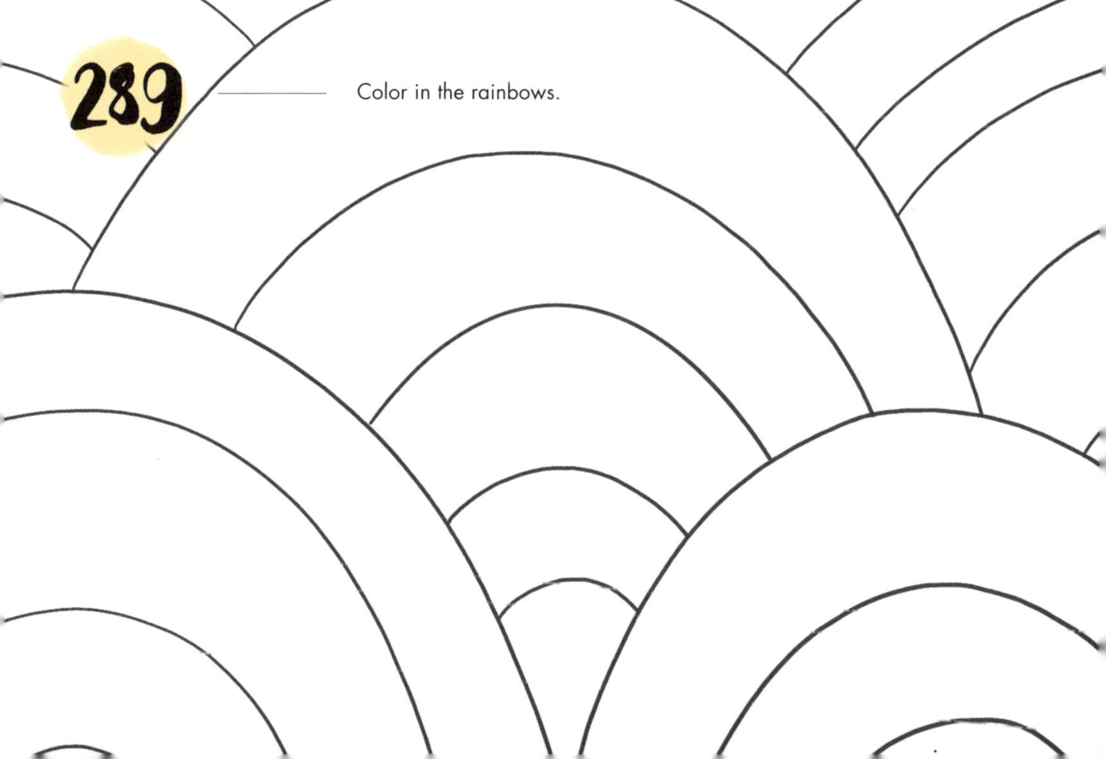

290

Paint the color of the sky at four different times. It could be different times of day, or during different weather conditions. Look for a variety of colors.

291 ——————

Use color and art to calm yourself when you feel stressed. Take a few deep breaths and choose some relaxing colors. Create a tranquil piece of art.

Tip: Don't worry what it looks like, just go with the flow and enjoy taking a moment for yourself.

292

Fill the page using colored pastels.

The mood of your drawing will be affected by the color palettes you choose. Design color palettes to describe each mood below. This is about how the colors make *you* feel—there's no wrong answer.

Tip: Consider using these palettes to evoke an atmosphere in future artworks.

Hopeful

Intimate

Content

Romantic

Tense

Excited

Tranquil

294

Create an expressive drawing of a scene—either from life or from a photograph. Allow yourself to react emotionally to what you see or the weather you experience, and choose colors and marks in response to how the scene makes you feel.

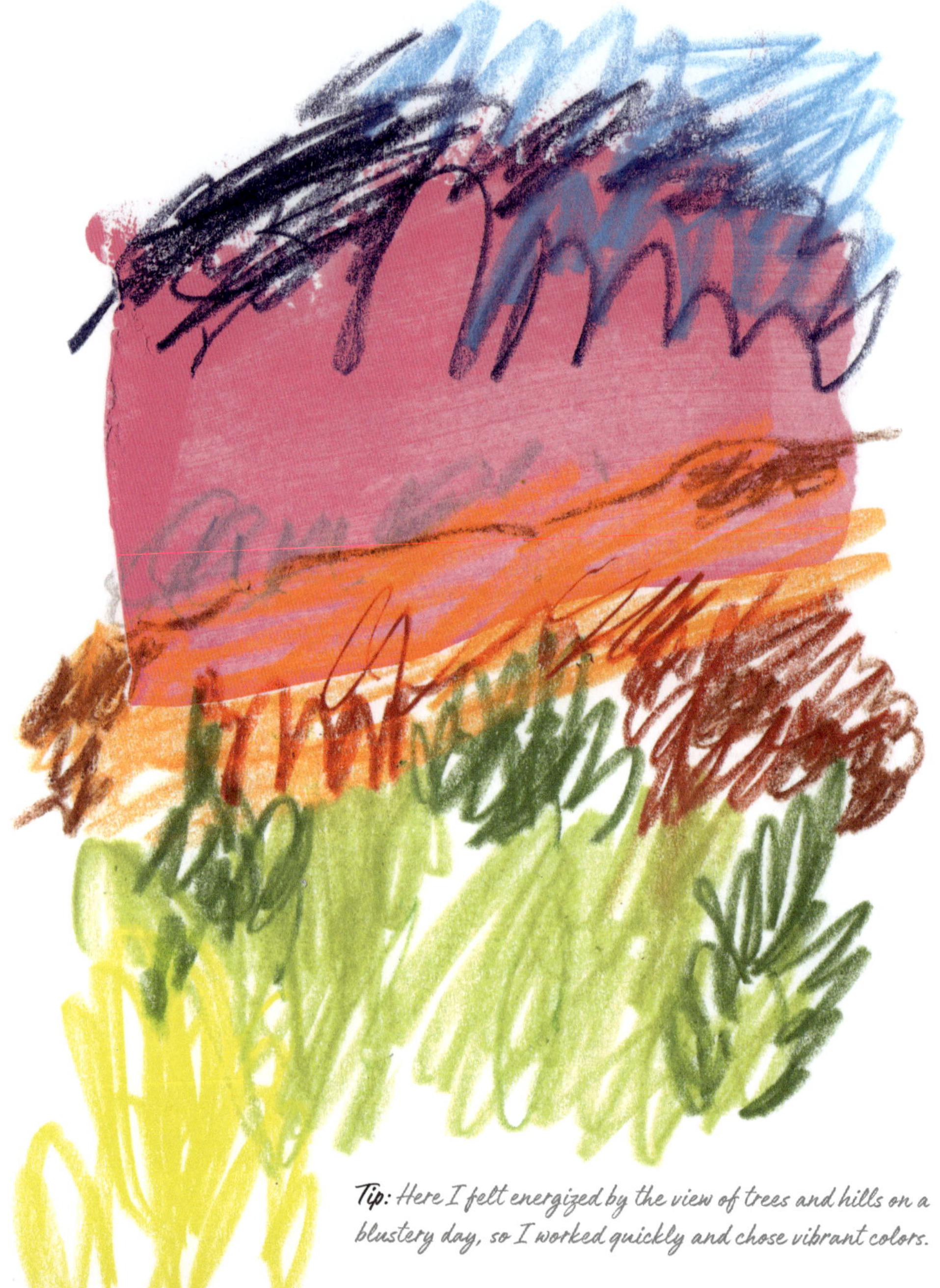

Tip: Here I felt energized by the view of trees and hills on a blustery day, so I worked quickly and chose vibrant colors.

 Design some colorful outfits. Consider adding texture, pattern, and print.

296

Create a portrait of yourself or anyone else from life or from a photo. Use sepia tones—oranges, browns, faded, and washed-out colors. Concentrate on capturing the areas of tone within the face.

Tip: Squinting your eyes while looking at an image can help identify which areas are light and dark.

You don't have to use a harmonious palette when creating art. Sometimes you may want to make something that is lively and eye-catching, and a color palette that features lots of contrast is perfect for that. Create collages that explore bold colors, jarring compositions and graphic shapes.

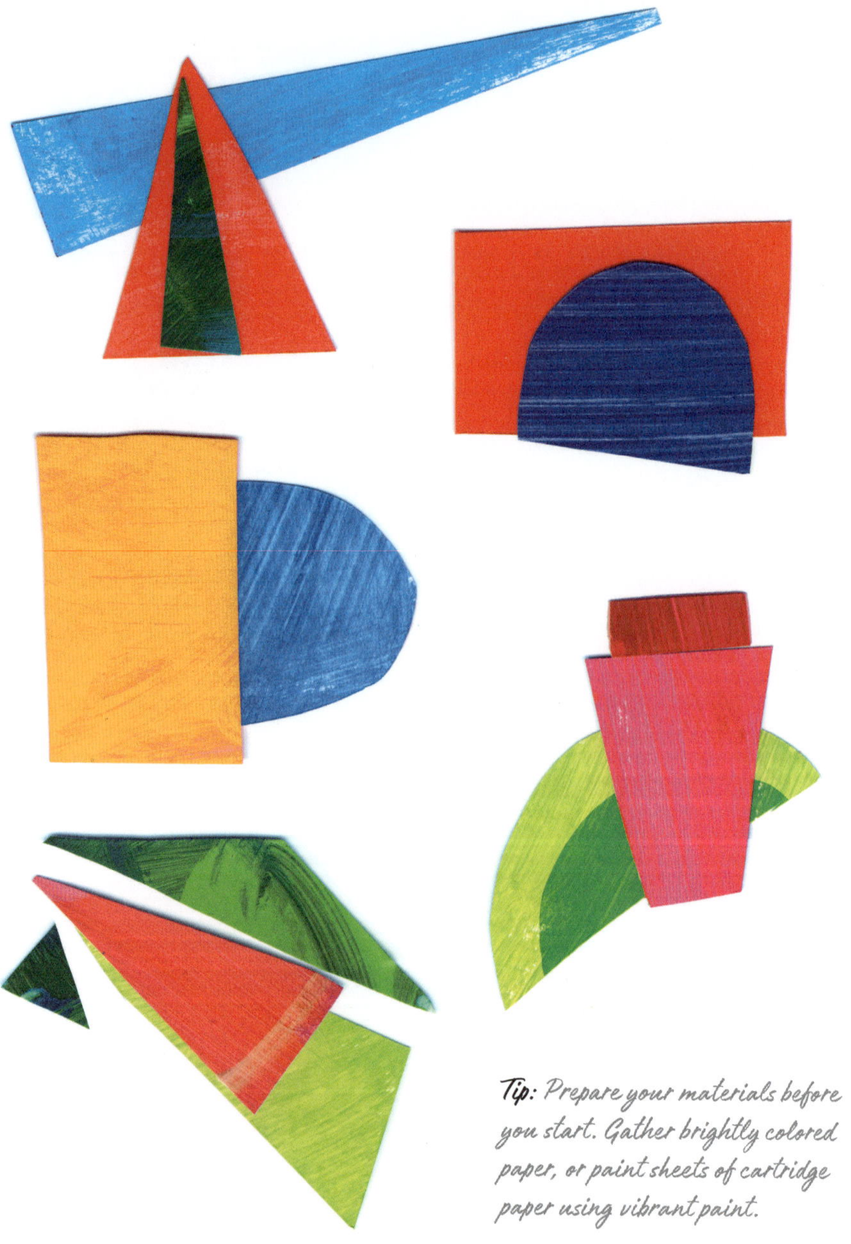

Tip: Prepare your materials before you start. Gather brightly colored paper, or paint sheets of cartridge paper using vibrant paint.

Sketch some landscapes (from life or imagination) using colors to help describe the atmosphere of the location.

299 —————— Draw three green things from observation.

300

It can be fun to paint with just a limited range of colors. This removes some of the decision making, giving you more opportunity to be playful. Create a piece of art using a small number of paint colors as a starting point. Begin by choosing three.

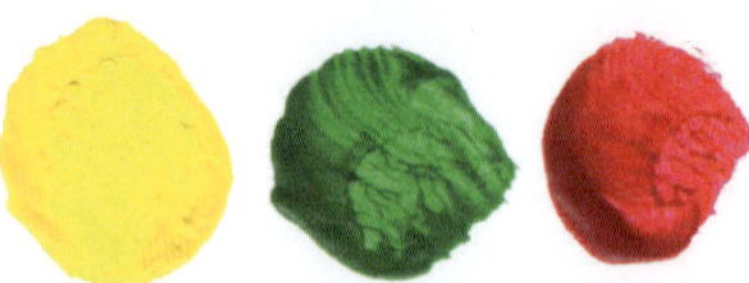

Then mix together those three colors in different quantities to form a range of colors.

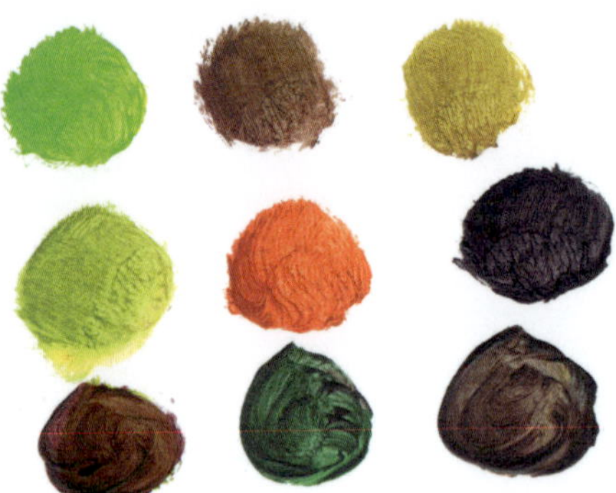

Paint an image using the colors in your palette. You don't need to make it look realistic, use any color you feel inspired by. It can be helpful to identify the light, medium, and dark tones within your palette and in the scene or object you are drawing.

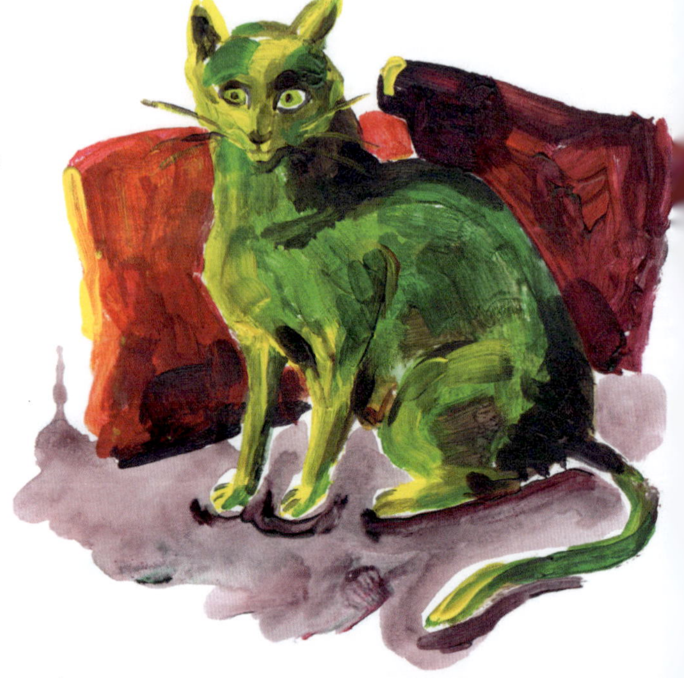

301

Observe the wing of this butterfly and create the other wing using any art material you like. Perhaps explore blending colors, or create a more abstract design using collaged paper.

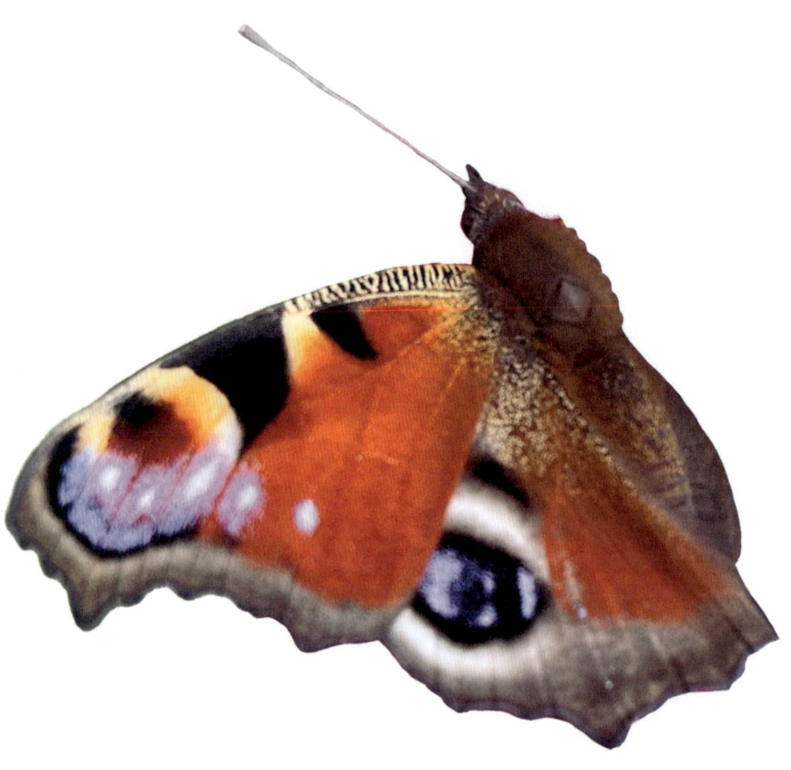

Create bold, simple shapes like these, then turn them into animals or people.

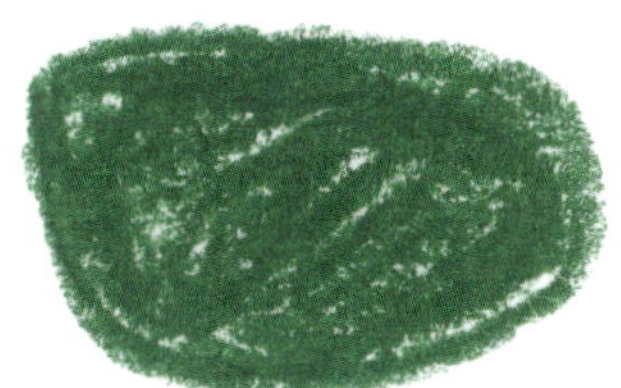

Color each of these images differently. Explore a variety of color combinations and enjoy using colors that aren't realistic.

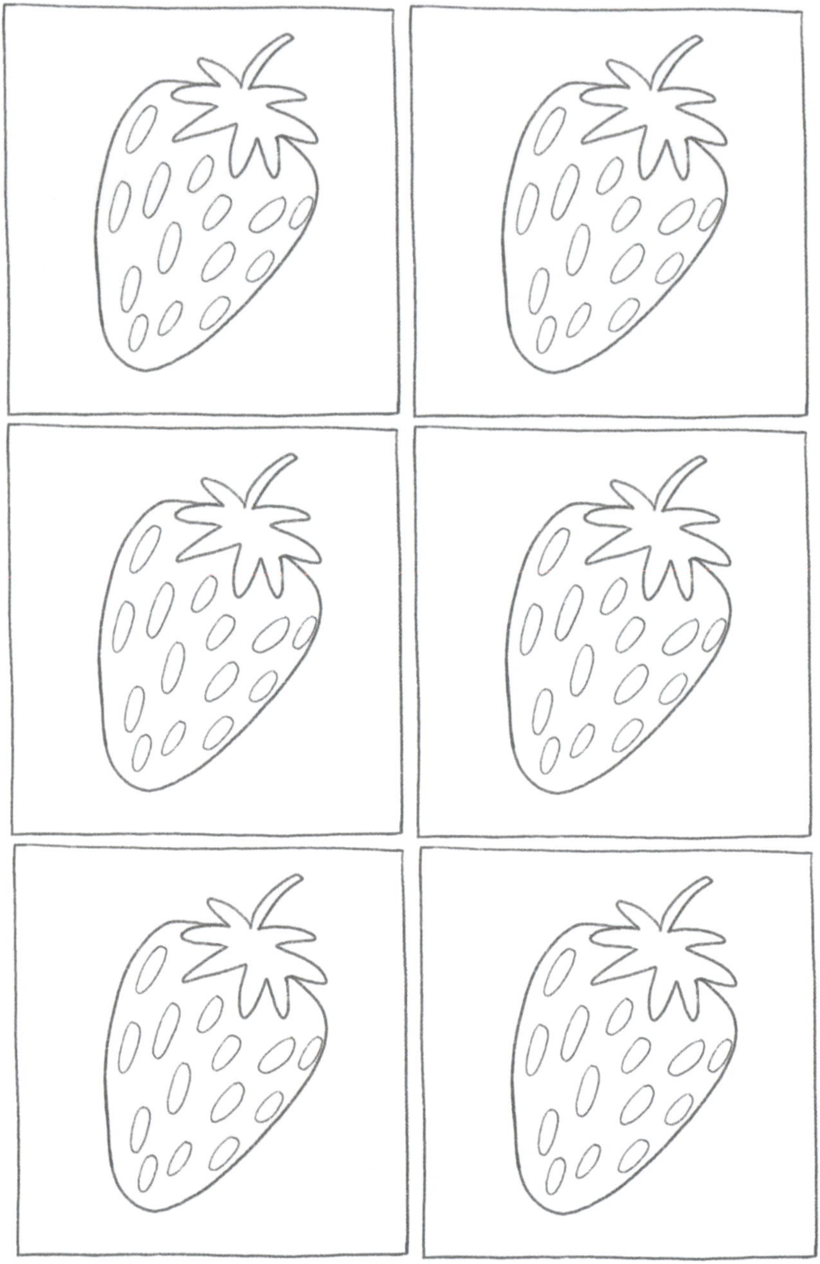

304

Draw an object using your favorite colors.

306 ———— Use mark-making and considered use of color
to express how you feel today.

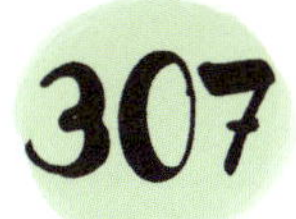

307

Color can be used to make bold compositions even more eye-catching. Draw three more objects, giving your artwork vibrant, colored backgrounds and consider unusual compositions.

Tip: Perhaps the object fills the space or is cropped in an interesting way.

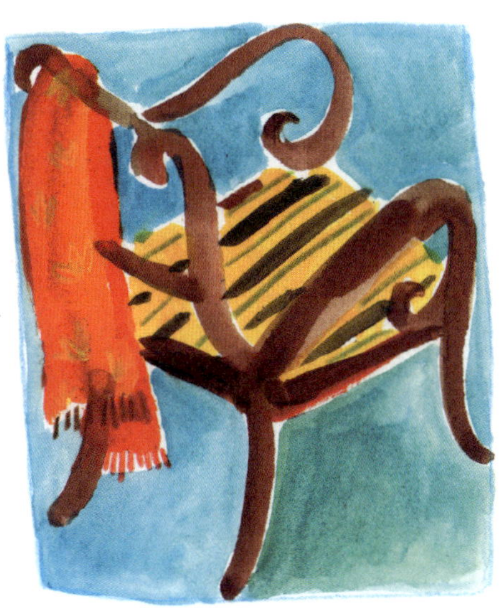

Fill the page with warm, earthy colors.
Perhaps it makes you feel calm and grounded.

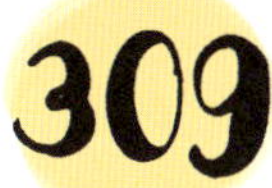

309 —————— Add the colorful surroundings to this scene—you'll be left with a white house that stands out against the background. Perhaps add colors to the doors too.

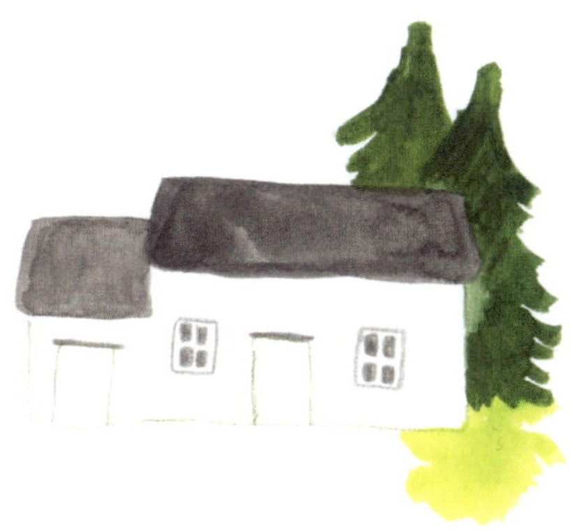

310 —————— Add colors to this design.

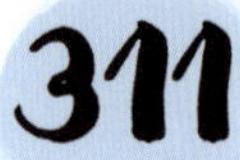

311 —————

Find a painting by an artist that you love, and study the use of color. Identify which colors are used in the piece and create your own version of it.

Tip: There's no need for this to be a detailed copy of the painting—it can be a simple representation.

312

Choose one (or a few) objects from nature and draw them, paying close attention to the variety of colors you can see if you really look carefully.

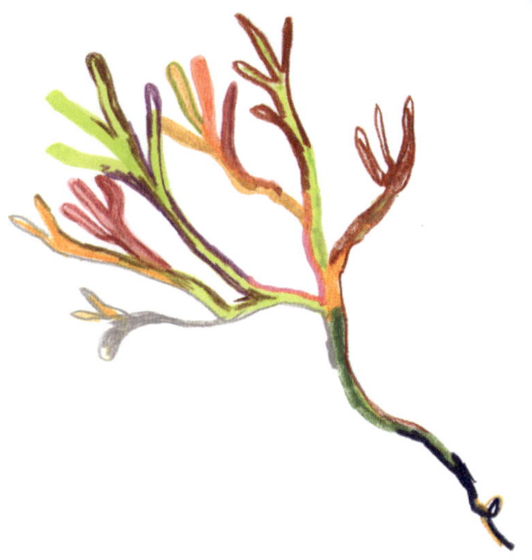

Create a woodland scene using collage.

Begin by painting sheets of cartridge paper with greens, blues, browns, and any other colors you think might be useful in your collage. Explore adding texture—you could blend colors together and try using dry brushes or bits of card to make marks in the paint. In this first stage, enjoy creating sheets of paper that have a patchwork of colors, rather than thinking too much about what areas you will use for your collage.

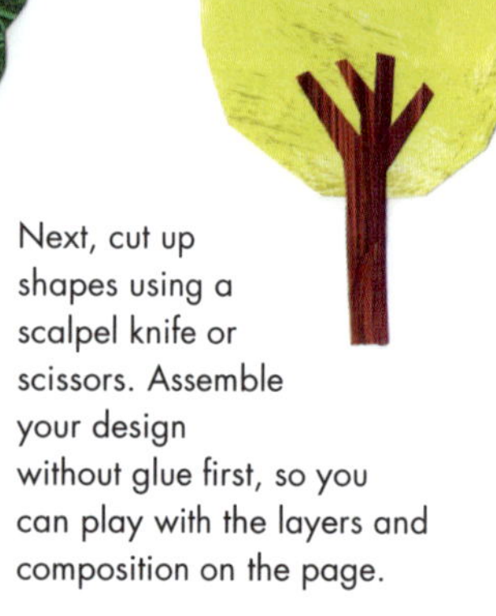

Tip: Acrylic or gouache work well, but you can use any paint you like. Be sure to let the paper dry fully before starting to cut it, otherwise the paper can rip.

Next, cut up shapes using a scalpel knife or scissors. Assemble your design without glue first, so you can play with the layers and composition on the page.

Tip: Add more details using pastels.

Once you have a layout you like, stick the elements in place using a thin layer of PVA glue. You might need to flatten your drying image underneath some paper and a heavy book to make sure the bits of paper dry without curling.

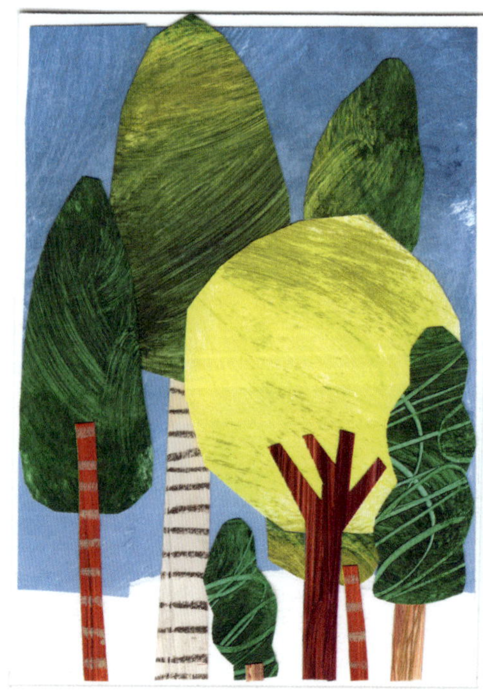

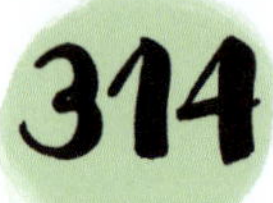

Look for color in unexpected places—pour a glass of water and draw it, paying particular attention to the colors you can see in the glass and liquid.

315

Make sketches of people using pairs of complementary colors. These can create an unsettling, dynamic image.

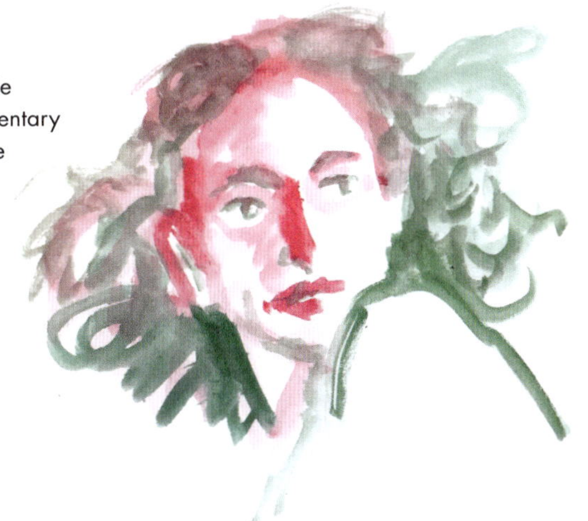

316

Lie down outside and spend some time looking up. Concentrate on the colors you can see. After 10 or so minutes, paint what you saw from memory. You may just remember big blocks of color, and that's great!

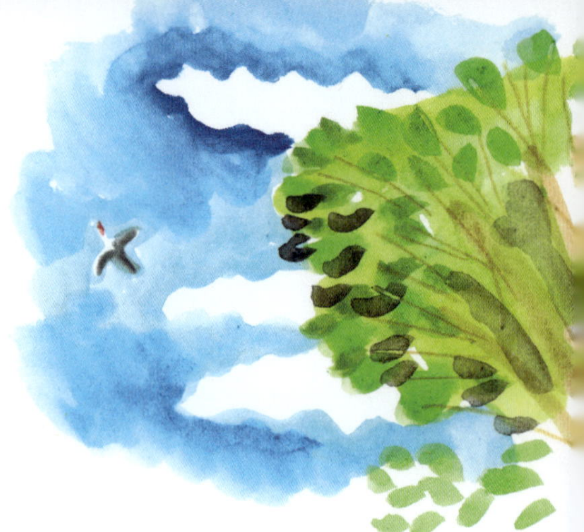

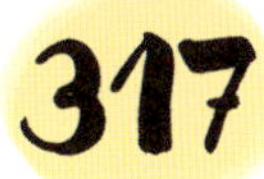

317 ———— Add more greens then turn the
image into a jungle.

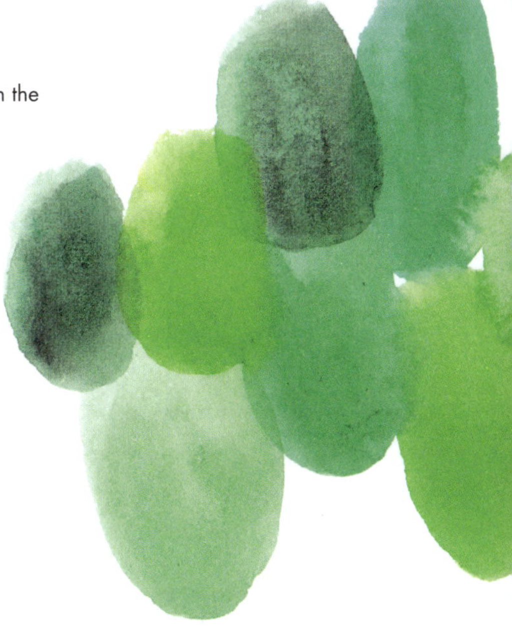

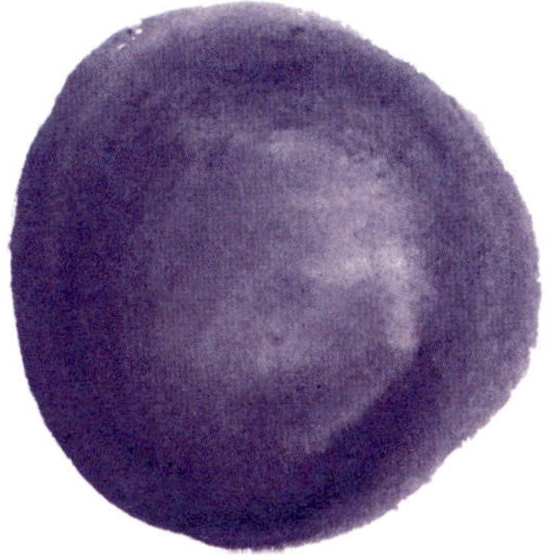

318 ———— Purple can evoke luxury, moodiness, spirituality, and magic.
Consider how purple makes *you* feel, and create an image based
on this shape.

If you use shapes and subjects that you really enjoy, your art can be joyful, colorful, and expressive. Choose an object that you love to look at and draw it lots of times on the opposite page. Delight in exploring its shape and using color playfully.

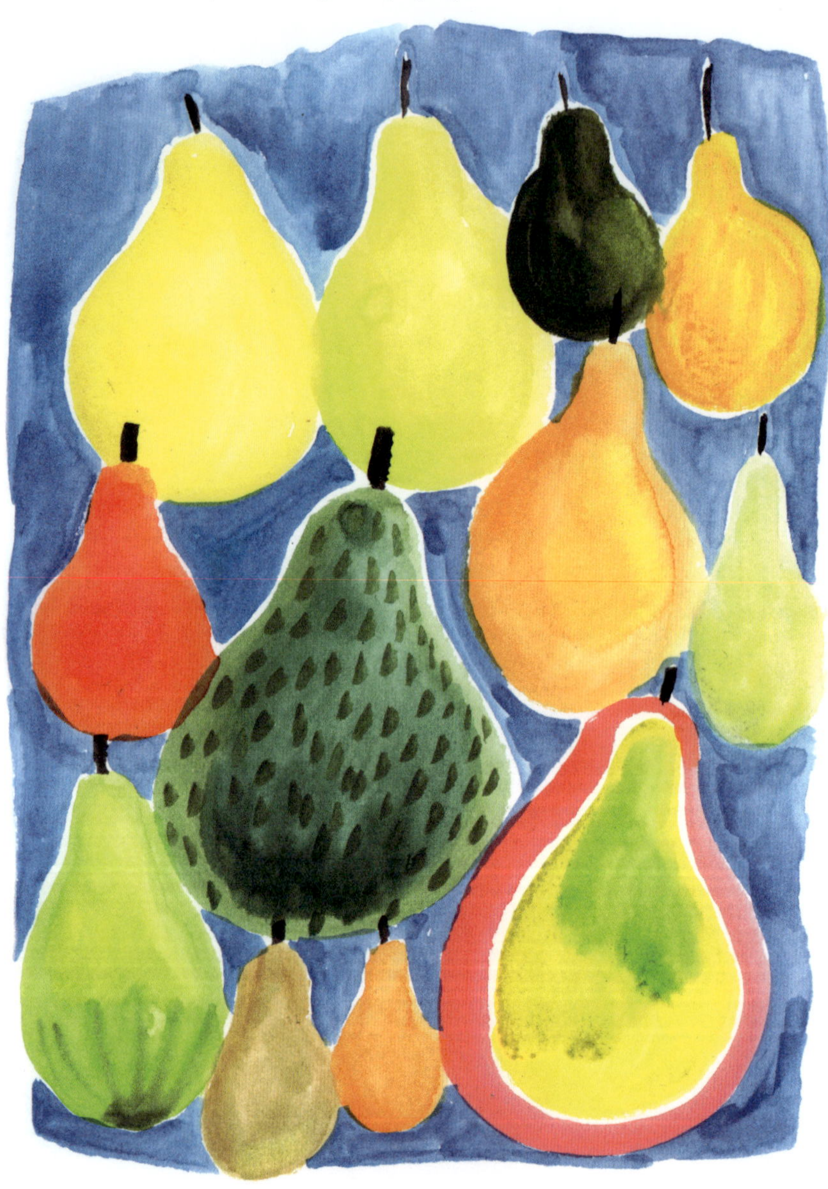

Tip: Learning to love using color can be tricky—but choosing subjects you enjoy will give you a good start.

320

Set up a small still life using household objects. Draw what you see using lots of confident marks.

Tip: Consider what you've learnt about shadows being colored rather than pure black.

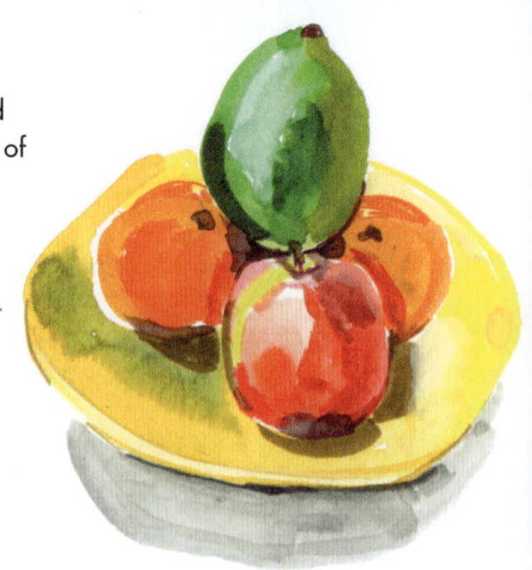

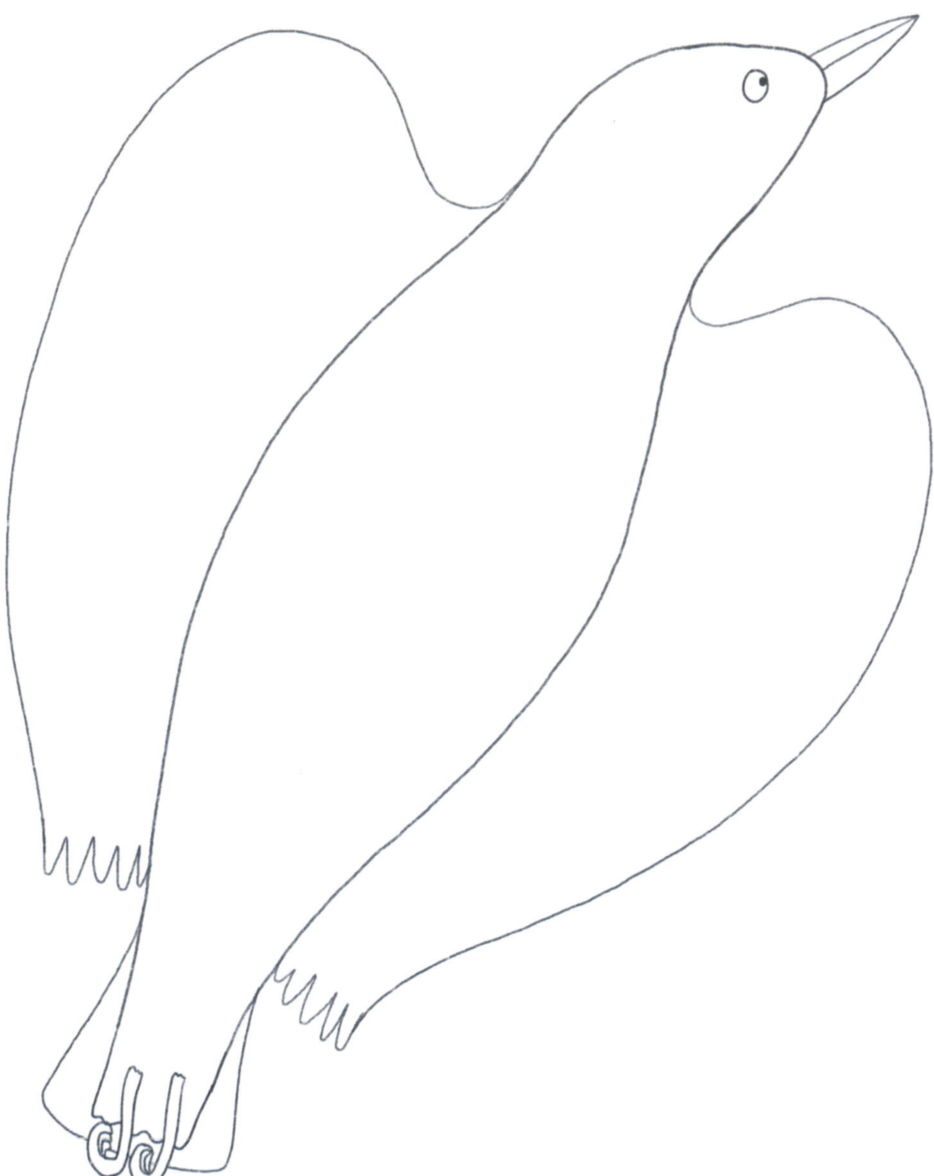

322

If we look into the distance, things that are further away—distant hills and buildings, for example—look less saturated. Add color to these hills, making the colors less saturated the further back they are.

323

Add colors that have a vintage feel to the grid.

Fill the page with blue and violet zigzags.

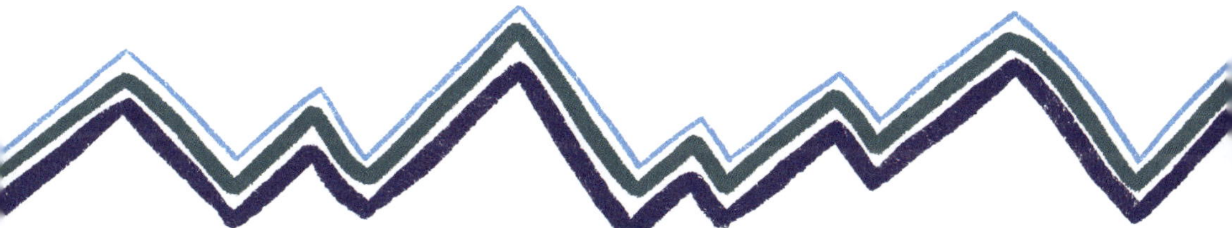

325

Visit a nursery, garden or park and, as you walk around, notice the color combinations that occur in nature. Look at flowers, stems, and leaves and see how the combinations of colors can be so beautifully balanced. Make studies of what you see.

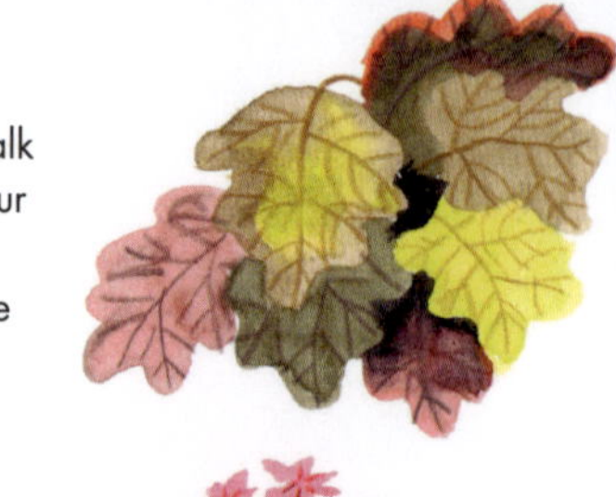

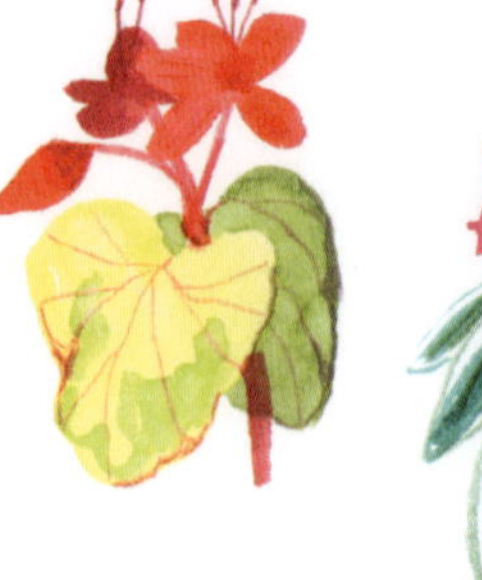

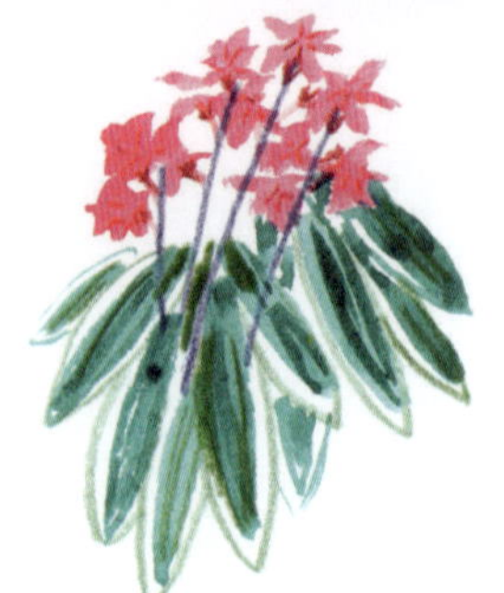

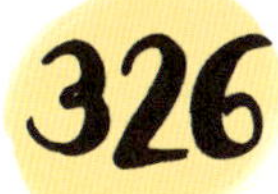

326

Using soft, muted colors—perhaps pastels and neutrals—add color to these eggs. Explore adding textures and allowing colors to bleed into each other.

Color this fruit using cheerful colors. Perhaps add a colorful, patterned tablecloth beneath them.

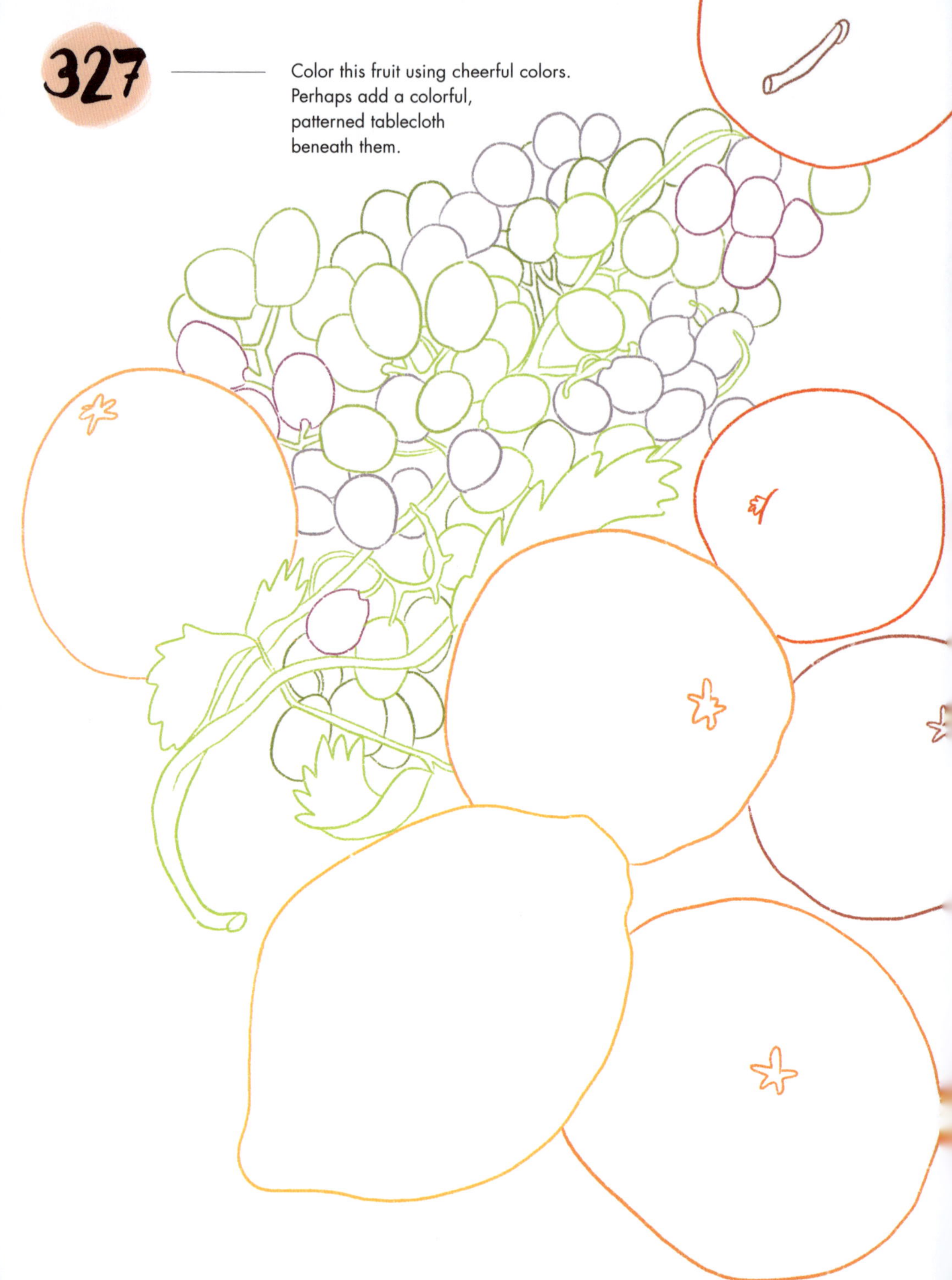

Draw five blue things from imagination.

329 ——————— Consider which colors evoke feelings of calm. Create an abstract drawing using serene shapes and colors.

330

Visit a woodland, park, or garden and draw what you see, using this background as a starting point.

Tip: Look for clean and dirty colors that you could add to your image. Perhaps there are a lot of dirty colors and one small pop of bright, clean color.

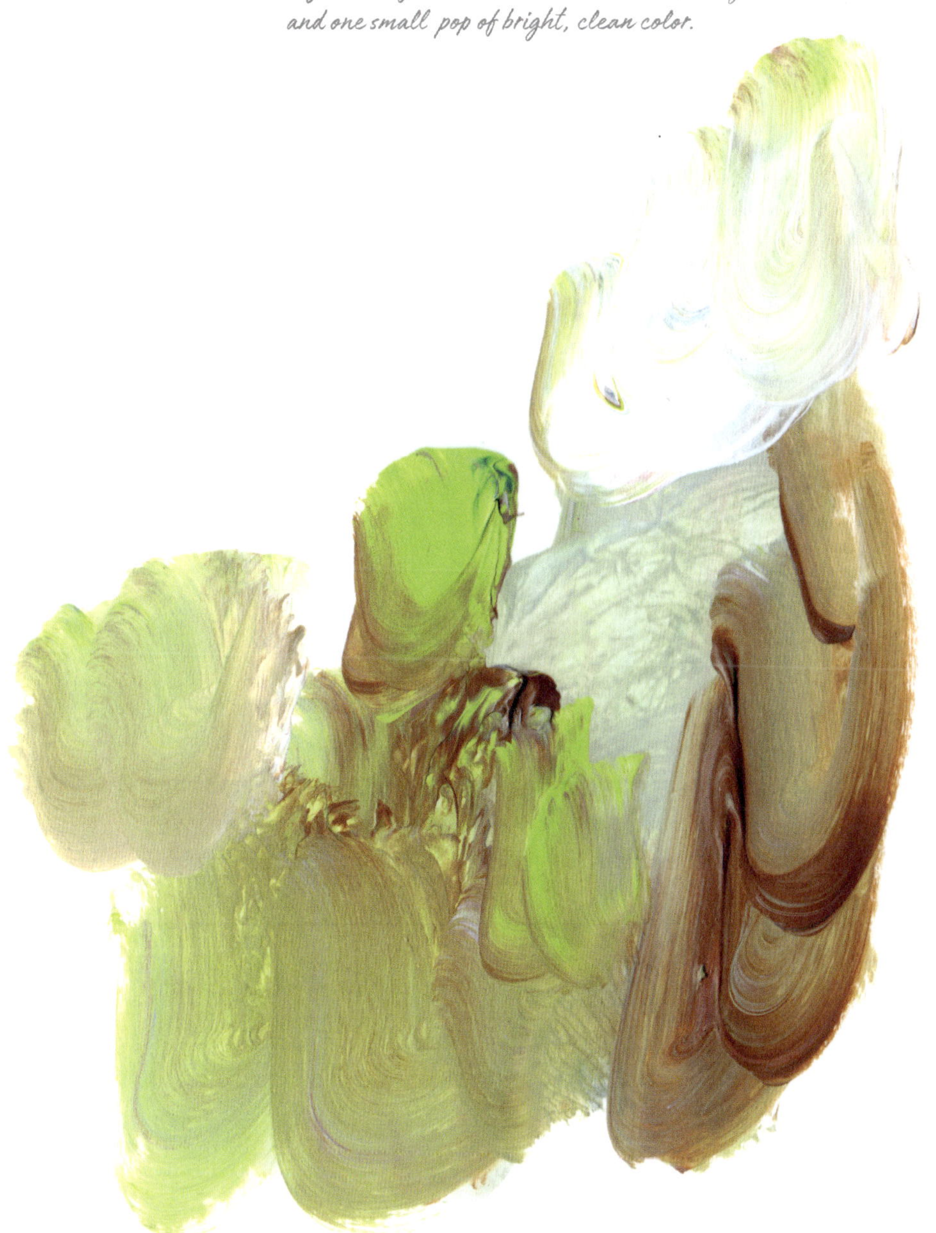

331 ———— Orange can evoke friendliness, happiness, and warmth. Be inspired by how orange makes *you* feel and create a piece of art based on this shape.

332 ———— Add an image to this turquoise.

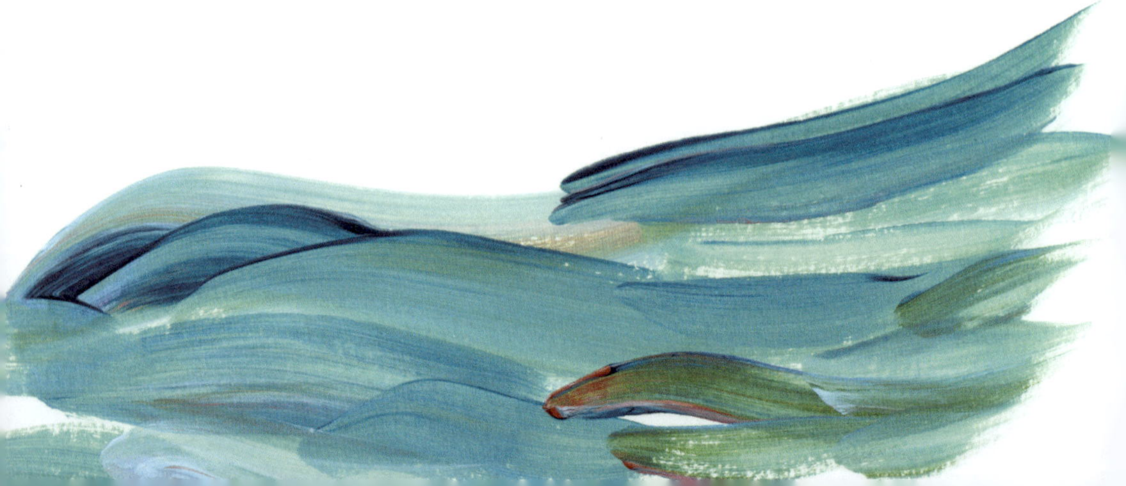

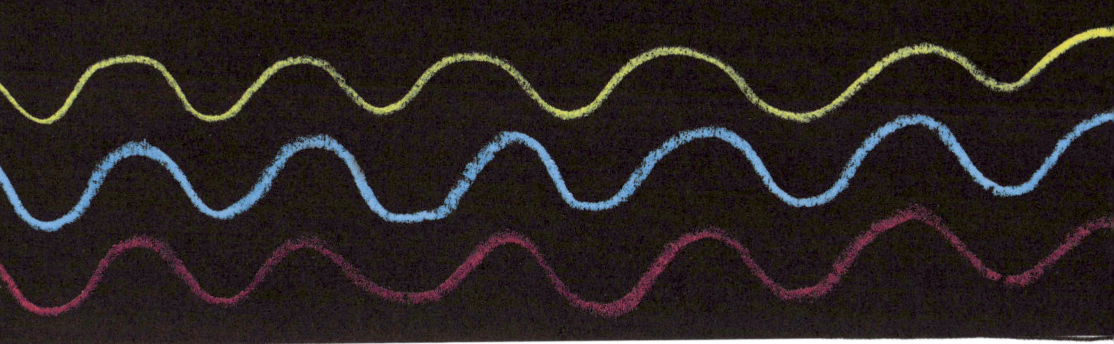

334

You can use color and shape to depict movement in your art.
Draw something kinetic—for example a firework—and use color to
illustrate how it travels through the air. It can be an abstract image,
rather than needing to be realistic.

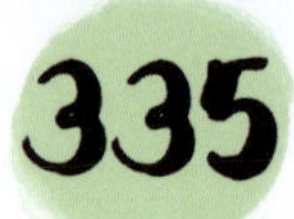

335

Draw an object or scene using a thick black or brown outline. Then add color to your drawing, making bold, confident marks using vibrant colors.

Tip: Starting with a bold outline will immediately make your art eye-catching!

336

Start by painting a wash of bright color across the page. Then add small amounts of other colors until you've filled the page. Enjoy choosing colors that work well together, and consider where you add marks so that your composition feels balanced.

Tip: Acrylic paint or gouache would be effective here. Or use watercolor for your background and pastels on top once the paint has dried.

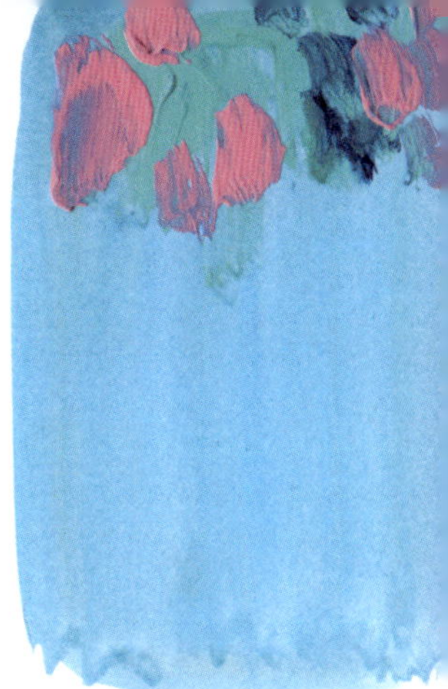

337 — Design a color scheme for a room in your house that evokes a specific feeling of your choice.

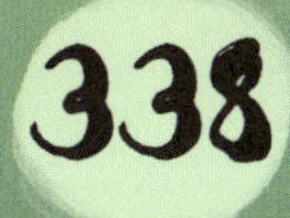

338 — Make a piece of art from observation, using these two colored backgrounds as starting points. Perhaps draw a potted plant that you can see, creating the pot in the bottom half and the plant in the top half.

339

Color the clouds
using moody colors.

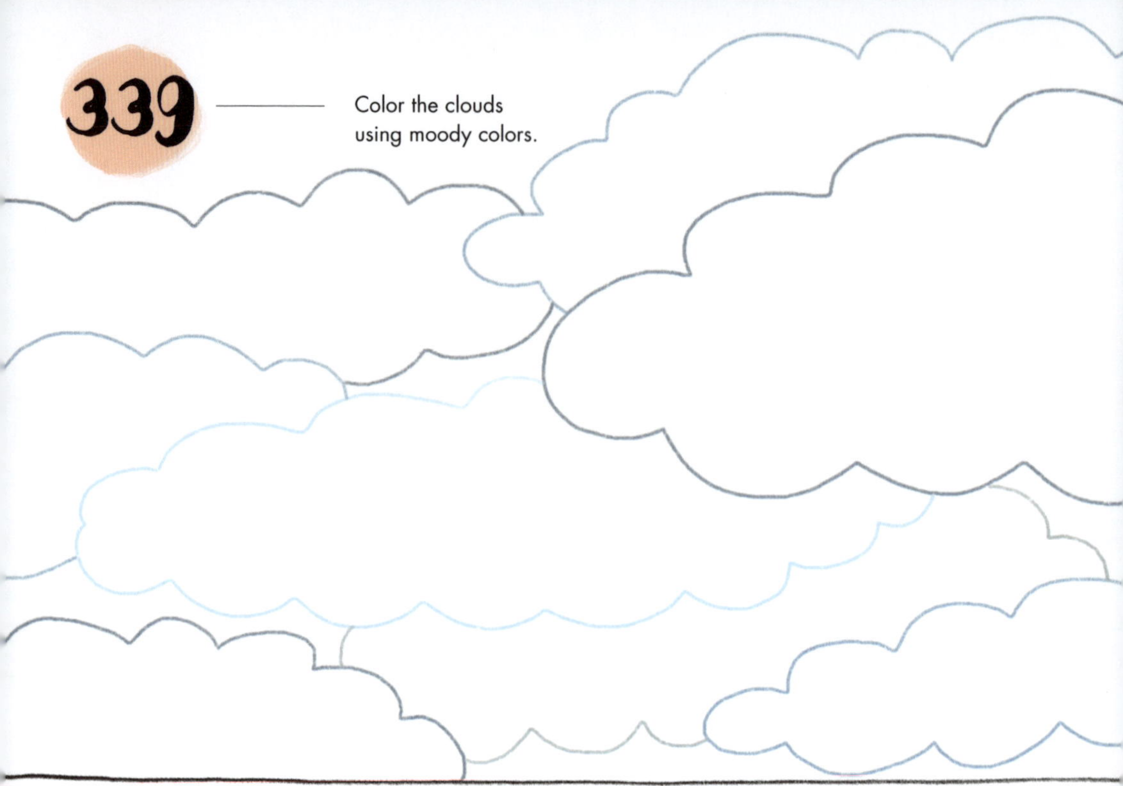

340

Design a pair of colorful shoes.

Choose two to five colored pencils, pens, or pastels and draw a person, concentrating on capturing their outline. There's no need to add tone or blocks of color, just enjoy letting your materials glide across the page.

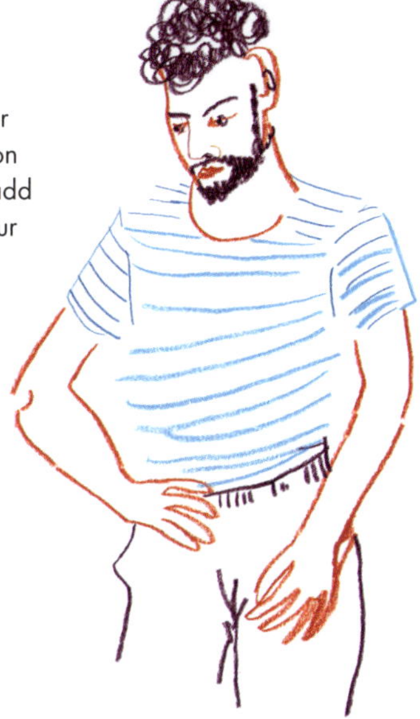

Draw a view from your home—inside or outside—using as many colors as possible. You could explore using a variety of materials too. Aim for your creation to be energetic and full of life.

Turn these green feathers into a bird.

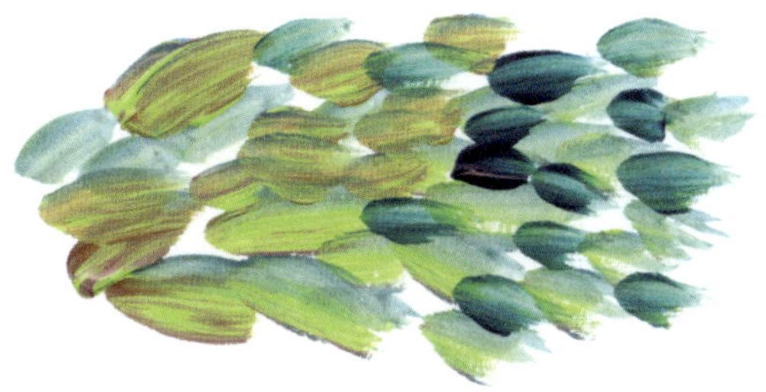

344

Create a palette of colors to describe your mood today.
Don't worry if you don't know exactly why you chose each color
– just go with your instincts.

It can be striking when a lot of one color is used confidently. Look around your home for a scene or object which includes a few similar colors, and use this as inspiration for a piece of art. Be bold and unapologetic with your use of one color—aim to create an arresting image.

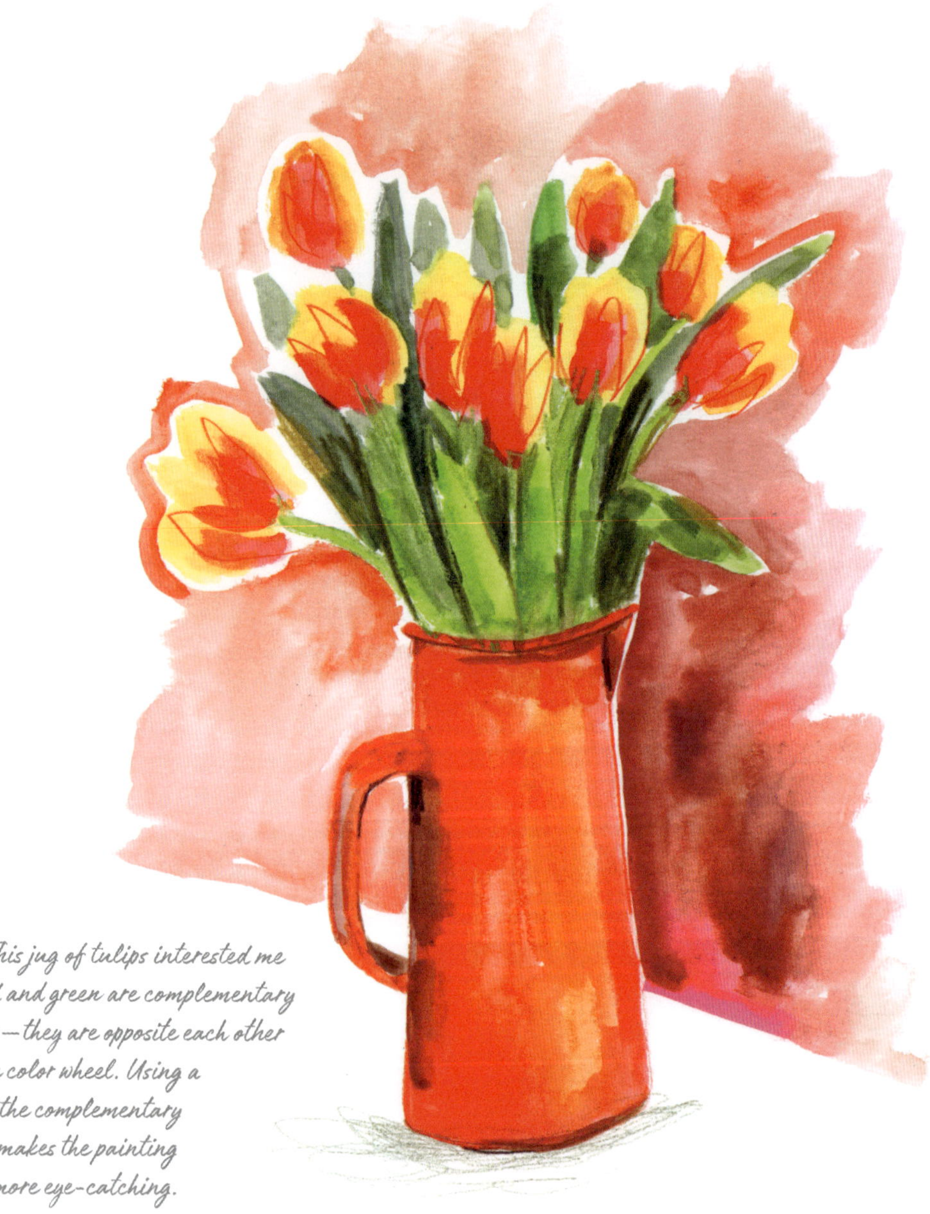

Tip: This jug of tulips interested me as red and green are complementary colors—they are opposite each other on the color wheel. Using a bit of the complementary color makes the painting even more eye-catching.

Continue adding triangles, then fill them in using any color you like.

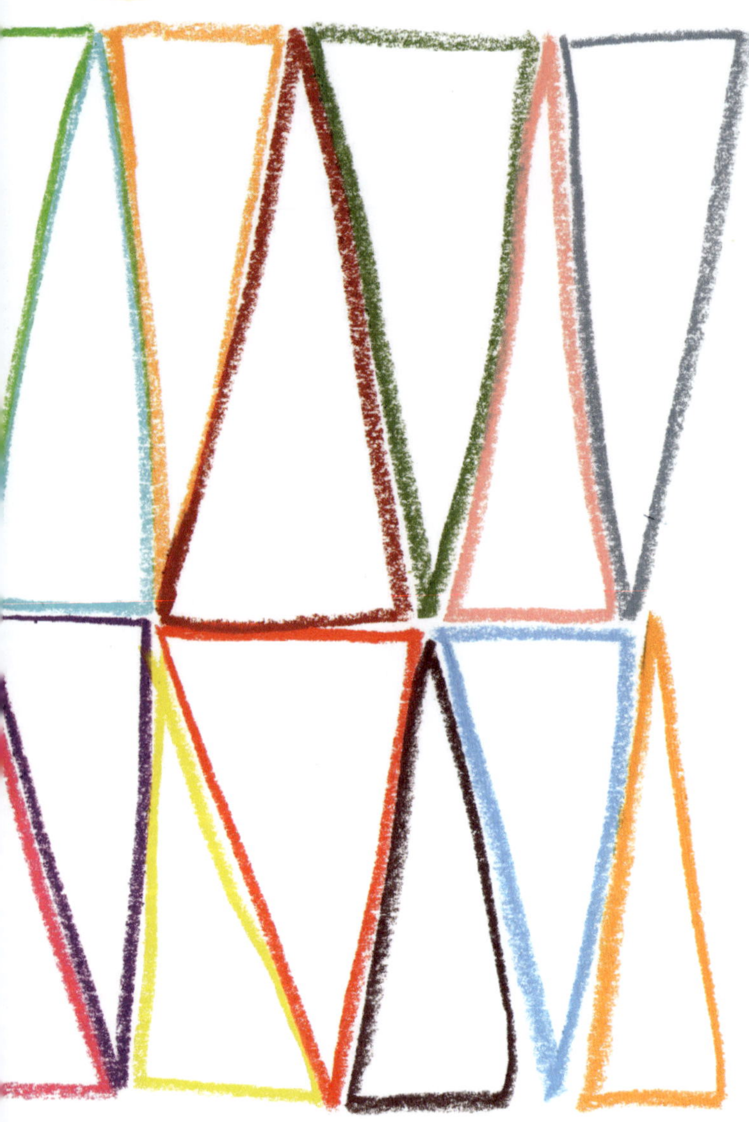

347

Inspiration for paintings can come from anywhere. There can be beautiful color combinations in industrial machinery, buildings, and everyday objects that catch your eye. Paint a view or scene that isn't traditionally depicted in art but interests you.

Explore bright, vibrant color combinations here. Draw a circle of color and then add a second color around the outside.

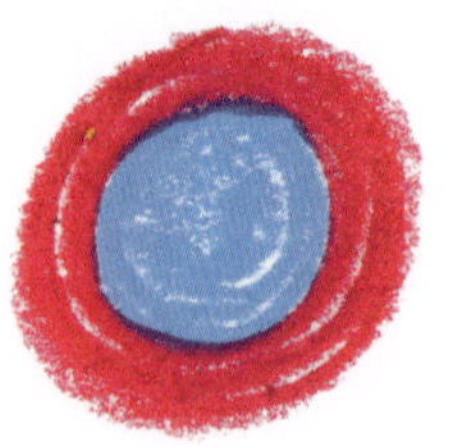 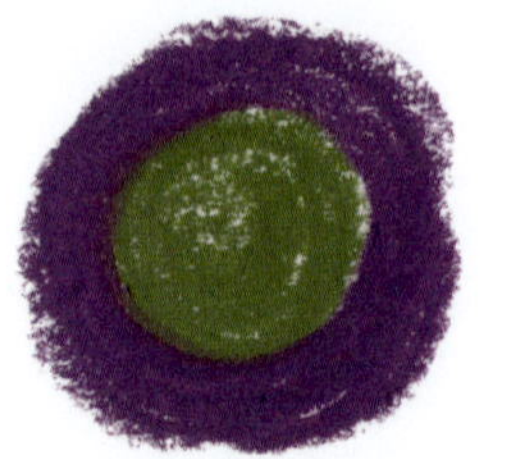 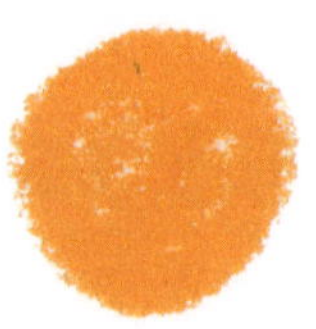 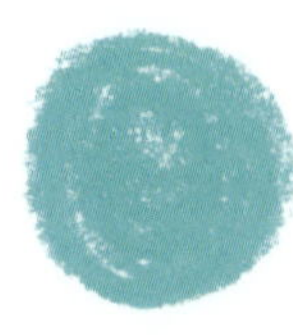

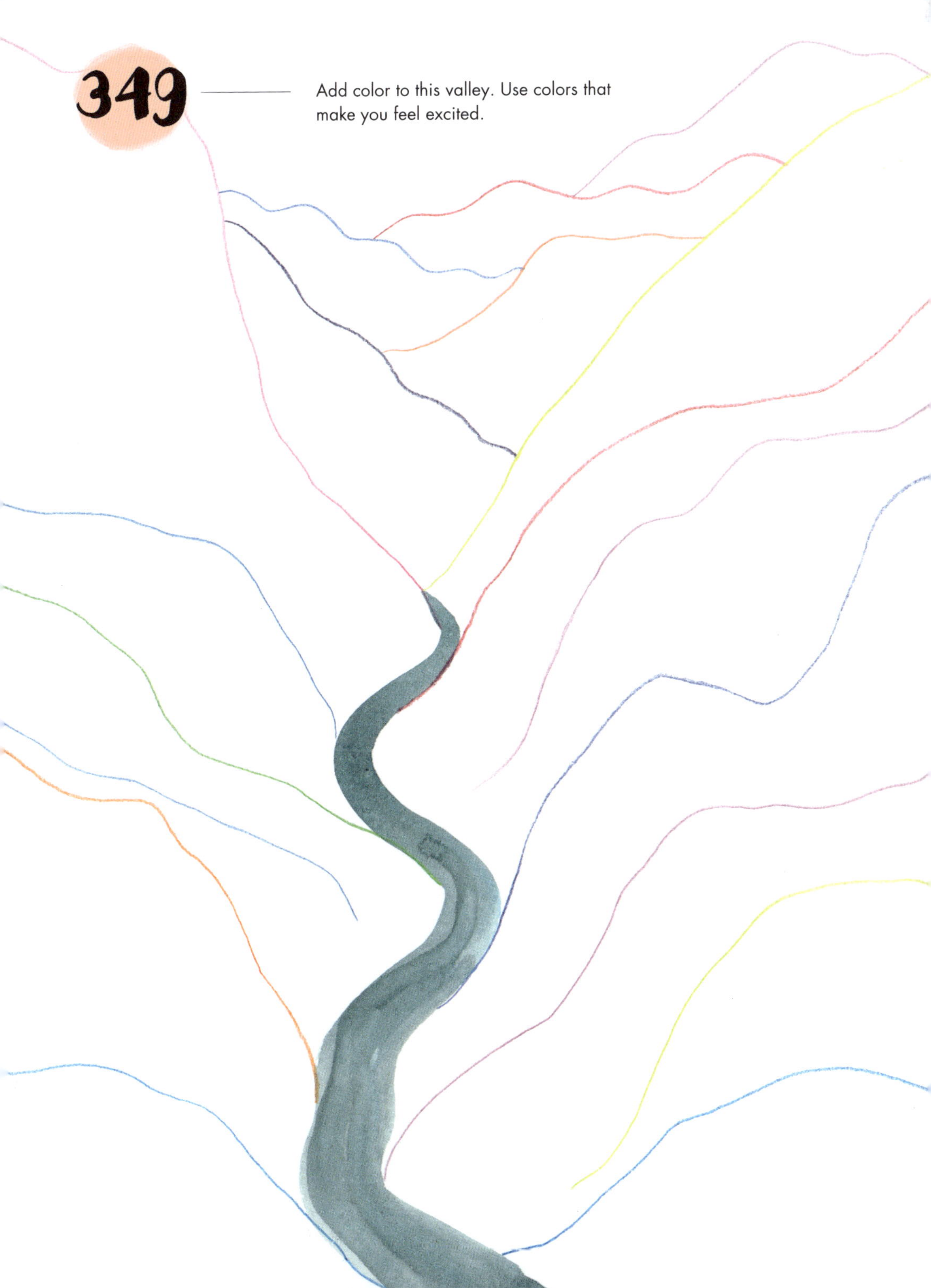

349
Add color to this valley. Use colors that make you feel excited.

350

Draw the same scene at different times of day and observe how varying the colors can be. The same view can be inspiration for many pieces of art, as the light and weather changes.

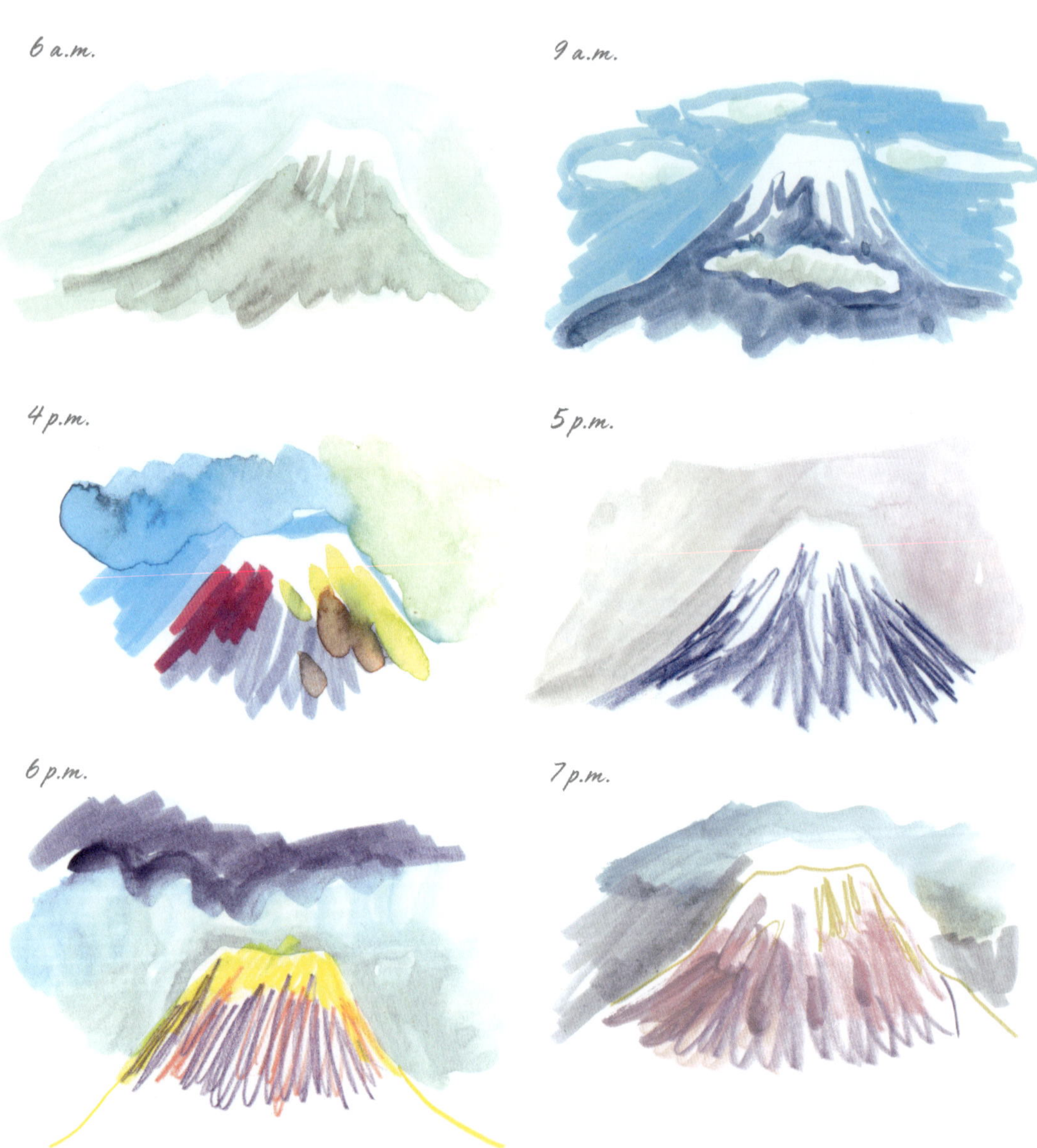

Tip: Light can change quickly, especially at sunrise and sunset! You may want to have some materials prepared in front of you, ready to quickly grab as soon as you need them.

There is more than one color in the sea and in a river or lake. Look at a body of water—in person or in a photo or video. Draw it, being sure to capture all the colors you observe. Consider how the weather has an affect on the tones you see in the water.

Fill the page with multicolored diamonds.

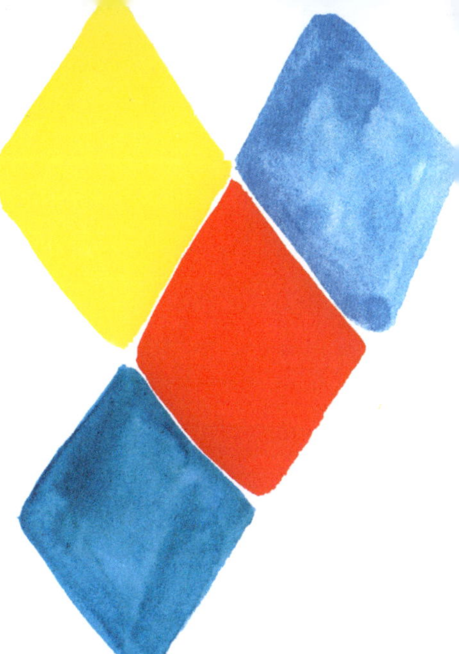

353 —————— The colors we wear can affect how we feel.
Design an exuberant costume here.

Paint a scene that features a lot of tone (areas of light and dark). Use color to depict tonal areas instead of grays and blacks.

Tip: Consider using tints and shades of colors, or perhaps complementary colors, to create striking shadows.

Add color.

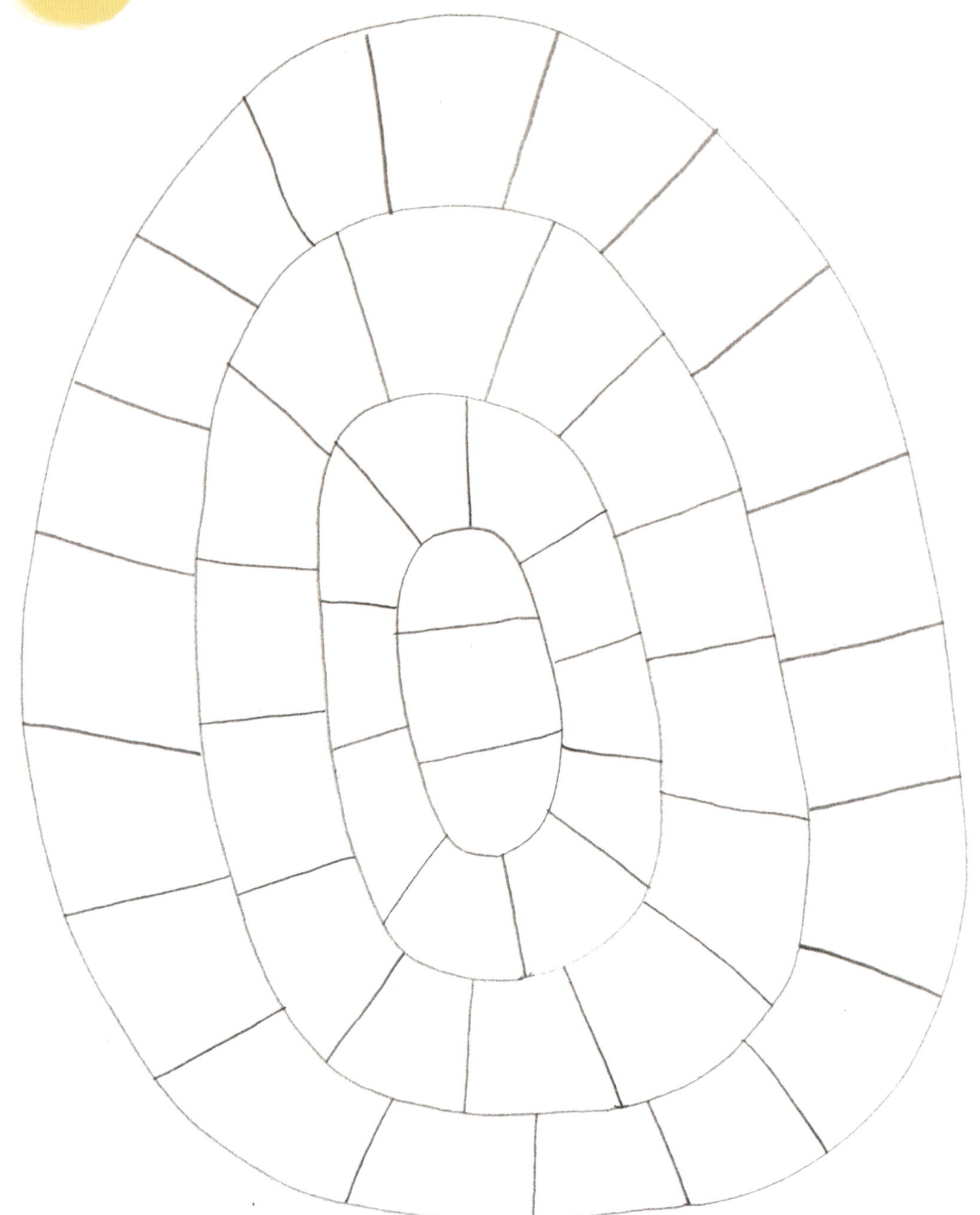

356

Paint a human figure using analogous colors to create a harmonious image. The colors you use don't need to be realistic, and can instead represent colors that are a similar tone.

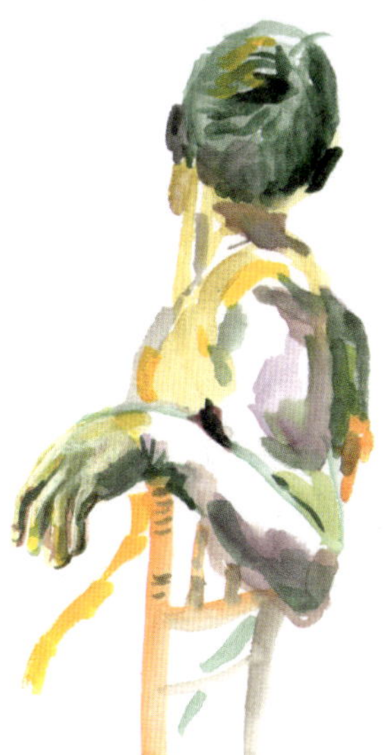

357

When painting, you don't need to mix paints before starting—and sometimes more spontaneous artwork can be created by using paints straight from the tube. Create a still life scene using objects or food from your home. It can be as simple as you like. Begin by looking carefully at the scene in front of you, and gather a palette of colors you'd like to use.

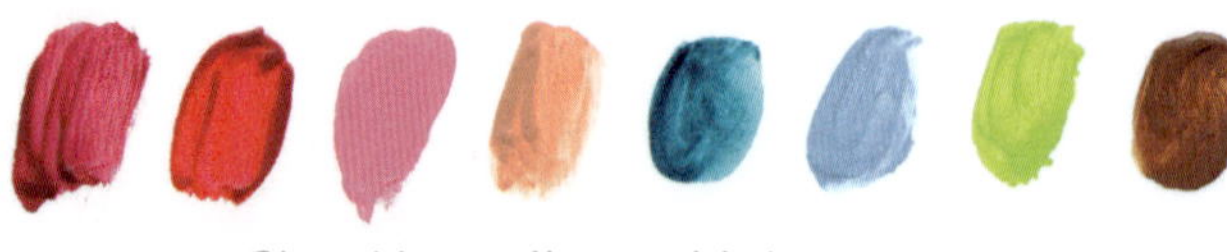

Straight from the paint tubes

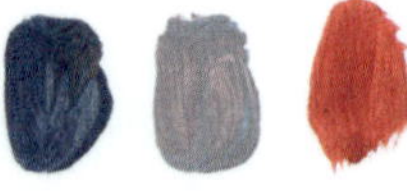

Mixed colors

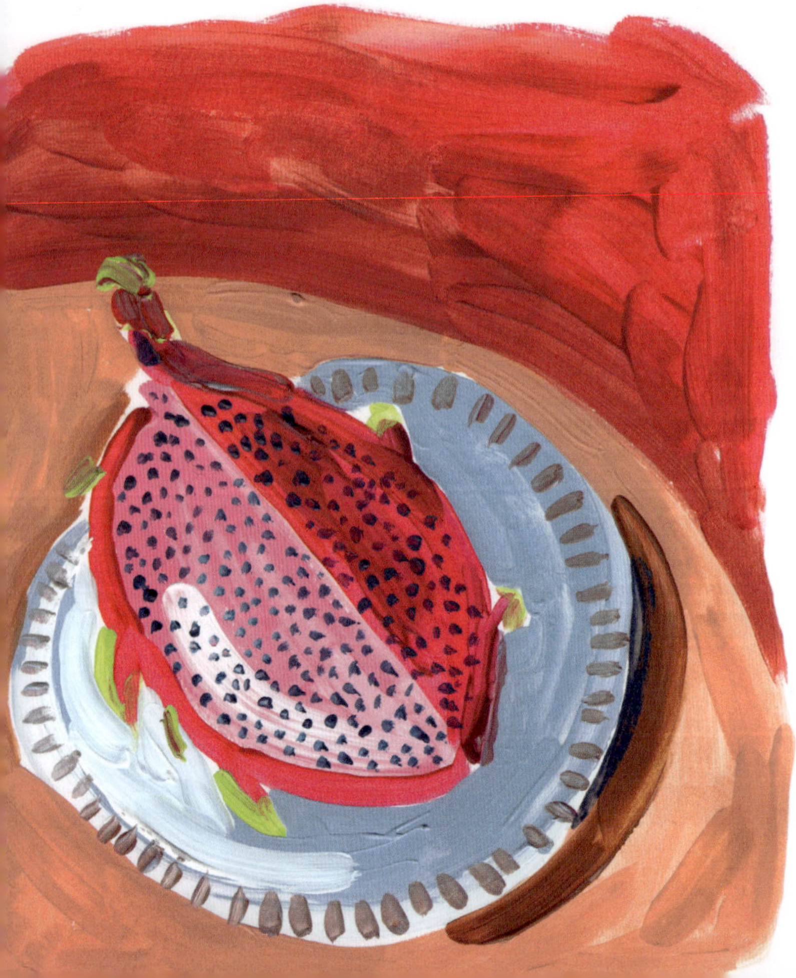

You may like to create some color studies first—refer back to activity 231 before starting, or just go for it and paint the scene. Use big, bold shapes and work quickly, enjoying the colors and the ease of using them straight from a palette.

Tip: Wash and dry your brush well between colors so that you keep them clean and prevent your colors from getting murky.

358 ———— Paint a sunrise.

359

Paint a sunset. Consider how the colors differ from those you chose for your sunrise.

360 ——————— Use neutral, earthy colors to create a relaxing, peaceful image.

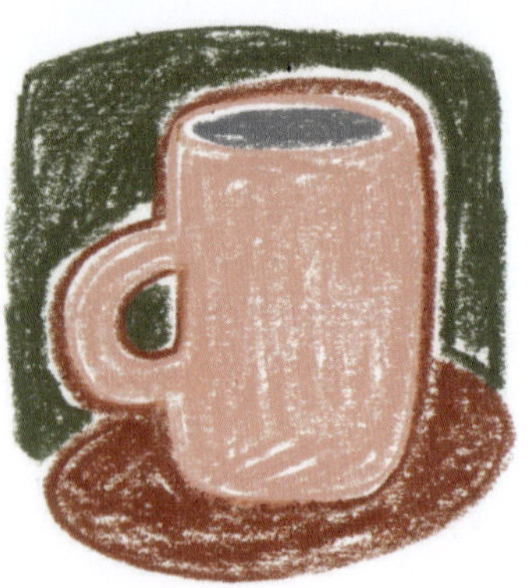

361

We may naturally assume that a drop of water always looks blue, but if we look more closely, a water droplet actually looks a similar color to the object it's on or in front of. Make a study of water droplets on a flower, based on the image below, paying particular attention to the colors.

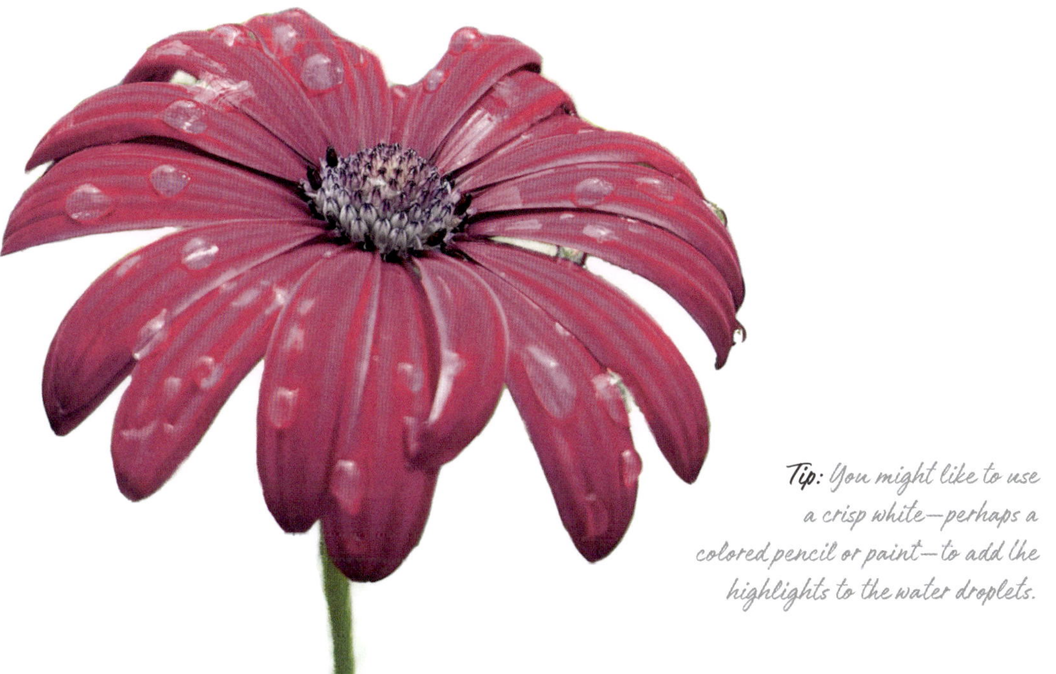

362

Use a pre-prepared, painted background to inspire a piece of observational art. Begin by painting color onto the white page, allowing it to dry completely. Choose any color you like, in any shape.

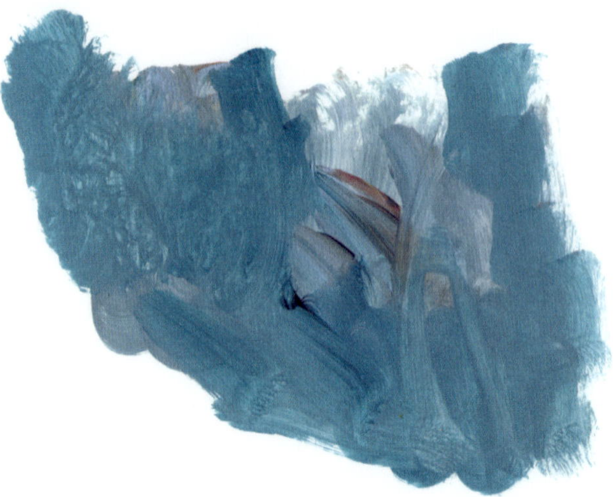

Then go for a walk with your colored page and create a drawing or painting on top of this color, using the color as inspiration for a background, or as part of your image.

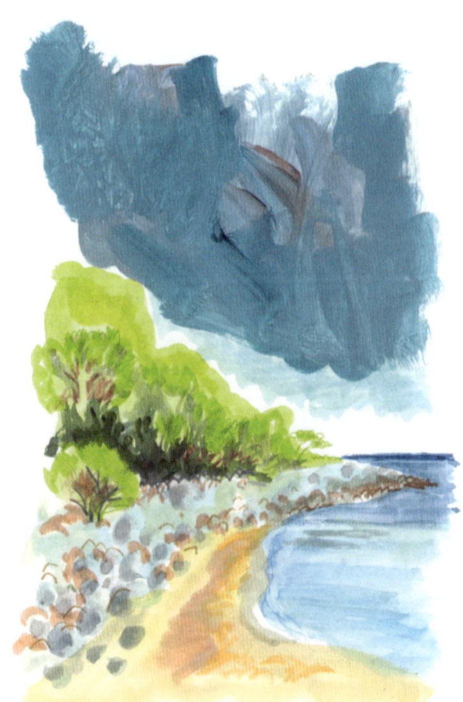

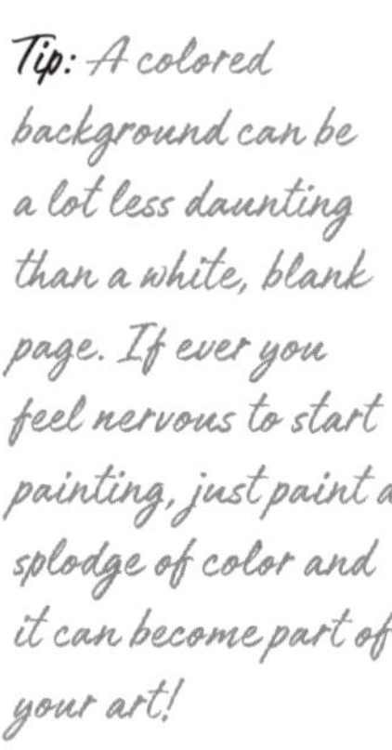

Tip: A colored background can be a lot less daunting than a white, blank page. If ever you feel nervous to start painting, just paint a splodge of color and it can become part of your art!

Create a nature-inspired pattern on a dark background.

364 ——————— Color is used carefully in the design of logos to evoke certain feelings and create an identity. Design a logo for an imaginary product using colors deliberately. What do the colors mean to you?

365

Share your creations, and the joy of color, by making some colorful greetings cards to send to your loved ones. Create an abstract piece of art using colors you love, and let it dry.

Tip: You may prefer to use a separate piece of card for your creations and use the opposite page to explore color palette options.

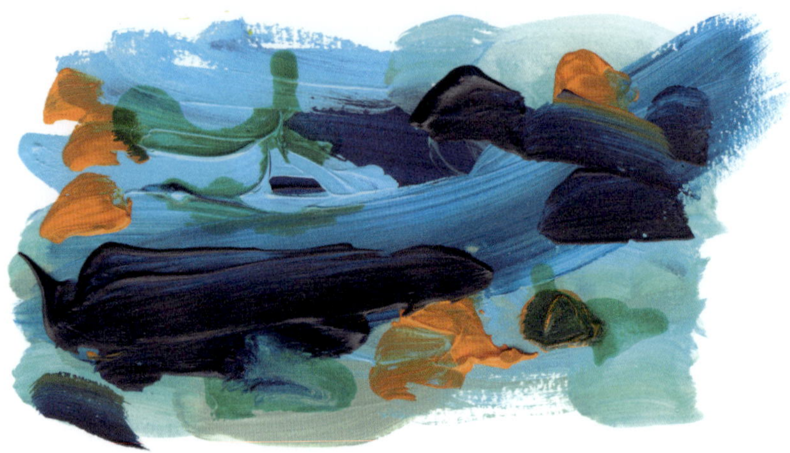

Then cut your colorful abstract into smaller, mini abstracts. Stick these onto a piece of folded card to create your greetings cards.

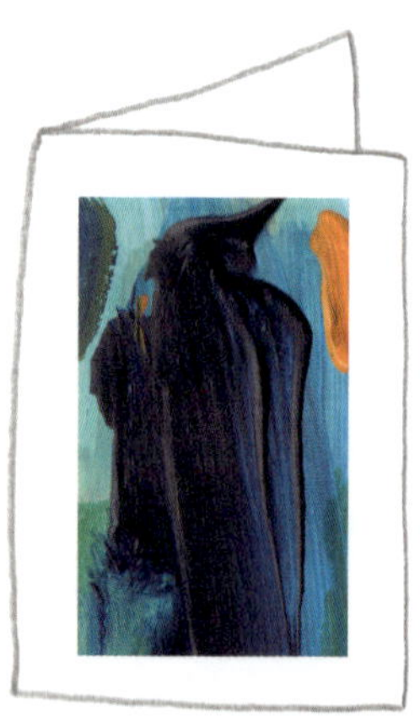

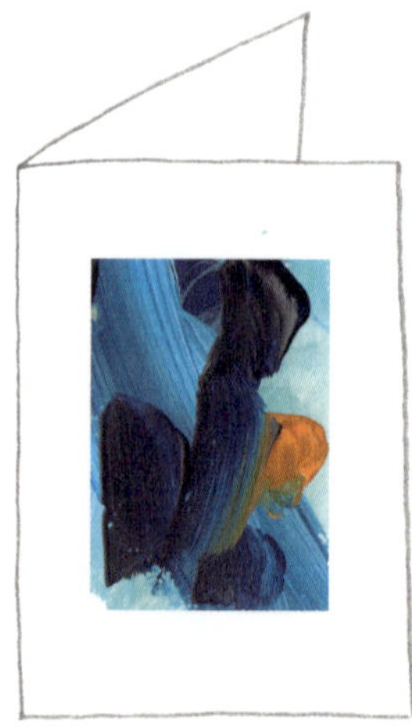

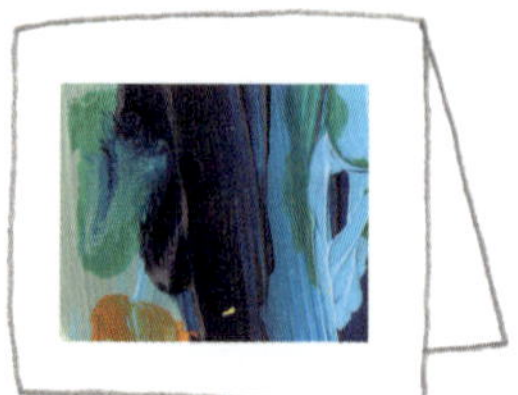

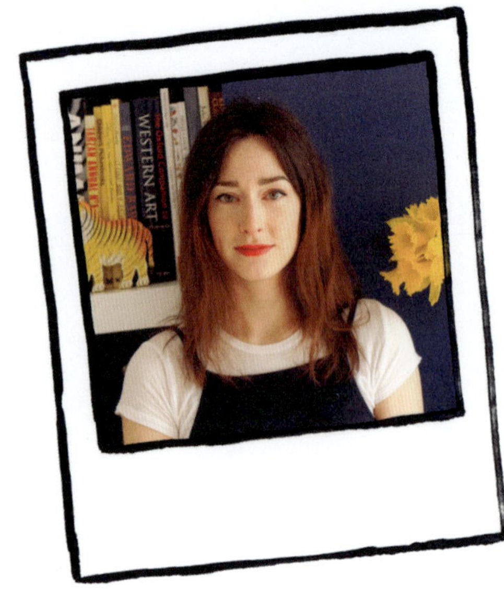

About the Author

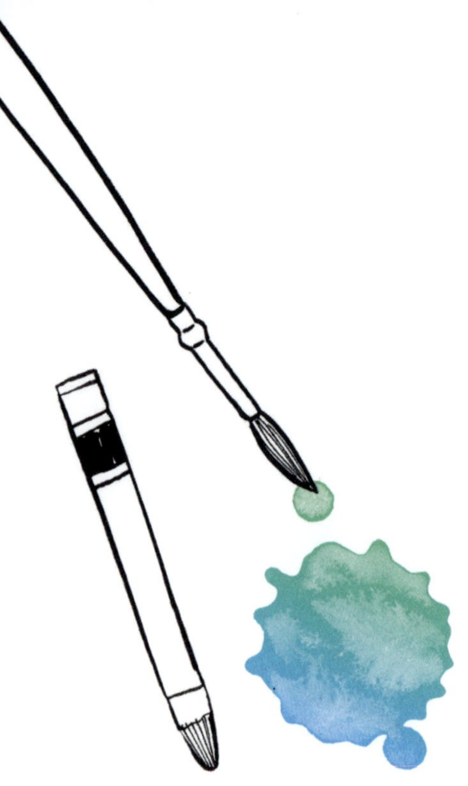

Lorna Scobie grew up in the English countryside, climbing trees and taking her rabbit for walks in the fields. She is an author, illustrator, and designer, now based in south-east London.

Lorna always has a sketchbook close to hand, just in case. She enjoys spontaneity in art, and the 'happy accidents' that can happen along the way. Her favorite place to draw is outside among nature, on trips around the world.

This is the sixth book in Lorna's *365 Days* series, following on from *365 Days of Art*, *365 Days of Drawing*, *365 Days of Creativity*, *365 Days of Art in Nature* and *365 Days of Feel-good Art*.

If you'd like to keep up to date with Lorna's work, she can be found on Instagram: **@lornascobie**

www.lornascobie.com

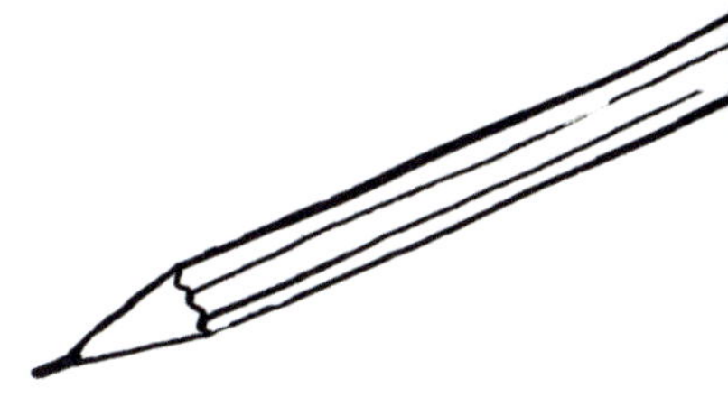

Thank you

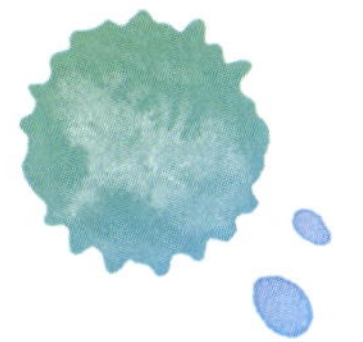

To Tom, Coco, Isla and Charlie—
for inspiring me to do what I love.
And to Kajal and Chelsea and my
super publishing team.

Dedicated to my mom, Emily,
who has always surrounded
me with joyful color and art.

Quadrille, Penguin Random House UK,
One Embassy Gardens, 8 Viaduct Gardens,
London SW11 7BW

Quadrille Publishing Limited is part of the
Penguin Random House group of companies
whose addresses can be found at global.
penguinrandomhouse.com

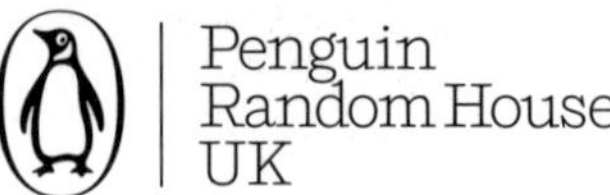

Text © Lorna Scobie 2025
Illustrations and photos © Lorna Scobie 2025
Author photo © Tom Scobie Cookson

Published by Quadrille in 2025

www.penguin.co.uk

A CIP catalogue record for this book is available
from the British Library

ISBN 9781837833672
10 9 8 7 6 5 4 3 2 1

Managing Director: Sarah Lavelle
Publishing Director: Kajal Mistry
Editorial Director: Harriet Butt
Managing Editor: Chelsea Edwards
Proofreader: Gaynor Sermon
Production Manager: Sabeena Atchia

Color reproduction by F1

Printed in China by C&C Offset Printing Co., Ltd.

The authorized representative in the EEA is Penguin
Random House Ireland, Morrison Chambers,
32 Nassau Street, Dublin D02 YH68.

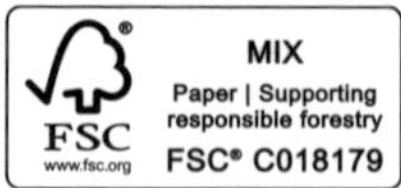